DRUGS AND JUSTICE

DRUGS AND JUSTICE

Seeking a Consistent, Coherent, Comprehensive View

Margaret P. Battin
Erik Luna
Arthur G. Lipman
Paul M. Gahlinger
Douglas E. Rollins
Jeanette C. Roberts
Troy L. Booher

With additional contributions from

David G. Dick
Dennis M. Fuchs
Karol L. Kumpfer
Kelly J. Lundberg

OXFORD
UNIVERSITY PRESS

2008

OXFORD
UNIVERSITY PRESS

Oxford University Press, Inc., publishes works that further
Oxford University's objective of excellence
in research, scholarship, and education.

Oxford   New York
Auckland   Cape Town   Dar es Salaam   Hong Kong   Karachi
Kuala Lumpur   Madrid   Melbourne   Mexico City   Nairobi
New Delhi   Shanghai   Taipei   Toronto

With offices in
Argentina   Austria   Brazil   Chile   Czech Republic   France   Greece
Guatemala   Hungary   Italy   Japan   Poland   Portugal   Singapore
South Korea   Switzerland   Thailand   Turkey   Ukraine   Vietnam

Published by Oxford University Press, Inc.
198 Madison Avenue, New York, New York 10016

www.oup.com

Oxford is a registered trademark of Oxford University Press

Library of Congress Cataloging-in-Publication Data
Drugs and justice : seeking a consistent, coherent, comprehensive view /
Margaret P. Battin ... [et al.].
p.   cm.
Includes bibliographical references and index.
ISBN 978-0-19-532100-5; 978-0-19-532101-2 (pbk.)
1. Drug control—United States.
2. Drug abuse—Government policy—United States.
3. Drugs—Law and legislation—United States.
I. Battin, M. Pabst
HV5825.D7793 2007
364.1'770973—dc22   2007000563

9 8 7 6 5 4 3 2 1

Printed in the United States of America
on acid-free paper

THE MANY FACES OF DRUGS: A PERSONAL PERSPECTIVE

Gentlemen, this is no Humbug!
—Dr. John C. Warren's exclamation on
October 16, 1846, after performing painless
surgery under ether anesthesia at the Massachusetts General Hospital[1]

It was a new, full can of ether; perhaps he jabbed the safety pin too roughly into the can, or else he wriggled it around too impatiently. The ether dripped onto the face mask more freely than usual; his hand kept slipping off the cone before he could get enough to satisfy himself. He turned a little toward the wall; that way, the edge of the windowsill maintained contact with the mask over his mouth and nose after his fingers released their grip. There was just enough pressure from the windowsill to

1. Peter J. Cohen and Robert D. Dripps, "History and Theories of General Anesthesia," in *The Pharmacological Basis of Therapeutics*, 3rd ed., Louis S. Goodman and Alfred Gilman, eds., (New York and London: Macmillan, 1965), 45.

hold the cone in place.... . The cause of
death would be respiratory failure, due to
aspiration of vomit, which would lead to
cardiac arrest.
—John Irving, *The Cider House Rules*[2]

These two introductory passages epitomize the vast panoply of drug dichotomies lucidly presented in this provocative, stimulating, and challenging book. The first, in only five words, represents the dawn of anesthesia, humanity's triumph over pain. The second chillingly describes the miserable and lonely death of Dr. Wilbur Larch from an overdose of the very same anesthetic. Although the author never explicitly states whether Larch's death was suicide or accident, both are well-known sequelae of addiction (drug dependence).

There are numerous terms that our language applies to drugs, each with its own nuance, each with its own impact, each leaving its own impression. "Medication," "pharmaceutical," "therapeutic agent," "herbal remedy," "natural remedy," "dietary supplement," "psychotropic agent," "anabolic steroid," "enhancing agent," "legitimate drug," "illegal drug," "prescription drug," "street drug"—all these terms (and many others) are encompassed by the term *drug*. It is not at all surprising that many, sometimes opposing, descriptions also apply to *drug use* and *drug users*. These concepts are integral to this book; indeed, it is unrealistic to attempt to formulate rational policies without understanding and acknowledging these subtleties. Let me illustrate just a few examples where these Janus-like perceptions of drugs are obvious.

For several years, I have taught two courses at the Georgetown University Law Center whose curricula exemplify society's ambivalence toward drugs. *Alternative and Complementary Medicine: Legal Issues* examines the many ways in which the law deals with unorthodox medicine, often with the aim of increasing access to these frequently unproven practices—including the perfectly legal sale and use of drugs classified as "dietary supplements." *Drugs, Addiction, and the Law: Policy, Politics, and Public Health* focuses on

---

2. John Irving, *The Cider House Rules* (New York: Ballantine Books, 1997), 515–16.

"illegal" drugs (as defined by the political process and not necessarily by objective science). The following news items demonstrate this disconnect between science and policy:

> When the Celtics' superstar Len Bias died, apparently from a crack overdose, Congress rushed to pass a bill making the sentence for possessing 5g of crack the same as the sentence for possessing 500g of cocaine. The death of someone so young with such a promising future reinforced the idea that the country was under assault by drugs. Congressional representatives returning to their districts to campaign over summer break got an earful from concerned voters. The outrage was especially great in Boston, the home of House Speaker Tip O'Neill, and when the Congress reconvened, drug legislation was a priority.[3]

> FORT LAUDERDALE, Fla.—A dietary supplement containing the herbal stimulant ephedra may have contributed to the death Monday of Baltimore Orioles pitcher Steve Bechler, Broward County Medical Examiner Joshua Perper said today, adding that such products should be banned from baseball and other sports.

> Perper said Bechler's apparent consumption of Xenadrine RFA-1, a product readily available at nutrition stores, may have acted in tandem with other health issues to precipitate the heatstroke and resulting multiple organ failure that caused Bechler's death less than 24 hours after he collapsed on the field during drills Sunday.[4]

In contrast to the draconian sentences often imposed for the manufacture and distribution of cocaine, the Food and Drug Administration's efforts to ban ephedra, a "legal" but often unsafe dietary supplement, remains under litigation; at this time, it is perfectly legal to sell and purchase the compound. In spite of our War on Drugs, "legal" dietary supplements and "illegal" drugs are both multi-billion dollar industries.

What factors might be responsible for this dichotomy in society's approach to the two stimulants, crack cocaine and ephedra? Why do we

---

3. Peter J. Cohen, *Drugs, Addiction, and the Law: Policy, Politics, and Public Health* (Durham, N.C.: Carolina Academic Press, 2004), 357n.5.

4. Dave Sheinin, "'We All Feel a Deep Sense of Loss'; Bechler's Death Casts a Pall Over Orioles," *Washington Post*, February 19, 2003, D1.

allow the sale of alcohol and tobacco, both responsible for far greater rates of mortality and morbidity than "illegal" drugs? No doubt, among the many factors responsible for the disjunction between scientific fact and public policy are the overwhelming influences of money and lobbying. However, another element of the human condition is more subtle and insidious—stigmatization.

> [S]tigma exists when the following interrelated components converge. In the first component, people distinguish and label human differences. In the second, dominant cultural beliefs link labeled persons to undesirable characteristics—to negative stereotypes. In the third, labeled persons are placed in distinct categories so as to accomplish some degree of separation of "us" from "them." In the fourth, labeled persons experience status loss and discrimination that lead to unequal outcomes. Stigmatization is entirely contingent on access to social, economic and political power that allows the identification of differences, the construction of stereotypes, the separation of labeled persons into distinct categories and the full execution of disapproval, rejection, exclusion and discrimination. Thus we apply the term stigma when elements of labeling, stereotyping, separation, status loss and discrimination co-occur in a power situation that allows them to unfold.[5]

The phenomenon of stigmatization exemplifies the extraordinarily important role of public perception. My grandparents told me that in their generation, tuberculosis was viewed as a disease of the ignorant, the immigrant, and the unclean. Today, in contrast, this disease is perceived simply as a serious bacterial infection (unless, of course, it is a surrogate for HIV/AIDS).

In order to personalize the pervasive role of stigma, imagine a party during which the host offers a cocktail to a guest. What might be the host's internal reaction to each one of the following responses?

5. Public Health Law," *Journal of Law, Medicine & Ethics* 30 (2002):179–81, quoting B. G. Link and J. C. Phelan, "On Stigma and its Public Health Implications," paper presented at *Stigma and Global Health: Developing a Research Agenda*, a conference convened by the Fogarty International Center at the National Institutes of Health, Bethesda, Md., September 5–7, 2001, available at: http://www.stigmaconference.nih.gov/LinkPaper.htm (accessed October 14, 2006).

- No thanks. I don't drink.
- No thanks. I cannot drink because I have a genetically induced deficiency of the enzyme aldehyde dehydrogenase, and alcohol gives me a terrible headache and red face.
- No thanks. I cannot drink because I suffer from *Jellinek's Disease.*[6]
- No thanks. I am an alcoholic.
- No thanks. I am a recovering alcoholic.

Stigma is only one of numerous public perceptions that should not be ignored by those responsible for formulating public policy. That drug-related legislation is often based far more on politics than science is, at least to me, tragic. It is equally discouraging, but not surprising, that members of the judiciary often view drugs through clearly divergent lenses:

> Although peyote serves as a sacramental symbol similar to bread and wine in certain Christian churches, it is more than a sacrament. Peyote constitutes in itself an object of worship; prayers are directed to it much as prayers are devoted to the Holy Ghost. On the other hand, to use peyote for nonreligious purposes is sacrilegious.... The record thus establishes that the application of the statutory prohibition of the use of peyote results in a virtual inhibition of the practice of defendants' religion. To forbid the use of peyote is to remove the theological heart of Peyotism.[7]
>
> To be a confirmed drug addict is to be one of the walking dead.... The teeth have rotted out, the appetite is lost and the stomach and intestines don't function properly.... In some cases membranes of the nose turn a flaming red; the partition separating the nostrils is eaten away—breathing is difficult.... Good traits of character disappear and bad ones emerge. Sex organs become affected.... Boils and abscesses plague the skin; gnawing pain racks the body. Nerves snap; vicious twitching develops.... Such is the torment of being a drug addict; such is the plague of being one of the walking dead.[8]

6. E. M. Jellinek, *The Disease Concept of Alcoholism* (New Haven, Conn.:, Conn.: College and Universities Press, 1960, 1962). Jellinek described the syndrome and natural history of alcoholism and, on the basis of his observations, termed it a disease.

7. *People v. Woody*, 394 P.2d 813, 817–818 (California Supreme Court, 1964).

8. Justice Douglas (quoting Lewis Thomas) in *Robinson v. California*, 370 U. S. 660, 672 (1962).

As with so many attitudes, the objects of stigmatization have not been constant throughout time or universal in every culture. Contrast, for example, a news article conveying today's attitudes toward athletes who use performance-enhancing drugs with an extraordinarily accurate and beautiful description of the use of cocaine by—of all people—Sherlock Holmes:

> SAN FRANCISCO (AP)—The chemist who created "the clear," a previously undetectable steroid, was sentenced Friday to three months in prison and three months' home confinement for his role in the BALCO drug scandal.
>
> Patrick Arnold was the last of five defendants convicted of steroid-distribution charges connected to the Bay Area Laboratory Co-Operative, a nutritional supplement company federal authorities exposed as a steroid distribution ring for top athletes.
>
> "The behavior reflected here is destructive and damaging to Arnold, damaging to the community and damaging to the nation as a whole," U.S. District Court Judge Susan Illston said. Arnold was ordered to report to prison by Sept. 19.
>
> "I'm very regretful for what I've done and especially since what it has precipitated in sports and society," Arnold said outside court. "I do believe there should be a level playing field, and that this whole things needs to be addressed."…
>
> "The defendant bears a heavy burden for his key role in effectively polluting professional sports with drugs which were designed to cheat the system," prosecutors said in court papers urging the prison term.[9]

> Sherlock Holmes took his bottle from the corner of the mantelpiece, and his hypodermic syringe from its neat morocco case. With his long, white, nervous fingers he adjusted the delicate needle, and rolled back his left shirt-cuff. For some little time his eyes rested thoughtfully upon the sinewy forearm and wrist, all dotted and scarred with innumerable puncture-marks. Finally, he thrust down the tiny piston, and sank back into the velvet-lined arm-chair with a long sigh of satisfaction.[10]

9. *Bismarck Tribune*, August 5, 2006, sports section. See also: Associated Press "Father of 'The Clear' Sentenced in BALCO Case," online at http://www.ktvu.com/balco/9629803/detail.html.

10. Sir Arthur Conan Doyle, *The Sign of the Four* (Tuesday, September 18, to Friday, September 21, 1888) in *The Annotated Sherlock Holmes*, edited by William S. Baring-Gould (New York and Avenel, N.J.: Wing Books, 1992), 610.

David Musto has cogently summarized the role of history on society's attitude toward some drugs:

> Dramatic shifts in attitude have characterized America's relation to drugs. During the 19th century, certain mood-altering substances, such as opiates and cocaine, were often regarded as compounds helpful in everyday life. Gradually this perception of drugs changed. By the early 1900s, and until the 1940s, the country viewed these and some other psychoactive drugs as dangerous, addictive compounds that needed to be severely controlled. Today, after a resurgence of a tolerant attitude toward drugs during the 1960s and 1970s, we find ourselves, again, in a period of drug intolerance.[11]

Drugs: Boon to Humankind or Forbidden Fruit?

Public perception of "the many faces of drugs" does not preclude objective science. Indeed, a rational and just policy depends on acknowledging, measuring, and evaluating the risks of drug-associated pathology. I strongly believe (as a physician who is intimately involved in the process of intervention and treatment of physicians who manifest the most destructive aspects of drug dependence) that these risks should neither be ignored nor falsely exaggerated. Regardless of society's perceptions, and regardless of what the law is (or should be), there *are* objective harms that can result from the use of many drugs (whether "legal" or "illegal"). This pathology is inherent in the substance itself and does not depend on its legal status. Alcohol overdose can produce vomiting; aspiration of vomitus often results in death. Opioids can cause death due to respiratory depression; it does not matter whether the drug is used "in the street" or in the operating room. Hallucinogens may result in death: the individual believes he/she can fly and jumps out the window. Cocaine can kill the user by triggering cardiac arrhythmias, stroke, and paranoid delusions. Drugs and alcohol are a major risk factor associated with domestic violence.[12] While these harms

11. David F. Musto, "Opium, Cocaine and Marijuana in American History," *Scientific American* 265 (1991): 40.

12. Demetrios N. Kyriacou et al., "Risk Factors for Injury to Women from Domestic Violence," *New England Journal of Medicine* 341 (1999): 1892.

are incontrovertible, they do not automatically justify either regulation or criminal sanctions. While the harm of permissiveness is obvious, the detrimental effects on our democratic society associated with an over-zealous criminal justice system—especially when fueled by prejudice and operating without any scientific justification—are far more insidious. Therefore, the challenge for our people, our elected lawmakers, and our judiciary is to decide when and whether these harms rise to a level where state action is justified.

While personal autonomy is highly valued and should not be lightly imperiled, a democratic society does not demand the unfettered exercise of personal autonomy in every aspect of life. Drugs, whether used to prevent disease, treat disease, maintain health, or affect the emotions, are not devoid of risk. Risks are not necessarily, and, indeed, not usually, confined to the individual; rather, they often extend to an entire society. In the emotional and contentious matter of drugs, it would be naïve to seek an *absolutely best* choice. Rather, we must be prepared to accept the *least worst choice*. In seeking to create a balanced, just, and scientifically reasonable policy, we must also accept that there are inherent risks both in commission and omission. Failure to regulate may constitute as much of a risk as imposing unjustified controls.

An overarching theme of this book is *justice*; I propose that the concept of a politics-free and neutral public health system—balancing the societal good with individual rights—might be the most appropriate and reasonable way to accomplish this aim.

Over a century ago, the Supreme Court issued a decision that has become a paradigm holding in the disciplines of public health law and medicine. In *Jacobson v. Massachusetts*, the 7–2 majority considered both constitutional principles and basic scientific knowledge in denying an individual's absolute right to refuse vaccination. *Jacobson* should not be viewed as a narrow decision, since its bedrock arguments can be applied to many issues in which individual autonomy and societal needs collide:

> [T]he liberty secured by the Constitution of the United States to every person within its jurisdiction does not import an absolute right in each person to be, at all times and in all circumstances, wholly freed from restraint. There are manifold restraints to which every person is necessarily subject for the

common good. On any other basis organized society could not exist with safety to its members. Society based on the rule that each one is a law unto himself would soon be confronted with disorder and anarchy. Real liberty for all could not exist under the operation of a principle which recognizes the right of each individual person to use his own, whether in respect of his person or his property, regardless of the injury that may be done to others.... Even liberty itself, the greatest of all rights, is not unrestricted license to act according to one's own will. It is only freedom from restraint under conditions essential to the equal enjoyment of the same right by others. It is then liberty regulated by law.

There is, of course, a sphere within which the individual may assert the supremacy of his own will and rightfully dispute the authority of any human government, especially of any free government existing under a written constitution, to interfere with the exercise of that will. But it is equally true that in every well-ordered society charged with the duty of conserving the safety of its members the rights of the individual in respect of his liberty may at times, under the pressure of great dangers, be subjected to such restraint, to be enforced by reasonable regulations, as the safety of the general public may demand.[13]

I believe it is appropriate to propose an *a priori* method to balance the interests and obligations of individuals and society. Although a balancing analysis is often considered essential when public health considerations demand State intervention, the process is difficult, emotional, and clouded with political considerations. Are there methods by which society might decide in a consistent, rational, and transparent way how to draw the line between individual rights and obligations?

The line between absolute autonomy and unfettered governmental intervention is not unwavering but depends on the circumstances. Thus, a philosophy of multifactorial analysis is appropriate when it is necessary to balance the benefits and burdens imposed by the law in the name of public health. Such an analysis raises a number of complex questions: What are the rights under review and who is involved? What is the magnitude of

13. *Jacobson v. Massachusetts*, 197 U.S. 11, 26 (1905).

the harm to individuals and/or society? What is the probability that this harm will occur? What type of harm is involved—physical harm to only one person? Physical harm to some members of society? Physical harm to all members of society? Harm to the "moral fabric" of society? What data might support the analysis of magnitude and probability of harm? What is the degree of state intrusiveness? What remedies may be imposed, either by the state or by civil authorities? How ought we to select those who will be subject to state action—before the fact in order to prevent harm, or after the fact, as a reaction to actual harm? Will these remedies be imposed on targeted individuals, or universally applied to all members of society? Is it always possible to evaluate and balance these factors?[14]

I come now to the end of my personal musings and welcome you to the reflections of the eleven authors—seven main authors, and four more in contributing roles—from a wide variety of disciplines who have jointly written this book. My thoughts, philosophy, and perspective are meant to serve as a further contribution to the project of this book, to discover how to develop theory, public policy, and practice that is not based on preconceived ideology or the difficult legacy of an erratic history, but on rational acknowledgment of scientific fact about the goods and evils of drugs—all drugs—across the board.

Peter J. Cohen, MD, JD

14. Adapted from Cohen, *Drugs, Addiction, and the Law*.

PREFACE

This resolutely interdisciplinary book attacks a central problem in theory, policy, and practice concerning drugs: the tendency of health professionals, government, academics, medical scientists, social scientists, clinicians, and the public to compartmentalize thinking about "drugs." Issues about drugs and drug use arise in at least seven areas concerning controlled and other substances:

- Prescription pharmaceuticals
- Over-the-counter drugs
- Alternative medicines and dietary supplements
- Common socially used drugs (alcohol, tobacco, caffeine)
- Religious-use drugs (e.g., peyote and ayahuasca)
- Sports-enhancement drugs
- Illegal recreational (street, club, and party) drugs

This book's working hypothesis is that issues about drugs will look quite different if examined across the board—that is, both with the full spectrum of drugs in mind and also from a truly interdisciplinary, integrative perspective. The rather insular professional and policy spheres within which drug issues are typically discussed involve different literatures, focus on different practical dilemmas, and employ different conceptions of the very point of theory and policy development. Even the understanding of such basic notions as "harm" and "addiction" varies from one field to another. To be sure, there is some overlap—for instance, in the discussion of the use of prescription pharmaceuticals like OxyContin or Adderall in illegal recreational situations, in political debates about marijuana as medical treatment, or in disputes about whether ephedra—the "dietary supplement" or "alternative medicine" comparable to the prescription drug ephedrine—should be restricted or allowed for sale on the open market. But in general, there is little cross-fertilization and cross-critique among the various spheres within which drug issues and policy are confronted. What is said about addiction to illicit drugs, for example, may be inconsistent with what is said about addiction to prescription pharmaceuticals or to over-the-counter stimulants; what is said about the health impact of sports-enhancement drugs like steroids or red blood cell augmenters may be inconsistent with what is said about common-use drugs like caffeine or herbal remedies or St. John's wort. Many practical questions arise:

- Is the rationale for restricting prescription drugs consistent with the absence of such restrictions for dietary supplements and herbal drugs?
- Is there any good reason why the same amounts of crack cocaine and powder cocaine should result in vastly different criminal punishments?
- Is the rationale for anti-doping programs in Olympic and professional sports medically coherent? Should it vary from sport to sport, or from amateur to professional venues?
- Why are members of a Native American church who are of Native American ancestry federally permitted to use peyote, but people not of this race and religion are not?
- Should risks of death count? Why is marijuana illegal if alcohol is not? Why is peyote illegal if tobacco is not?
- Why can't physicians prescribe certain hallucinogens that may be effective in the treatment of alcoholism?
- Is coffee addictive? Does the answer vary depending on the definition of addiction? And if coffee is addictive, why shouldn't it be regulated as a drug?
- Should testing for safety and efficacy be required for dietary supplements and herbal medicines as it is for prescriptions and over-the-counter drugs before they may be marketed for human use? If so, what weight, if any, should be given to data from other countries or to the "millennia of experience" claimed for use of traditional medicines from other cultures?
- Why is "self-medication" permitted and even admired in some fields (e.g., "natural medicines") but not in others (e.g., sports drugs and illegal drugs)?

This book seeks to lay the foundation for achieving greater consistency, coherence, and comprehensiveness in the discussion of drug issues, including both theoretical issues and practical questions like those above. This is an urgent project. As Douglas Husak observes, "what passes for conventional wisdom in one discipline is flatly contradicted in another."

Our objective in this project, as we shall explore in detail, is to identify apparent inconsistencies in theory, policy, and practice about drugs; to diagnose what is at the root of these inconsistencies and consider whether some may be justified while others not; and to show what would be involved in developing a coherent body of theory, policy, and practice that is also comprehensive, that is, that covers all pharmacologically active substances. Doing this will contribute to our ultimate goal, working toward greater justice in the way the world manages drugs. We certainly do not intend to offer a complete theory of drugs, nor yet another candidate for a comprehensive policy of drug reform—many have been proffered in the already enormous literature on drugs. Rather, we want to look at the underpinnings of what such theory, policy, and practice must have in order to count as being *just*. An interdisciplinary and interagency discussion, as well as substantially increased interaction among academics, policymakers, practitioners, and clinicians, is necessary to achieve this goal, even partially. What we hope to provide is a suggestive and stimulating sketch of what must happen for such a discussion to work.

If facing these inconsistencies in order to achieve a more coherent approach were taken seriously in the actual formulation of policy, it could have potentially far-reaching effect. What is distinctive about this project is the very broad view it takes in breaching these comparative insularities, and the way in which it attempts to explore issues of justice in theory, policy, and practice across this very wide expanse.

This book is the joint product of an interdisciplinary group that formed in 2003 at the University of Utah to consider issues of justice in the way that drugs are used and controlled in society. We were fortunate to have a unique constellation of experts: a pharmacotherapist/clinical pharmacologist specializing in pain management and editor of one of that field's premier international journals; a trial court judge known nationally for his work on drug courts; a medicinal chemist (now dean of a college of pharmacy) who is a specialist in dietary supplements and herbal remedies;

a physician-anthropologist who is a world-renowned expert on religious drugs and author of a best-selling work on illegal drugs; two experts on addiction, one of whom is a former director of the Center for Substance Abuse Prevention at the U. S. Department of Health and Human Services and the other an experienced substance-abuse clinician; a law professor whose area of expertise is illegal drugs and who has been involved in high-profile litigation in this area; a pharmacologist/toxicologist who was the Medical Director of Doping Control for the 2002 Winter Olympics; and several philosophers who specialize in various areas of ethics, political theory, and bioethics. With one exception, none of the working group is a native Utahn; we just happen to have been in Utah at the same time.

It is a lively and extremely interesting group. Meeting over a period of several years, we have been exploring ways in which our current thinking about drugs of all sorts, from prescription pharmaceuticals to illegal street drugs, is encapsulated within distinct professional, clinical, legal, policy, and practical fields of interests, sometimes called spheres or silos. The "silo mentality" phenomenon, as it is often called, makes intercommunication difficult or impossible in both professional and public discourse, and we found that our working group was subject to it as well. At the beginning, we often talked past each other—the doctors in the working group made one set of assumptions, the psychologists another, and the lawyers still another, and at the same time those who worked primarily with prescription drugs made quite different assumptions from those who worked principally with illegal drugs. But once we realized what conceptual dislocations were at the root of our troubles and our discussion flourished, we began to think about how to enable theorists, clinicians, policymakers, law enforcement officials, and the general public to take a much broader, more fully comprehensive look at drugs—not just illegal drugs, not just medical-use drugs, but drugs of all sorts. We have talked a lot, and in the process discovered that not only do we sometimes disagree, but that we often disagree not just for personal or political reasons (some of us are liberal, some conservative, some libertarian) but for quite subtle, foundational reasons. Exposing the complexities of such agreements and especially the deeper disagreements will, we believe, be of service to each discipline as well as to policymakers and practitioners attempting to resolve the world's difficulties with drugs. It is for this reason that we decided to write this book.

Our project of exposing and exploring the depth of disciplinary disagreements about drugs has made it imperative to avoid formats that reinforce territorial, discipline-bound approaches to a problem. Perhaps the most problematic of such formats is the collection of conference papers. It isn't that conferences aren't desirable or that interdisciplinary discourse isn't possible; indeed, some volumes of collected papers, whether originating in a conference or not, are extremely useful, like James A. Inciardi and Karen McElrath's *The American Drug Scene* (which includes forty-one authors from an enormous range of fields), or Jefferson Fish's *How to Legalize Drugs* (thirty authors, also from many fields). These collections are invaluable. But when different chapters are written by different authors, each chapter tends to reflect the background assumptions of its author's field, and these assumptions are rarely challenged, let alone brought into real conflict.

To avoid that approach, this book is a multi-authored volume designed to speak with a single, integrative voice. It is, as we said, resolutely interdisciplinary, a monograph rather than a volume of discrete, individual papers. It is the product of a core writing group (the seven authors on the cover) and four additional participants (shown on the title page), as well as a number of others who have made further contributions, also at various times part of the working group. Together, the working group (many of whom double-count) includes two physicians, three lawyers, two pharmacists, three philosophers, two pharmacologists, a medicinal chemist, a psychologist, an anthropologist, and a judge. We have committed ourselves to work together all or almost all the time on this book, and no chapters are exclusively solo authored. It has been a genuine pleasure in the interests of deeper exploration. Though actually written primarily by the seven principal authors, each chapter is in a sense by *all* of us, insofar as each serves to try to reveal the tensions among our various fields and our subtly differing conceptions of the issues that we experience all the time.

Our hope is to display the value of such an integrated approach. The silo mentality manifests itself within disciplines, within government, between government and academia, and between all of these and the public. To be sure, the term itself is in growing disrepute in business lingo, replaced by trendier terms like "bucket" that seem to emphasize inclusiveness and teamwork, but the mentality of exclusive division, separation, noncontact and self-containedness that "silo" suggests—whether thought of as grain elevator or missile launcher—is still very much alive in drug contexts. All this "siloed" communication must be connected or re-connected if anything close to a just approach to drug theory, policy, and practice is to be achieved. After all, academia and its many research centers are typically compartmentalized by drug area—legal pharmaceuticals, alternative medicines, illegal drugs, and so on. Government agencies are also compartmentalized under a congressionally enacted system of different bureaucracies that each set drug policy within a stipulated area. Both are siloed, but in somewhat different ways. Because they speak in different terms and under different background assumptions, it is not always possible for these research centers and agencies to interact adequately among each other to strive for a coherent and comprehensive approach to drug management and regulation. Interaction between policymakers, practitioners, and academia is often starkly polarized, not only by ideological differences but by less obvious conceptual differences. We in the working group hope that this book will contribute to the possibility of bridging such gaps in the interests of consistent, coherent, comprehensive theory, policy, and practice about drugs of all sorts.

The book begins with a short description of the terrain, revealing just how many different aspects of our lives are affected by drugs—illegal drugs, common-use drugs, prescription drugs, sports and religious drugs, as reflected in popular culture. This pervasiveness begins to explain why an "across-the-board" approach is crucial. Chapter 1 highlights the need for attentiveness in detecting inconsistencies both within and between different disciplines to ensure that something as basic as the very terms and concepts in which drug issues are discussed are not being used in subtly but importantly different ways, thus making real communication about drug issues problematic. This is not to say that each discipline should not at times define important drug issues in its own way, but rather that each must be able to understand what the others are saying—how other disciplines approach drug issues, and what their view is from within. Drug issues look quite different when one has in mind prescription drugs rather than illegal drugs, or illegal drugs rather than common-use ones, and while many of the theoretical problems overlap, there are some very real differences. Chapter 1 concludes by identifying three characteristics that any theory, policy, or practice would need to have in order to be considered *just*—consistency, coherence, and comprehensiveness—demonstrating that a conceptually adequate look at drugs must be fully integrative, including the insights of medicine, law, pharmacy, philosophy, psychology, criminology and criminal justice, addiction research, and many other fields. Indeed, an adequate account of drugs must be integrative in two ways: it must look at *all* drugs in all classes, and it must look at them from the perspective of *all* fields that have to do with drugs, in whatever institutional setting those fields call home.

Chapter 2 provides a brief historical account of how drug policy reached the contemporary state of affairs–how it came to be this way. It is a troubling history, riddled with apparent inconsistencies that have their roots in a variety of historical events, including policymaking influenced by racism, xenophobia, and other reactions to political incidents. Chapter 2 also shows the results of this erratic history, identifying the mechanisms currently in place for regulating and controlling drugs.

Chapter 3 contends that advocacy of any specific drug policy must at least implicitly involve arguments about what principle or principles are appropriate bases for drug policy—principles like autonomy, moralism, paternalism, procedural justice, and so on—and what constitutes satisfying these principles and the tensions involved in the underlying assumptions. Here, as elsewhere, we do not attempt to take sides about which principles should govern drug policy, but we do try to sketch the broad alternatives for theoretical frameworks that theoreticians, policymakers, and practitioners should keep in mind when discussing drug issues. The core challenge to the status quo stems from a recognition that different agencies appear to be guided by differing principles about how drugs should be understood and regulated, resulting in seemingly inconsistent policies among them.

The next two chapters use some of the strategies of conceptual analysis to take an in-depth, somewhat technical look at two of the most basic issues in drug theory and policy, "addiction" and "harm." It finds conceptual fissures in each, often undetected splits over what should be included within a concept, what count as its central cases, and where its borders should be drawn. As chapter 4 shows, terms like "addiction" and "dependence" mean one thing in a given area of professional and public discussion, and something subtly but importantly different in another. These variations contribute substantially to difficulties in discourse and action over drugs.

The examination of harm in chapter 5 begins with the ways in which "primitive thinking" about drug-related harm still lingers in current thinking. In particular, this chapter explores the ancient view that it is the drug itself (rather than drug use) that causes harm or is even evil, although virtually every drug has the potential to produce both benefit and harm. For this reason, discussions that focus on drugs themselves are importantly incomplete, and we identify examples of this incompleteness in public discussion. Chapter 5 then focuses on the concept of harm itself, identifying how different institutions—representing different silos of thinking about drugs—do not even agree about what constitutes the harms that drugs can cause, what kinds of harm justify various forms of drug regulation and control, or what saliency the prospect of harm should have vis-à-vis prospective benefits. This lack of agreement persists even though these institutions are all in some sense committed to preventing or reducing the harm caused by drugs. Chapter 5 also recognizes that notions of benefit—the conceptual complement of harm—are even more variously treated. In some areas of drug use, like prescription drugs, benefits are the central focus and harms a comparative side concern; in other areas, like illegal drugs, harms are virtually the sole focus and benefits, if there are any, are not considered at all.

Chapter 6 then poses a series of puzzle cases about drugs that put these conceptual concerns into practice. This chapter is a kind of recreation after the hard work of the previous ones, though the dilemmas it raises are by no means easy to solve.

Finally, chapter 7 harvests the fruits of the explorations in the previous chapters by focusing on specific theoretical, policy, and practical dilemmas that show how and why the uneven, uncertain, unstable conceptual basis for our thinking about drugs exacerbates many of these dilemmas. It poses three scenarios of consistent, coherent, and comprehensive policies at opposite extremes—one an essentially autonomist scenario, the second a medical-model scenario, and the third a comprehensive, super-regulatory one—among which, we conjecture, actual policies will play out. We do not advocate adopting any one of these rather extreme versions of possible policies, but pose them to demarcate the area in between, within which any realistic solution must take place. The risks of disciplinary hyperspecialization loom large, which can only make things worse. We conclude that cross-disciplinary discussion about many basic issues in drugs—for example, self-medication, the use of mind-altering drugs, the prohibition of drug use, enhancement, and pain and pleasure—is essential, and that both enforcement and reform measures must take into account drug concerns across the board.

One may consider what each respective field of thought about drugs can take away from this conceptual exploration—what lessons it can learn. To do so is to put siloed, disciplinarily compartmentalized work in all areas of reflection, policymaking, and practice about drugs on firmer conceptual ground. This project aims to enrich disciplinary specialization, not destroy it, by considering just what the lessons of a fully comprehensive view of drugs might be for each of the fields involved; and we hope that the various fields can begin to listen to what other disciplines have to offer.

As noted, our working group includes philosophers, psychologists, pharmacologists, toxicologists, lawyers, doctors, and a judge: now the question is not so much what the respective disciplines bring to this discussion, but what can each discipline take away? What lessons can the separate disciplines learn from this broader view? Some of these lessons will be rather painful, a series of lessons that may need to be learned by all these fields if movement is to be made in the right kind of direction: toward theory, policy, and practice that is more consistent, more coherent, and more comprehensive. Particularly painful lessons may be in store as we survey the current state of policy about drugs. But in critiquing the seeming array of contradictions that drug policy now involves, this project ultimately aims to encourage the development of drug theory, drug policy, and programs and practices about drugs that can start on the way to becoming more just.

The literatures on drugs are huge. Within them, there have been many distinguished attempts to address drug issues. Examples include Douglas Husak's *Drugs and Rights*, Peter J. Cohen's *Drugs, Addiction, and the Law*, Glen Hanson and Peter Venturelli's *Drugs and Society,* Norman Fost's and Tom Murray's work on sport drugs, work on addiction by a long list of authors, including David Courtwright, Howard Rachlin, George Ainslie, Avram Goldstein, and many others. The best-selling *Illegal Drugs: A Complete Guide to Their History, Chemistry, Use and Abuse* which includes extensive accounts of religious-use drugs, is by Paul Gahlinger, a member of our working group. A number of writers focus on specific drugs: David Courtwright on opium, John Kaplan on heroin, Arnold Trebach on heroin,

Dominic Streatfield on cocaine, Martin Booth on opium. David Musto's historical work is of signal importance in understanding the issues confronted here, as is Steven Duke and Albert Gross's *America's Longest War* and Robert J. MacCoun and Peter Reuter's perceptive *Drug War Heresies,* but like many other volumes that could be mentioned with admiration, these all focus primarily on one aspect of the larger picture we are painting. Of the many think tanks and policy centers that focus on issues in drugs, including impressively interdisciplinary groups like the National Center on Addiction and Substance Abuse at Columbia University, for example, most still focus on one range of drugs or drug concerns. But with very few exceptions, these literatures on drugs are just that—literatures, in the plural—and there is little that examines all areas of drugs in a cohesive way.

We believe that there is not another book quite like this—that is, no book on drugs that has such broad scope, both as a matter of interdisciplinarity but also in the range of drugs it covers. We do not want to replace any of the classic existing works or supplant any of these discussions. Indeed, we admire them for their often extraordinary contributions to the discussion of some very difficult issues, and we want to ensure that other professionals in other silos, as well as other parties concerned with drugs of any sort, actually can and will read them in an open way. In short, we want to see if and how the differing concerns they all address might be examined in a more consistent, coherent, across-the-board way.

We would like to thank a number of people who have contributed in various ways to this project, some in brief ways, some in very sustained ways, but all valuable: Ryan Spellecy, Keri L. Fakata, Darren Bush, Scott Rogers, Mike W. Martin, Bruce Landesman, Leslie Francis, Chrisoula Andreou, Steve Gardiner, Rocky Anderson, Glen R. Hanson, and Charles B. Smith. We are also grateful to our various research and graduate assistants over the years: Mary-Jane Forbyn, Carolyn Wills, Monika Piotrowska, Pepe Chang, Emily Asplund, Diana Buccafurni, Shannon Atkinson, Mark Olsen, and Bethany Rabe.

CONTENTS

CONTRIBUTORS

Prescription Pharmaceuticals and Over-the-Counter Drugs

ARTHUR G. LIPMAN, PharmD: Professor of Pharmacotherapy, College of Pharmacy, Adjunct Professor of Anesthesiology, School of Medicine, Director of Clinical Pharmacology, Pain Management Center, University of Utah Health Sciences Center; Editor, *Journal of Pain & Palliative Care Pharmacotherapy*

Alternative and Complementary Drugs

JEANETTE C. ROBERTS, Ph.D., MPH: Professor of Pharmaceutical Sciences, Dean, School of Pharmacy, University of Wisconsin, Madison

Common-Use Drugs

KELLY J. LUNDBERG, Ph.D.: Clinical Associate Professor of Psychiatry, Director, Assessment and Referral Services, Department of Psychiatry University of Utah

Religious-Use Drugs

PAUL M. GAHLINGER, MD, Ph.D.: Medical Director, Davis County Jail, Farmington, Utah; Adjunct Professor of Family and Preventive Medicine, University of Utah; Author of *Illegal Drugs: A Complete Guide to Their History, Chemistry, Use, and Abuse*

Sports-Enhancement Drugs

DOUGLAS E. ROLLINS, MD, Ph.D.: Professor of Pharmacology and Toxicology, Executive Director, Sports Medicine Research and Testing Laboratory, University of Utah; Medical Director of Doping Control, Winter Olympics 2002

Illegal Drugs

DENNIS M. FUCHS, JD: Judge, ret., Third District Court, State of Utah (includes Third District Drug Court)

KAROL L. KUMPFER, Ph.D.: Professor, Health Promotion and Education, University of Utah; Former Director, Substance Abuse and Mental Health Services Administration, Center for Substance Abuse Prevention, U. S. Department of Health and Human Services

ERIK LUNA, JD: Hugh B. Brown Presidential Endowed Chair in Law and Professor, S. J. Quinney College of Law, University of Utah; Co-Director, Utah Criminal Justice Center, University of Utah College of Law, College of Social and Behavioral Science, and College of Social Work

Philosophy, Bioethics, and Law

MARGARET P. BATTIN, MFA, Ph.D.: Distinguished Professor of Philosophy, Adjunct Professor of Internal Medicine, Division of Medical Ethics and Humanities, University of Utah

TROY L. BOOHER, JD: Attorney, Snell & Wilmer L.L.P., Adjunct Professor, S. J. Quinney College of Law, Adjunct Professor of Political Science, Adjunct Instructor of Philosophy, University of Utah

DAVID G. DICK, Ph.D. (cand.): Department of Philosophy, University of Michigan

DRUGS AND JUSTICE

DRUGS "ACROSS THE BOARD": TOWARD A CONSISTENT, COHERENT, COMPREHENSIVE VIEW IN DRUG THEORY, POLICY, AND PRACTICE

Drugs in Culture and Life

Drugs are everywhere, both figuratively and literally. At any given moment, a large percentage of people nearly everywhere in the world are using one or more drugs as a medical requirement, a lifestyle choice, or to satisfy a desire or an addiction. The consequences of drug use, from prescription pharmaceuticals to illicit substances, are felt on a daily basis by the individual and society at large, and drugs as a topic of discussion or symbol for politics permeate many aspects of virtually every country, everywhere around the globe. Publicly debated issues in recent years have included, among many others:

- steroids in sports
- medical marijuana
- extremely lengthy drug sentences
- undiagnosed and unmedicated mental illness in public and in prison
- legal access to hypodermic syringes and needle-exchange programs
- injury and death resulting from "dietary supplements"
- costs and benefits of specialized drug courts
- efforts to suppress poppy growth in Afghanistan and cocaine production in Latin America
- pharmaceutical controversies surrounding marketing claims versus scientific evidence
- use of over-the-counter drugs like cough medicines as recreational drugs and decongestants as precursors for synthesizing methamphetamines, or as stimulants for sports performance enhancement

- chronic police corruption connected to illegal drugs
- prosecutions for religious use of hallucinogens
- the use of antipsychotics to render criminal defendants competent to stand trial

Such accounts may seem to belong within focused areas of discussion; a story about steroid use in sports falls within the general range of performance-enhancing drug use in athletics, for instance, or an account of clinical trials of antidepressants falls within the apparently quite different area of pharmaceutical drugs. Furthermore, each seemingly distinct area has its own history, literature, and legacy of traditional stories, problems, and legal conundrums. For example, drugs have long been associated with professional sports, whether it was chewing tobacco in baseball or diuretics in horseracing, almost always associated with attempts to enhance performance in the sport. To be sure, not all drugs issues in sports are unique to the arena of athletics—in the United States, Major League Baseball fans will recall famous cases of cocaine addiction, for example, Dodger pitcher Steve Howe in the 1980s and Mets all-stars Dwight Gooden and Darryl Strawberry in the 1990s. But the central issues in sports have involved the use of various drugs to try to boost speed, endurance, strength, or other factors in performance. After baseball sluggers Barry Bonds and Jason Giambi were called before a grand jury investigating illegal distribution of performance-enhancing drugs and former player José Conseco revealed rampant steroid use in his tell-all book *Juiced*, the House Government Reform Committee summoned baseball commissioner Bud Selig and a handful of major league stars to testify before Congress about steroids in America's national pastime. This investigation and analogs in other professional and Olympic sports are only part of the most recent chapter in a long history of drug use in sports aimed at a distinctive purpose: to enhance performance in competition and thereby provide the player or team an edge.

Some drugs are seen as "recreational" (also described as "street," "club," and "party" drugs, as well as "drugs of abuse"), a term applied to various illegal drugs used primarily to produce altered psychological states. Recreational drug use also has a long and colorful, though often tragic, history. Widespread drug use in this general category has included the psychedelics of the youth counterculture in the 1960s and 1970s, the reckless, sometimes conspicuous consumption of cocaine in the 1970s and

1980s, the "crack epidemic" of the 1980s, the emergence of "heroin chic" in the 1990s, and the "meth epidemic" of the early 2000s. Recreational drug use is often portrayed in popular culture and music. For example, probably the best known musical cliché of recent decades was "sex, drugs, and rock' n' roll," while the *Billboard* charts have been filled with songs involving drugs, such as Eric Clapton's *Cocaine* or the Rolling Stones' *Sister Morphine* and *Mother's Little Helper.*[1] Popular culture portrays not just recreational drug use but tragedy associated with drugs, for example, the deaths of guitarist Jimi Hendrix (possibly suicide, but most likely overdose), singers Janis Joplin (accidental heroin overdose) and Jim Morrison (heroin and alcohol), actor River Phoenix (GHB), Kurt Cobain (probably suicide, but possibly overdose), the rapper O.D.B. (cocaine and tramadol), and, always the king, Elvis Presley (prescription drug abuse, the entire pharmacy).

In an ostensibly different category, common-use legal drugs, especially alcohol and tobacco, are also a staple of modern culture, portrayed in films from Secret Agent 007's vodka martini, "shaken, not stirred," to the seemingly artful cigarette smoking of movie icons such as Humphrey Bogart, James Dean, and the entire "Rat Pack," to the suicidal alcoholism of *Leaving Las Vegas.* A number of famous actors, musicians, and writers have had their alcohol problems or alcohol-related deaths played out in public: Led Zeppelin drummer John Bonham, Truman Capote, Bix Beiderbecke, Errol Flynn, Billie Holliday, and Dylan Thomas, for instance. No one has tallied the sports heroes, musicians, and actors and actresses who have died from the effects of tobacco smoking, though the number of deaths among the U.S. population at large is estimated at 400,000 a year. This statistic likely underestimates the damage caused by cigarettes, given the now-established harm caused by second-hand smoke.[2]

Of course, not all common-use drugs are understood as dangerous or associated with tragedy. Coca-Cola is touted as the ubiquitous American drink, and while coca has been replaced as the principal active ingredient, Coke still delivers a drug, caffeine, that can be habit-forming or,

---

1. The "helper" was most likely prescription secobarbital, a favorite of many in the entertainment industry and general population at the time, a small yellow tablet used for anti-anxiety: *"Although she's not really ill, there's a little yellow pill…."*

2. "New Surgeon General's Report Focuses on the Effects of Secondhand Smoke." June 27, 2006. http://www.hhs.gov/news/press/2006pres/20060627.html.

on some accounts, addictive (a point discussed in chapter 4). So-called "energy drinks," the fastest-growing sector of the U.S. domestic beverage industry, are associated with health and performance, but may also be habit-forming or even addictive. As a November 2005 headline in the *New York Times* asked, "A Jolt of Caffeine, By the Can—Energy Drinks Are the Rage, But Are Some Youths Hooked?"[3] In yet another category, religious-use drugs appear to occupy a relatively separate sphere of concern. From an anthropological perspective, religious-use drugs, largely but not exclusively hallucinogens, can be seen as serving important symbolic functions and have been ritually utilized almost everywhere throughout history and across virtually all societies. For millennia, drug ingestion has been a key aspect of life in many indigenous groups and is still considered crucial in various ceremonies—for example, in Native American tribal worship, consumption of peyote and tobacco can be a means of achieving heightened spirituality. Some see this pattern repeated across the globe in "civilized" societies; for example, many Christian churches employ wine as a key sacrament during religious services, and wine is central to Jewish observance as a symbol of joy. Other drugs used in religious contexts include ayahuasca, bufotenine, marijuana, dimethyltriptamine, LSD, ibogaine, and coca.

Occupying what may seem to be a still different sphere of concern about drugs are substances touted as health aids, including herbal remedies and alternative medicines. These are referred to as "dietary supplements," but they are also variously known as nutritional supplements and "neutraceuticals." Together with chiropractic, acupuncture, and homeopathy, they form the majority of what is called Complementary and Alternative Medicine (CAM). Herbal remedies are sold in health food and general nutrition stores for a large range of ailments, from liver dysfunction to constipation, and for health enhancement of all sorts, from softer, smoother skin to increased sexual prowess. While some of these preparations are innocuous in the sense of having virtually no pharmacologic activity, others are comparatively potent drugs marketed as "dietary supplements" available without restriction to any purchaser.

---

3. Melanie Warner, "A Jolt of Caffeine, By the Can," *New York Times*, November 23, 2005, C1.

Finally, though certainly not least in scope or importance, there is the drug sphere that involves pharmaceutical compounds developed primarily for medical treatment, health maintenance, and preventive health purposes. These include medications in many different dosage forms that are produced by manufacturers ranging from huge multinational firms (often called "Big Pharma") to smaller, specialized compounding firms, which then produce or recompound drugs tailored to a smaller market or to individual needs. The world of medical drugs is immense—but, as will be explored, not entirely distinct from the worlds of drugs used in social settings, self-treatment and health promotion settings, sports, religion, and clandestine pleasure.

Drugs used in sports, religion, medical settings, social settings, and illegal recreational contexts have tended to be discussed in different areas or professional spheres. That is part of the problem we wish to explore. It is not the only problem that makes it difficult to think consistently and coherently about drugs—other conceptual fissures will be discussed as well—but the compartmentalization of drug issues is a major, primary concern, what is sometimes called "silo thinking."

"Silo Thinking"

Careful scrutiny of contemporary drug theory, policy, and practice in all areas, from prescription pharmaceuticals to illegal recreational drugs, reveals numerous apparent inconsistencies and pervasive incoherence. This results, in part, from a kind of silo thinking in which attention to drug theory and drug policy, however sophisticated in its own realm, is encapsulated within distinct professional, practical, and economic spheres or "silos." Silos are descriptively and prescriptively dense but stand isolated from each other in an empty landscape. In other words, people in one area of drug theory, policy, or practical programs have plenty to say to each other about the way things are and the way things should be with respect to drugs, but they don't talk much across the open spaces between their areas of focus. Not only do they not talk much between their fields, for reasons to be explored, they *cannot* really do so.

This silo mentality of compartmentalized thinking may indeed result, in part, from the erratic way in which drug policy has developed over the years, a history to be sketched in the next chapter. It may also be the natural tendency of experts and sophisticated professionals in any field to talk primarily with each other, to address the concerns central in one's own field, to rely on the data assembled within that field, and to grant the conceptual assumptions fundamental to that field. However, the silo phenomenon is a dangerous one in an area as volatile and politically charged as drug theory, policy, and practice. Despite attempts to replace the negative "silo" image with more inclusive metaphors like "bucket," silo remains the more accurate metaphor for the compartmentalization still prevalent in thinking about drugs.

Consider the recent debate over the relationship between federal drug laws and the medical use of marijuana. Some of it involves medical and scientific questions: *Is marijuana more effective than prescription drugs in relieving certain patients' symptoms?* Some of it involves predictive psychosocial questions: *Does marijuana use lead to the use of other, arguably more serious, drugs?* Some of it involves value-laden questions: *Is marijuana harmful to the person who uses it, or to others, or to society as a whole?* To untangle this debate, it is vital not only that legal, psychological, sociological, scientific, clinical, and epidemiological professionals communicate, but that those experts within the various drug silos—those who focus on prescription drugs, those who focus on common-use drugs, and those who focus on illegal drugs—all understand one another, wherever it leads. As will be discussed, an erratic history of policy development has contributed to silo thinking, and this in turn reinforces the erratic pattern of policies that has arisen. As a result, it is difficult for drug experts in one area, such as prescription pharmaceuticals, to talk clearly with drug experts in other areas, such as common-use and illegal drugs—so difficult, in fact, that real resolution cannot easily be achieved. It is this resolution-thwarting cycle with respect to drugs that needs to be challenged.

This book urges a broad, synoptic look at the full range of theory, policy, and practice surrounding pharmacologically active substances—not just illicit drugs or medical-use drugs, but the full spectrum of drugs. These include:

- Prescription pharmaceuticals
- Over-the-counter drugs
- Alternative medicines and dietary supplements
- Common socially used drugs (alcohol, tobacco, caffeine)

- Religious-use drugs (e.g., peyote and ayahuasca)
- Sports-enhancement drugs
- Illegal recreational (street, club, and party) drugs

In addressing these different types of drugs and the ways in which they are used (and abused), practitioners, investigators, and scholars within each discipline read different literatures, focus on different practical dilemmas, and operate under different assumptions about the very reason for theoretical discussion and practical policy construction. They employ distinct conceptions of foundational terms like "harm" and "addiction." Certainly there are some areas of overlap, but generally there is little cross-fertilization and cross-critique among the various professional and practical spheres—the independent silos—within which drug issues and policy are confronted and defined.

What is distinctive about the inquiry proposed here is the very broad view it takes in explaining this topic and the way it explores issues of justice with respect to drugs. This inquiry is framed as an interdisciplinary search for ways to make current drug theory, policy, and practice more consistent, coherent, and comprehensive; this is prerequisite to the development of just theory and just policy. It is *justice* in drug matters that is the goal—admittedly, an aspiration not easily achieved, and indeed, one that past historical patterns speak against. Yet both theory and policy, as well as the practices that follow from them, could clearly be far more just than they are now, and in charting a course and supplying some of the groundwork for moving in this direction, we hope to take steps—necessary, indispensable steps—toward that goal.

Basic Criteria for Justice in Drug Theory, Policy, and Practice

Justice, it can be asserted, should be a primary concern of any drug management or control policy, an integral aspect of the theory of drug abuse, and a primary consideration in medical drug access and use. The role of justice is to balance competing interests in an equitable way. However, much of current drug theory and policy as well as practice lacks three necessary (but perhaps insufficient) criteria that would jointly contribute to the possibility of justice: consistency, coherence, and comprehensiveness.

Consistency describes a relation between statements or, in practical applications, between policies, rationales for policies, and the like—specifically, whether they contradict one another. Inconsistency appears to be at work when some drug-related crimes carry harsher punishment than others and yet involve substances that do not seem to warrant the difference, for example, or when drugs designated as dietary supplements are exempt from the laws and regulations that pertain to medical drugs, even though they are marketed with health-related claims.

Coherence describes the relationship among a group of statements or claims, requiring not only that they be consistent but also that they properly relate to each other, that they be involved in the same dialogue, and that they be mutually supporting. A coherent theory is one that "hangs together," more or less, as it is analyzed and applied. For example, the very classification of a substance as a "dietary supplement" rather than a "drug" may raise issues of coherence, as this classification involves at least these two broad areas of practice and policy and raises the issue of whether this separate categorization contributes to, or detracts from, a coherent policy.

Comprehensiveness describes the proper scope of theory and policy—in particular, whether the theory or policy is too narrow or too broad, as is evident in many accounts of theories and policies concerning drugs altogether. Indeed, even some definitions of the term *drug* itself may undermine rather than contribute to overall comprehensiveness. For instance, defining "drug" as a substance that is used in the "cure, mitigation, prevention, or treatment of a disease in man or other animals, with the exception of foods," would be both too broad and too narrow. Although water, for example, is neither a food nor a drug, it is essential and often prescribed as rehydration to help treat dangerous medical conditions, and the production of bottled water and "natural" water is regulated.

Consider some of the often-discussed apparent failures of consistency and coherence, indeed of injustice, in recent and current drug policy in the United States:

- Some crimes involving crack cocaine receive harsher penalties than similar offenses involving powder cocaine, where similarity is based on the drugs' virtually identical chemical structure and the possession or distribution of the same amount of each drug. Under federal statute, for instance, an individual must possess 500 grams of powder cocaine in order to trigger a five-year mandatory minimum sentence, while someone who possesses only 5 grams of crack cocaine receives the same obligatory sentence.[4]

- For a number of years, federal law counted the weight of the carrier medium impregnated with LSD in determining the applicable sentencing range. A first-time offender caught selling 100 doses of LSD in sugar cubes received a sentence of 188–235 months, but if the offender had sold the stash on blotter paper, which is not as heavy, the punishment would have decreased to 63–78 months. If the offender had sold the LSD in gelatin capsules, the sentence would have been 27–33 months—and if it were sold in pure form, the term would have been just 10–16 months.[5] In each scenario, the amount of intoxicant was the same, yet the length of imprisonment changed.[6] The vehicle and the dosage form can affect the time to onset and maximum effect, but do not affect the mechanism of action of the drug.

- In the world of elite Olympic athletes, the first violation of the prohibition against use of anabolic steroids may result in a one-year suspension and a second violation a lifetime suspension. For professional football players in the National Football League, at least as of 2006, the first violation results in a four-game suspension and thus allows a player to continue to compete during that year.

- According to national surveys, it is about as easy for a high school student to obtain illegal drugs as it is to obtain alcohol. Ironically, of course, the law will allow her to purchase alcohol in just a couple of years but will never permit her to buy or possess the other drugs.[7]

---

4. See 21 U.S.C. § 841(b)(1)(B). At the time this book was going to press, the U.S. Sentencing Commission once again recommended "modifications to the statutory penalties for crack cocaine offenses" and "prompt congressional action addressing the 100-to-1 crack-powder drug quantity ratio." See "U.S. Sentencing Commission Votes to Amend Guidelines," April 27, 2007, available at http://www.ussc.gov/PRESS/rel0407.htm; also see chapter 7.

5. See *Chapman v. United States*, 500 U.S. 453, 458 n.2 (1991).

6. The U.S. Sentencing Commission eventually changed the relevant sentencing rule to limit the carrier medium's effect on sentences for LSD-related crimes. See *U.S. Sentencing Guidelines Manual* § 2D1.1 (application note).

7. 2003 *Sourcebook of Criminal Justice Statistics* 173 tbls. 2.83 & 2.84, available at http://www.albany.edu/sourcebook/pdf/t283.pdf; http://www.albany.edu/sourcebook/pdf/t284.pdf.

- A person from Maine with Micmac Indian ancestry is permitted to use peyote for religious reasons, though it grows at least 2,000 miles away, while a non-Native sacramental user of the substance living in Texas, who may have peyote growing on his property, would be prohibited from consumption.
- In some states, carisoprodol (Soma, the muscle relaxant) is listed as Schedule IV controlled substance.[8] Under federal law, however, it is not a controlled substance, although the active metabolite of carisprodol, meprobamate, is a federal Schedule IV controlled substance.
- There are sometimes stunning differences in drug punishment across and within various jurisdictions. At the low end of the punishment spectrum, for instance, Colorado makes possession of less than one ounce of marijuana a petty offense subject to a $100 fine. In New York, possession of up to 25 grams of marijuana is a civil (rather than criminal) violation. In the middle range, possession of under an ounce of marijuana in Utah is a misdemeanor punishable by no more than 6 months in jail, but cultivation of marijuana is a felony with the possibility of up to 5 years imprisonment. Under this latter scheme, moving marijuana from your garden to your pocket reduces your risk from a felony conviction and prison term to, in all likelihood, a fine. At the upper end of the punishment spectrum, for instance, Montana allows the theoretical possibility of a life sentence for producing more than a pound of marijuana or more than thirty plants.

On their face, then, the disparate results in these examples seem blatantly unjust—they do not appear to treat like cases alike, as the basic Aristotelian principle of justice would demand. Such cases suggest the problems involved in ascertaining whether policies and claims made in the defense of policies are consistent, whether they could fit together within a coherent picture, and whether all relevant cases are considered. Above all, they challenge our conceptions of justice in dealing with drugs of all sorts.

Part of the objective in this project, then, is to identify apparent inconsistencies in talk and policy about drugs, and to show what would be involved in developing a coherent body of theory and policy about drugs that is comprehensive—that is, one that covers all drugs, across the board.

8. See, e.g., Ga. Code Ann. § 16–13–28.

The apparent inconsistencies that abound in theory and policy about drugs provide the starting place, the irritant, so to speak, that provokes this inquiry, though some of these inconsistencies may turn out to be justified while others may not. The real challenge for those in every field of concern about drugs is to see how these considerations might be blended into a coherent whole. This is not an easy task, and neither a complete theory of drugs nor another candidate for a comprehensive drug policy will be offered here; many have been advanced in the already enormous literature on drugs. Rather, the central idea of this project is to look at the underpinnings of apparent inconsistencies, of what would be required for coherence, and what it would take to make drug theory and policy genuinely comprehensive. Doing this is a small step toward the ultimate goal, contributing to greater justice in theory and policy about drugs.

Of course, this leads to a fundamental objection: Are consistency, coherence, and comprehensiveness really desirable in drug theory and policy? Examples and anecdotes such as those cited above illustrate a few simple ways in which drug policy lacks these characteristics. But why should anyone care? It is not obvious, one might argue, that having a drug policy that is more consistent, coherent, and comprehensive is thereby better and more just than the current policy. Given limits of resources and knowledge, society might for instance choose to prohibit a number of risky substances, maybe regulate some substances, and allow market forces to control still others. All of this might be a result of some criteria like perceived harm, or historical development, or sheer happenstance. And perhaps this is acceptable, given that, for example, the harm principle doesn't require prohibition, it just permits it.

Or consider another sort of objection to the claim that drug theory, policy, and practice ought to be consistent, coherent, and comprehensive. Imagine, for example, the following simple hypothetical situation: *All drugs become legal and available over-the-counter.* What was once kept behind the counter and available only with a prescription is now displayed in the aisles—cholesterol-reducing statin drugs next to sunblock, for instance, and antibiotics and amphetamines next to antacids. Not only would the "counter" be removed, but additional drugs also would be available, such as marijuana and heroin. Of course, the neighborhood pharmacy would have to close for several months for remodeling, but when all is complete, formerly prescription-only drugs will have been brought out from behind the counter and street drugs will have been brought indoors. Such a policy certainly is consistent, coherent, and comprehensive—it treats all drugs the same, it is easy to understand, and it applies equally to all drugs however defined. Yet in all likelihood, such a drug policy would be deemed indefensible by many, if not most, parties. So would its contrary, that *no drugs would be legal or available over-the-counter, by* ℞ *or any other way.* It is important to remember that simply adhering to consistency, coherence, and comprehensiveness as guiding values may not by itself lead to better drug policy, one that has greater practical value or, for that matter, any political chance of being adopted. Thus, it is necessary to identify other principles that should guide decision-making, articulating why it is a criticism, not a mere observation, to charge a policy with lacking consistency, coherence, or comprehensiveness.

This, in turn, requires a more detailed examination of each of these criteria. First, however, it is necessary to provide some conception of what is being talked about—what is a drug, anyway?—which will provide a foundation for assessing these criteria.

What Counts as a Drug and Where Does a Drug Count? A Policy View

Not only does talk about drugs vary widely from one sphere or "silo" to another, but the definition of "drug," especially as used in policy contexts, itself may exhibit inconsistencies. The term is often value laden and means different things to different people and within different professional spheres, for example, law and medicine.[9] The origin of the word is from the Old French *drogue,* which came from the Middle Dutch *druge vate,* "dried" or "dry-vat," perhaps referring to dried plant medicinals. Some people equate "drugs" with "medicines," whereas others consider drugs as "bad" and medicines as "good" or offer a similar dichotomous caricature. Although not necessarily justifiable, these differences may be completely understandable. Are drugs good? Physicians prescribe drugs to cure or ameliorate illness, and the drug industry that develops and manufactures

---

9. Husak provides a very useful account of medical and legal definitions of drugs as well as of characterizations of drugs used in other contexts. Douglas N. Husak, *Drugs and Rights* (Cambridge: Cambridge University Press, 1992), 19–27.

these prescription drugs is one of the largest, most profitable, and important segments of the U.S. and global market. Yet at the same time, children are taught that drugs are bad through programs such as Drug Abuse Resistance Education (DARE) and nationwide public-relations campaigns aimed at reductions in substance abuse; they are taught to *"just say no to drugs."* Recognizing these differences in perceived meanings of the term "drug," clinicians today are often advised to use the words "medicine" or "medication" rather than "drug" when describing therapeutic substances, under the assumption that the negative connotations of the term "drug" can decrease patient adherence to prescribed medication regimens. Drug manufacturers speak of themselves as the "pharmaceutical industry," perhaps to distance themselves from another highly lucrative drug industry, the illegal one, that also flourishes in the United States and around the world. Whether a therapeutic agent is "medicinal" is often controversial and contentious, and a distinction that attempts to differentiate between compounds that are "curative" and those that compensate for "biological deficiencies" also will often be challenged.

Complicating matters further, the official definition of the term "drug" varies among nations and even within a given country. In the United States, the term "drug" is defined in the first instance by the federal government and, derivatively, by organizations such as the United States Pharmacopoeia (USP), an independent body of health professionals. The USP publishes the United States Pharmacopoeia–National Formulary (USP-NF), a primary resource on drug standards in the United States. The USP-NF defines drugs as:

1. substances recognized in the official U.S. Pharmacopoeia;
2. substances intended for use in the diagnosis, cure, mitigation, treatment, or prevention of disease in humans or other animals;
3. substances (other than food) intended to affect the structure or any function of the bodies of humans or other animals; or
4. substances intended for use as a component of any substances specified in (1), (2), or (3) above, but does not include devices or their components, parts, or accessories.

Certainly, there is a degree of circularity in these definitions: "drugs" are classified by the USP as those substances recognized as "drugs" in the USP. And although most U.S. jurisdictions adopt terms mirroring those used by the federal government, legal terms may differ from state to state, as each jurisdiction has the power to define for itself what will or will not be deemed a drug (or type of drug) for purposes of its laws.

Not only is there no one universally accepted definition of the word "drug," it is also difficult to categorize drugs in a reasonable way. Where should a particular drug count in a classificatory scheme that serves as a basis for policy? Inconsistent drug classifications within an incoherent classificatory system may seem to be a fertile source of injustice in drug policy. But it may also (or instead) be the case that differing classificatory systems are inconsistent with each other, although internally more or less consistent and coherent. Mapping out the various classification systems and their internal categories is a major project in seeking greater justice in drug matters, and it is by no means obvious that an overall classification system that avoids internal inconsistencies and is a coherent whole can be devised.

In the United States today, as will be explored in greater detail in chapters 2 and 3, many legally manufactured and distributed drugs are tightly regulated, while other drugs, including dietary supplements and herbal remedies, are virtually exempt from regulation. Drugs may be regulated under the prescription legend, as controlled substances, as dietary supplements, under special laws for alcohol and tobacco, and within particular regulations for competitive sports. These regulatory schema are overlapping: an individual drug may be included in more than one regulatory scheme. For example, dextroamphetamine is a prescription drug, a controlled substance, a banned substance in certain sports, and allowed in some herbal substances in its analogue form.

Many substances with abuse potential—including numerous drugs—are assigned to one or more of five different controlled substance schedules under the federal Controlled Substances Act of 1970. Schedule I controlled substances (C-I) are those determined to have no legitimate medical application and they can only be used legally under approved experimental protocols. Drugs in Schedules II through IV (C-II, C-III, and C-IV) are largely prescription pharmaceuticals for which there is evidence of abuse potential. Schedule V controlled substance drugs (C-V) are largely non-prescription agents, for which it is presumed that there is little or no abuse potential.

Dietary supplements are an especially curious category. They are not officially categorized as drugs and by statute are exempted from regulation applying to drugs (though they are often popularly called "herbal drugs" or "natural drugs"). Yet dietary supplements are recognized as pharmacologically active substances that can be called "natural remedies" to promote, for example, "immune health." Nor do alcohol, caffeine, and tobacco consistently fall under the same regulatory schema, and they are not understood in the same way as other drugs. From a policy point of view, alcohol is a common-use drug and not a controlled substance. More precisely, ethanol and methanol are defined as drugs in the USP-NF but are regulated by separate agencies that do not treat them as "drugs" but instead as sources of taxation, as will be discussed in chapters 2 and 3. The frequent policy expression "alcohol and drug abuse" is accurate in referring to two distinguishable forms of substance abuse from one point of view, but redundant from another.

The USP definition of "drug" does not include substances that have not yet been accepted as such by medical authorities. In effect, this means that these substances have not been approved for use as medications by the federal Food and Drug Administration. The substances are treated as a special class of agents under investigation, defining them as "new drugs." They cannot be prescribed or used legally in humans except under specific clinical protocols that meet stringent criteria for safety and require informed consent, which then permits a special investigational license, known as an "investigational new drug exemption" (IND). This exempts the experimental agent from the new drug restrictions for purposes of the specific protocol. Once the clinical research has been completed under the IND, the sponsor files a New Drug Application (NDA) with the federal Food and Drug Administration. When the FDA approves the application, the agent is no longer a "new drug" and instead is licensed for human use as a drug.

Some substances—alcohol, nicotine, and caffeine, for example—are inconsistently defined as drugs in the federal code despite having many of the same properties as substances that are classified as controlled substances. Some substances (like ephedrine) are classified as prescription drugs if they go through the FDA approval process, while the same substance is exempt from approval and review as a drug when marketed as a dietary supplement (such as ephedra, an herb with the active substance ephedrine)—that is, unless there is evidence of exceptional risk to society. Furthermore, the same substance can be readily obtainable as a plant product (e.g., the ephedra in ma-huang or "Mormon Tea"). Consider also heroin, which, when injected or ingested by humans, is metabolized within minutes into morphine. In the United Kingdom, heroin is a legal pharmaceutical drug known as diamorphine, prescribed by physicians as a strong pain reliever. In the United States, however, heroin in an illegal Schedule I controlled substance with no accepted medical use, but morphine is a widely used Schedule II controlled substance useful in treating pain and terminal dyspnea.

Furthermore, the numbered rankings of the Schedule's classifications raise questions as to whether, for instance, the disparate classification of marijuana (Schedule I) versus cocaine (Schedule II) proves meaningful or instead remains as a historical artifact and ongoing political artifice. It could be argued that this arrangement is plausible because cocaine has legitimate medical uses, especially in nasal surgery, but marijuana is not currently recognized by the federal government to have medical uses; or it could also be argued that it is inaccurate in that at least one of these drugs is misclassified or that the bases of classification (e.g., "potential for abuse") are misguided.

Needless to say, the term *drug* is both complex and relentlessly normative. Thus one obvious source of inconsistency and silo thinking about drug theory and drug policy arises from the inability to provide a single, robust account of exactly what constitutes a drug in the first place, or where specific drugs belong in a classificatory scheme. Clarifying these terms, concepts, and classificatory schemes, or at least delineating when and why different versions are being used, is an indispensable task in developing more just drug theory and drug policy.

The Role of the English Language

It is also important to recognize the role of the English language in facilitating this inquiry. English uses the term "drug" ubiquitously and colloquially for all the categories of substances we are examining across the board, from prescription drugs to over-the-counter drugs to herbal drugs to religious-use drugs to sports-enhancement drugs to illegal drugs. The only exception is that alcohol, tobacco, and caffeine are less likely in colloquial English to be spoken of as "drugs" or as "common-use drugs," though this way of labeling them is not resisted. In using the term "drug" so broadly, English makes the inquiry we are conducting plausible from a conceptual level as well as from a pharmacological point of view—English-speakers are accustomed to referring to all these substances as drugs.

In contrast, this inquiry will seem more difficult conceptually in many other languages. Dutch, for example, has no word for "drug" that is used across the board; it uses *drog* only for illegal drugs, subdividing them into "hard drugs" (e.g., heroin) and "soft drugs" (e.g., marijuana). Dutch uses *medicijn* (from the French, *médecine*) for pharmaceutical drugs or *Geneesmeddel*, literally "healing substances." Most languages involved in Olympic sports use the term "doping" (a term from South Africa) for sports-enhancement drugs; the United States adopted this term at a comparatively late point. German uses *Droge* ("drug") and also *Rauschgifte* ("narcotics" or "drugs," from a root meaning "intoxication" or "elation-poisons") for illegal drugs, *Genussmittel* (literally "enjoyment substances") for common-use drugs, *Medizin* for prescription and over-the-counter drugs, and *Kräutermedizin* ("herb medications") for herbal drugs. Mandarin Chinese uses the very negative term 毒品 *du pin* ("poisonous item") for illegal drugs, including opium, heroin, and marijuana. It uses 药品 *yao pin* ("medical item") for medicinal drugs, including drugs similar to Western prescription drugs. It should be noted that China does not have a full-fledged prescription legend system; while some drugs can be bought only in a hospital, many drugs that are prescription legend in the United States can be bought on the open market in China, much as over-the-counter and dietary supplements are in the United States. Chinese uses 兴奋剂 *xing fen ji* ("stimulating item") or sometimes 违禁药品 *wei jin yao pin* ("illegal medical item") for sports-enhancement drugs.

Thus the inquiry pursued here would be more difficult to envision and to carry out in Dutch, German, Chinese, or many other languages than in English. That the term "drug" is not used across the board in many languages may help avoid some underlying confusion in those languages, but it does not facilitate comprehensive inquiry of the sort conducted here. For better or worse, however, even the English language is changing in this area. Physicians now frequently use "medication" rather than "drug" to avoid the value-laden connotations of the term "drug"; OTC drugs are referred to as "medications," and herbal drugs are called "remedies" and many other terms. Nonetheless, all pharmacologically active substances will be referred to here under the broad English language heading of "drugs."

Justice in Drug Theory, Policy, and Practice

Formulation of the basic principle of justice is traditionally attributed to Aristotle. In its purely formal understanding, the principle of justice requires that one *treat like cases alike*. This basic principle identifies all three of the requirements of consistency, coherence, and comprehensiveness as prerequisites for justice in drug policy: what is done in a specific case must not contradict what is done in a relevantly similar case; what counts as like and unlike cases must "fit together" in a coherent account or system, and all relevant cases must be considered. But what makes Aristotle's principle intuitively appealing—the fact that it applies to all cases— also makes it unhelpful in practice. It is so abstract as to not provide much guidance in real-world, applied matters, and it gives no guidance about the scope of the problem.

Consider an example cited earlier: the hundred-fold difference in sentences for the same quantity of powder cocaine and crack cocaine appears inconsistent because they are merely different forms of the very same drug with the same active ingredient. Presumably, a drug policy will be consistent only if it treats both substances alike, given their largely indistinguishable chemical composition, as demanded by the basic Aristotelian principle of justice. Yet this does not directly follow, as the two forms of cocaine may differ significantly in relevant respects despite their chemical similarity. For instance, perhaps one form is (1) linked to more violent criminal behavior, (2) linked generally to greater social harms, or (3) more widely available and thus a greater threat. If so, then it might be perfectly consistent to treat them differently despite their chemical similarity. In fact, this is the precise type of reasoning that has led courts to find disparate sentences justified. For example, in 1990 the Eighth Circuit concluded that the difference is not "arbitrary or irrational" because "[m]embers of Congress considered cocaine base to be more dangerous to society than cocaine because of crack's potency, its highly addictive nature, its affordability, and its increasing prevalence."[10] On this point, the court quoted the claim made by one U.S. Senator in support of the 100-to-1 ratio:

> Because crack is so potent, drug dealers need to carry much smaller quantities of crack than of cocaine powder. By treating 1,000 grams of [freebase] cocaine no more seriously than 1,000 grams of cocaine powder, which is far less powerful than freebase, current law provides a loophole that actually encourages drug dealers to sell the more deadly and addictive substance, and lets them sell thousands of doses without facing the maximum penalty possible.[11]

But why is such reasoning just? This same conclusion would not seem defensible if, for instance, crack turned out to be sold more on Tuesday and powder cocaine on Thursday. In other words, not all differences justify different treatment. Until it is known what makes two cases relevantly alike or relevantly different, there is little use for the principle of justice that requires like treatment of like cases and different treatment of different cases.

One type of consistency, *internal consistency*, can help locate these relevancy criteria. For a policy to be internally consistent, it must not frustrate its own stated purpose in its application. If the stated purpose of making certain drugs illegal is to protect the user from the drug, then treating crack and powder cocaine differently seems internally inconsistent, given their chemical equivalence and similar biological effects. However, if the stated purpose is more specifically to protect the urban poor from dangerous substances, and impoverished city dwellers are found to gravitate toward crack cocaine instead of the powder form, then there is no internal inconsistency in treating the two drugs differently. Similar comparisons can be made between distilled alcohol, wine, and beer and their occasionally disparate treatment, or among various types of over-the-counter and prescription analgesics.

Internal consistency is the easiest type to identify because the subject matter provides the relevancy criteria—the stated purpose—by which to test for consistency, but it rarely is helpful when analyzing drug policy. Often, a policy's stated purpose is precisely what is deemed objectionable when it is claimed that a drug policy is inconsistent.

---

10. *United States v. Buckner*, 894 F.2d 975, 978–79 (8th Cir. 1990).

11. Id. at 979 [quoting Sen. Alfonse D'Amato, 132 Cong. Rec. S8092 (daily ed. June 20, 1986)].

Consider, for example, a drug policy that has as its stated purpose the eradication of "addiction." The appropriateness of this purpose, as well as its achievement by the policy, will depend crucially on the selected understanding of this term. If the notion of *addiction* is informed by the diagnostic manual used by psychiatrists and psychologists to provide uniform criteria for mental illness—currently, the fourth edition, text-revised, of the American Psychiatric Association's *Diagnostic and Statistical Manual* (the DSM-IV-TR), which, as will be discussed in chapter 4, takes addiction intrinsically to involve harm to its subject—then the rationale for eliminating addiction will be obvious, with the purpose of a policy intended to reduce addiction fulfilled when harmful, compulsive behaviors have subsided. However, if the notion of addiction is informed by theorists like Graham Oddie[12]—who take addiction to be a formal relation characterized by a subject's compulsive and sometimes uncontrollable desire to seek and engage in his addiction, be it work, exercise, or heroin—then the rationale for eliminating addiction is not obvious, since harm is not a necessary part of addiction. An advocate of this second notion may find internally inconsistent a drug theory or policy that classifies uncontrollable, harmful habits differently than uncontrollable, beneficial habits. As a result, any disagreement between each type of theorist over the consistency of current drug policy on addiction is likely to be about whose (or what) criteria should be used to judge consistency.

This makes it clear that an in-depth examination of drug theory and policy must also explore whose (or what) criteria to use to judge consistency in any given circumstance. In other words, the search for consistency in drug policy is at least partially a search for rationales or values that *should* shape drug policy in the given circumstances, not simply descriptive claims about whether contradictions exist. Thus the question is which (apparent) inconsistencies are justified by a more general appropriate principle, and which are not. Trying to answer this question is part and parcel of what it means to pursue justice in the area of drug theory and drug policy. Because this subject matter affects so many different spheres, the search requires engagement in an interdisciplinary dialogue. Knowing that crack and powder cocaine are chemically similar only *begins* the

12. Graham Oddie, "Addiction and the Value of Freedom," *Bioethics* 7(5)(1993): 373–401.

discussion, and it still is necessary to determine whether there exists an inconsistency that demands attention after a fully informed, multiperspective analysis of the issue.

A just theory and policy must also be coherent, otherwise it is not really intelligible as either a theory or policy. Coherence requires not only that a theory or policy be consistent, but also that its parts all relate to each other, that they are involved in the same dialogue, and that they are mutually supporting. In other words, a coherent theory or policy hangs together in such a way that its rationale is apparent and easily evaluated. Coherence is desirable for all the reasons consistency is desirable, but developing a coherent drug policy requires a deeper inquiry into the types of rationales that should shape drug policy.

To illustrate apparent incoherence in drug policy, consider another example mentioned earlier, ephedra, a substance derived from plants containing ephedrine. Under the Dietary Supplement Health and Education Act of 1994 (DSHEA), ephedra is classified as a "dietary supplement" and thus largely removed from FDA regulation, even though ephedrine has been—and still is—available as a prescription drug. By 2004, it had come to light that ephedra had been associated with a number of fatalities. It was redescribed as a "dangerous" drug that can be abused, and the FDA initiated legal action that led to the withdrawal of ephedra from the market—though only after a professional athlete died, Baltimore Orioles pitcher Steve Bechler. That action was overruled in 2005 by a federal trial court decision. Ephedra was again marketed as a dietary supplement without much governmental oversight, while pharmaceutical manufacturers continued to market ephedrine in accordance with the stringent FDA requirements for a prescription pharmaceutical—same drug, very different package. In 2006, however, a federal appellate court ruled for the FDA, holding that the agency had correctly interpreted the Food, Drug and Cosmetic Act (and thus DSHEA) to require a risk-benefit analysis in determining whether a dietary supplement presents "an unreasonable risk of illness or injury."[13]

Does there seem to be a basic inconsistency here in the treatment of this drug, ephedra? Government regulation of dietary supplements after the passage of DSHEA in 1994 does not protect consumers in

---

13. *Nutraceutical Corporation v. Von Eschenbach*, 459 F.3d 1033 (10th Cir. 2006).

advance—that is, it does not assure a favorable risk-benefit ratio when the product is used according to labeling—yet government regulation by the FDA does. Ephedra has been marketed in both ways. As will be examined more fully in later chapters, DSHEA still presumes that supplement manufacturers will develop appropriate standards and police themselves accordingly, as the Act does not provide the FDA regulatory authority over supplement manufacturers unless and until there is evidence of "unreasonable risk." Yet DSHEA permits supplement manufacturers to make "structure or function" claims,[14] such as "promotes healthy cardiovascular functioning," an assertion about efficacy that the FDA would not permit a *pharmaceutical* manufacturer to make without adequate scientific evidence.

Is the rationale for this policy the protection of the consumer, the protection of the manufacturer, both at the same time, or neither? Indeed, does the seemingly inconsistent treatment of ephedra, despite the recognition of risk, alert us to more general issues about the system of drug regulation altogether? Are parts of it, or perhaps all of it, incoherent in the end—that is, does it simply not hang together as a unified policy? Some scholars have recently challenged DSHEA's apparent incoherence: "If dietary supplements have or promote such biological activity, they should be considered to be active drugs. On the other hand, if dietary supplements are claimed to be safe because they lack or have minimal biological activity, then their ability to cause physiologic changes to support 'structure/function' claims should be challenged, and their sale and distribution as products to improve health should be curtailed."[15] The DSHEA regulations make it difficult for consumers of supplements to know what type of substance they are purchasing and difficult for manufacturers to know what types of claims they can make. DSHEA seems to lack not only consistency, but also a coherent rationale. And DSHEA itself may be part of an overall system that itself lacks coherency, in that its components do not fit together in a mutually supporting whole.

14. See 21 U.S.C. § 343(r)(6)(A).
15. Phil B. Fontanarosa, Drummond Rennie, and Catherine D. DeAngelis, "The Need for Regulation of Dietary Supplements—Lessons from Ephedra," *Journal of the American Medical Association* 289(2003):1568–70.

Finally, for theory, policy, or a set of practices to be just, they must be comprehensive—they must cover or include all relevant cases and situations. Thus, when drug theory and drug policy are at issue, justice requires that they encompass all relevant spheres across the board, including prescription pharmaceuticals, complementary and alternative drugs, over-the-counter drugs, common-use substances including alcohol, caffeine, and tobacco, religious-use drugs, sports-enhancement drugs, and illegal recreational drugs. Comprehensiveness may fail for any number of reasons, however, ranging from professional competition among distinct disciplinary silos to the use of different underlying assumptions and definitions about what qualifies as a "drug" in the first place.

It may seem necessary to require agreement on a definition of the term "drug" before attempting to develop a consistent and coherent drug policy. But requiring agreement on such a definition before analyzing drug policy may get it exactly backward. Whether drug policy is comprehensive depends upon whether it speaks to all that it should, namely, all "drugs." Does this include, for example, herbal remedies and dietary supplements? Does it include the "active ingredient" (though it is never labeled this way) in widely used stimulant beverages like coffee, tea, energy drinks, and colas? Whether a drug policy speaks to all drugs in all spheres of drug discussion and drug use depends upon a determination of what purpose—or purposes—drug policy should serve.

In other words, whether the distinctions made by chemists, health professionals, social scientists, psychologists, lawyers, et cetera, will define the proper scope of a particular drug policy also determines whether the drug policy is comprehensive—whether it encompasses all that it should in all spheres of discourse on drugs and their use—and thus whether it can count as just. The conceptual problems raised by this definitional circle pervade all the issues that will be addressed in this book. Both drug theory and drug policy differ within the various, often insular silos of discussion, from prescription pharmaceuticals to illegal recreational drugs, yet considerations of *comprehensive* applicability have not been seen as fully relevant or even considered at all. The proper coverage of drug theory and drug policy should be established by determining how drug theory and policy ought to be designed and implemented in practice—that is, what would be fully just—not before such judgments are made.

This is not to presuppose that improving drug theory, policy, and practice requires that different spheres of discussion converge upon a single set of terms and attached distinctions. Perhaps there is justification for various professionals in various silos adopting different definitions. For example, one goal of the criminal justice system is to protect members of society by punishing certain conduct pursuant to certain mental states and thereby dissuading others from engaging in similar behavior. Because of this goal, professionals in criminal justice might give preference to a definition of the term "addiction" that focuses upon the potential harmful effects to others and the possibility of general deterrence rather than the actual harm to the individual (or others) and the lack of self-control on the part of the offender. In contrast, the primary goals of the mental health profession involve the improvement of the biopsychosocial functioning of the individual. For this reason, professionals in mental health fields may find it preferable to use a definition of the term "addiction" that focuses either upon the potential harmful effects for the individual, or the general lack of self-control (whether or not it produces harmful effects), or both. The definitions that emerge from within these different professions will probably lack consistency and comprehensiveness when viewed from the outside, but this is not necessarily a problem and they are not truly inconsistent *if* the different policy goals of the various spheres of discussion justify different definitions.

Nonetheless, the interdisciplinary discussions needed to assess consistency, coherence, and comprehensiveness remains theoretically underdeveloped. When professionals employ different definitions of drugs and drug policy, they risk "talking past one another" instead of incorporating and responding to each others' arguments. To ensure that professionals are engaging one another in their discussions, it is important to recognize that varying concerns within different spheres may in fact lead to different distinctions. Moreover, mutual understanding permits critical internal and external review of a field's premises and accepted doctrine. For instance, examining why those in criminal justice have concerns distinct from those in the mental health profession may help experts within each sphere to take a critical look at how they define the scope of their own discussions. Perhaps a better understanding of addiction's effect on individual self-control will encourage professionals in criminal justice to reassess assumptions about personal responsibility for addiction-related behavior, including drug-related crime, or conversely, the law's conception of culpable wrongdoing may help shape the way mental health experts structure, analyze, and extrapolate their research and the consequences for public policy. More generally, while differing policy goals within the various spheres may justify different definitions for terms, in at least some cases the distinctions may serve no meaningful objective at all and may instead hamper fruitful discourse and collaboration.

Rather than different disciplines merely pointing out how current policy in their own (and other) areas fails to respect their favored distinctions, what is needed is a serious "inter-silo" discussion to determine the proper purpose or purposes of drug theory and policy. Unless the exploration of this possibility is interdisciplinary and comprehensive, the theory and the public policy that results could well be a mere outlining of antecedent positions rather than resolving disputes or even sharpening and refining the overall discussion. To be sure, it should not be assumed in advance that this will be possible, or that it is even desirable in the end to settle on a single account of drug issues and a single purpose for drug policy. But a broad search, no matter how ambitious, is part of what it is to seek justice in drug theory, drug policy, and drug-related practice.

A focus on drug theory, drug policy, and drug-related practice, across the board, cannot be a static entity. Rather, it is constantly evolving and shifting underfoot, as drugs move in and out of scheduled classifications, as legal penalties change, and as public opinion shifts. In his seminal work on the origins of narcotics control, David Musto sees the history of drug policy as a series of shifts back and forth between liberal, permissive attitudes and conservative, intolerant stances.[16] Whether society might currently be poised at the point of yet another such shift or not, it is still appropriate to seek justice in policies of today and tomorrow. Thus, the following seeks to illuminate better ways to think about present arrangements, including the many current inconsistencies, so that future changes in drug theory, policy, and practice can be designed to produce a more coherent result that is also more just. A large step toward justice in drug issues involves

16. David F. Musto, *The American Disease: Origins of Narcotic Control*, 3rd ed. (New Haven, Conn.: Yale University Press 1973; New York: Oxford University Press, 1987, 1999).

identifying apparent inconsistencies, providing greater overall coherence, and bridging gaps in comprehensiveness. This would be equally relevant whether a policy shift looming ahead was from liberal to conservative or from conservative to liberal; policies can be unjust at either extreme, and for that matter also in between. By looking at the underpinnings of drug theory, drug policy, and the myriad diverse practices about drugs across the board, this volume seeks to provide a first step toward this end.

The aim of this book, then, is to illuminate the ways in which current thinking about drugs, both legal and illegal, discussions of drug issues, formulations of drug policy, and various practical drug-related programs can become more just. That is the whole purpose of this book. It will not be speaking for or against specific policies or ways of thinking about drugs, except to point out sometimes small, sometimes gross inconsistencies between one way of thinking about drugs and another, or incoherencies in an overall view, or failures to achieve anything like a comprehensive, well-reasoned view. But what it does have in mind—contributing to greater justice in drug theory, drug policy, and drug-related practice by exploring the disarray in foundational assumptions—is already a tall order.

2

HOW DID IT COME TO BE THIS WAY?: THE HISTORICAL DEVELOPMENT OF DRUG REGULATION

Drug policy and practice in the United States include a sometimes baffling web of drug regulation. Some drugs are legally banned and subject to stiff criminal sanctions; other drugs can be prescribed by medical professionals subject to varying degrees of restriction and oversight; still other drugs are directly available to the public with controls only on the purity of the product and the claims made by the manufacturer. Drugs are often treated differently across and within jurisdictions, with, for instance, the punishments for illegal recreational drugs depending on the various legislatures or the prosecuting entity. Some drugs are almost completely free or exempted from regulation (such as caffeine), or are restricted based solely on the age of the consumer (such as tobacco and alcohol). And some drug use is regulated primarily by private parties rather than government, such as sports-enhancement drugs and, to some degree, religious-use and workplace drugs.

It is not always appreciated that this kaleidoscope of regulation is a relatively recent phenomenon. Most drug controls have been enacted over the course of the twentieth century in a largely piecemeal way, without a comprehensive plan for the entire spectrum of substances. The regulatory structure in the United States (and in many other countries) is a patchwork that has evolved in response to specific issues, or in reaction to perceived problems, at the time, but only rarely revised in light of demands for greater consistency or coherence as a comprehensive system.

Indeed, throughout history, as David Courtwright's able *Forces of Habit* has documented,[1] drugs generally have not been a significant

1. David T. Courtwright, *Forces of Habit: Drugs and the Making of the Modern World* (Cambridge, Mass.: Harvard University Press, 2001).

concern of government except as a potential basis for taxation and revenue. For the most part, intoxicating substances have been viewed as a minor vice rather than as the bane of society. To be sure, the world has seen periods of legal prohibition and even draconian enforcement—such as the execution of tobacco users in the Russian and Ottoman Empires during the seventeenth century or the strangulation of opium purveyors in eighteenth-century China[2]—but these regulatory adventures almost always quickly failed at their abolitionist goals. Similarly, from the fifteenth to the seventeenth centuries in Europe, roughly 500,000 people were executed for witchcraft that often involved the use of psychoactive plants and medicinal herbs, some of which were employed by midwives for the control of pain and hemorrhage during childbirth.[3] But again, official regulation has been the exception; the unrestricted availability of drugs has been the rule.

One might ask, then, how did it come to be this way? What accounts for the piecemeal regulation that characterizes the current situation? Who were the regulators and what were they reacting to? Why did twentieth-century policymakers make regulation of drugs such a high priority? The following sections will offer brief sketches of the origins and status of regimes for various categories of drugs in the United States. This account will be developed in a category-specific way, from illegal drugs to common-use drugs to prescription-legend and over-the-counter drugs, to herbals, sports, and religious-use drugs. Of course, these histories are to a considerable degree interrelated, even though their outcome has been our currently "siloed" picture of drugs as occupying discrete, largely independent categories. These distinct histories, in much more detailed form, will be familiar to those who work in various professional spheres involved with drugs of various sorts, but comparatively few readers will be familiar with the full historical picture across the board.

2. See David Boaz, "A Drug-Free America—or a Free America?" U.C. Davis Law Review (24)(1991): 617.

3. Michael J. Harner, ed., *Hallucinogens and Shamanism* (New York: Oxford University Press, 1973).

Illegal Recreational Drugs

In the United States, the origins of modern drug criminalization stretch back over a century and a half, to a point when many currently banned substances were legal and widely available. Opium, one of the first popular narcotics, was commonly used in eighteenth-century America for a variety of medicinal purposes, from dysentery and rheumatism to cholera and lockjaw. The drug was liberally recommended by doctors, who described opium as "God's Own Medicine," something that "the Creator himself seems to prescribe."[4] Morphine, first derived from opium in 1803 and named after Morpheus, the Greek god of dreams, also was freely used as a stronger palliative with fewer direct side effects. Another opium derivative, first synthesized in 1874, was dubbed "heroin" because it heightened the sense of self-worth and gave the user a sense of heroism, a euphoric feeling. Heroin was used in relieving any number of illnesses, particularly those related to the upper respiratory system: coughs, congestion, asthma, bronchitis, and catarrh. Along with these opioids, cocaine was lauded as a stimulant and anesthetic, as well as a treatment for psychological and physical disorders including depression, anxiety, sexual disorders, hay fever, sinus problems, headaches, and, ironically, opium addiction.[5] Only prior to the turn of the twentieth century did the medical world conclude, after protracted debate, that these drugs were not innocuous cure-alls, but addictive and dangerous substances.

Against this background of wide availability and few if any restrictions, a handful of factors helped spur a drug regime of legal regulation and criminal prohibition. During the Civil War, injured soldiers were treated with morphine, facilitated by the invention of the hypodermic needle, and many of them would return home with the so-called "soldier's disease," morphine addiction. The general public also faced the potential of inadvertent addiction, as stores and mail-order manufacturers offered these drugs without

---

4. H. Wayne Morgan, *Drugs in America: A Social History, 1800–1980,* (Syracuse: Syracuse University Press, 1981); the quotation is from Oliver Wendell Holmes, "Currents and Counter-Currents in Medical Science," *Medical Essays 1842–1888* (Boston: Houghton, Mifflin, 1895), 202; David F. Musto, *The American Disease.* (New Haven: Yale, 1973; New York: Oxford University Press, 1987).

5. Robert Byck, ed., *Sigmund Freud: Cocaine Papers* [*Über Coca*, 1884] (New York: New American Library, 1974). Freud advocated the use of heroin for cocaine addiction.

a prescription, often in the form of patent medicines and popular beverages. For instance, the aptly named Coca-Cola contained cocaine from 1886 to 1903, when the company removed the coca-leaf derivative as the active ingredient and replaced it with caffeine. Children constituted a significant proportion of the addict population during this time period, with, as Karl Marx observed, oblivious parents "dosing children with opiates" to induce calmness.[6]

These concerns contributed to another major factor behind drug prohibition, the rise of the American Progressive Movement in the late nineteenth and early twentieth centuries. Led by a league of social reformers and ministers, the movement advocated a type of "legal moralism" stipulating that a nation's morals should be shaped by and embodied in national legislation, including the use of criminal prohibitions to stamp out vices that accompanied modernity. Drugs were deplored as the "creator of criminals and of unusual forms of violence"[7] with publications describing the drug culture of "[l]ate hours, dance halls, and unwholesome cabarets."[8] Progressives sought to purge the immorality and resulting social burdens.

Less altruistic concerns were also at work, including overt racism. The earliest drug laws were passed by local governments in the American West to protect white society from the dangers of, among others, Chinese railroad laborers, whose opium consumption was blamed for crime, violence, lascivious behavior, and other social ills. And although addiction in black communities prior to drug prohibition was relatively infrequent, reports of the time suggested that African Americans were "naturally most readily influenced" by drugs and "therefore among them we have the greater number of addicts."[9] Some claimed that blacks taking cocaine had "no

---

6. Edward M. Brecher and the Editors of Consumer Reports, *Licit and Illicit Drugs* (Boston: Little, Brown & Co., 1972), 5, citing Karl Marx, *Capital*, I, 399; online at http://druglibrary.org/schaffer/Library/studies/cu/cu1.

7. "Report on the International Opium Commission and on the Opium Problem as Seen Within the United States and Its Possessions," S. Doc. No. 61–377, at 2 (1910), quoted in Erik Luna, "The Prohibition Apocalypse." 46 DePaul Law Review 483 (1997).

8. Troy Duster, *The Legislation of Morality: Law, Drugs, and Moral Judgment* (New York: The Free Press, 1970), 11.

9. Morgan, *Drugs in America*, 92 (quoting a 1903 report by the American Pharmaceutical Association).

regard for right or wrong,"[10] while one myth held that African Americans using the drug were impervious to .32 caliber bullets, causing southern police departments to adopt .38 caliber firearms.[11] This style of racial propaganda has been repeated throughout America's history of drug prohibition, with, for instance, the movement to ban marijuana in the 1930s based in large part on images of "reefer-mad Mexicans" and alleged sexual abuses of white women by minority men.

This is not to say that there were no legitimate concerns about the use of what are now illegal drugs. For example, heroin can cause respiratory depression, cocaine can produce cardiac arrhythmia, and excessive alcohol use can lead to coma, aspiration, or even death. The point here is rather that these harmful potentials were rarely the sole or even primary impetus behind the movement to criminalize drugs in the United States, which at least suggests that certain drugs may not be categorized appropriately given their potential to do harm. It is for this reason that it is important to keep in mind the original motivations behind the criminalization of drugs.

The movement toward drug prohibition also involved issues of international relations. After the Spanish-American War, U.S. administrators of the newly acquired Philippines were confronted with problems of both drug consumption and trafficking on the archipelago. At the same time, China was struggling with rampant opium use and addiction that had been fueled by British trade policy, employing sometimes draconian means to deal with a drug crisis that was associated with the Empire's social, economic, and military deterioration. To address these problems, American missionaries in the Far East convinced U.S. officials that an international conference was necessary to stamp out the evils of narcotics, and as a consequence, a series of multilateral meetings produced protocols calling for an international ban on narcotics. One of the delegates to these meetings, Dr. Hamilton Wright, became the driving force behind drug prohibition in the United States. Often described as the "father of American narcotics laws," he led the campaign using all of the aforementioned

---

10. "Importation and Use of Opium: Hearings Before the House Committee on Ways and Means," 61st Cong. 12 (1911) (statement of Dr. Christopher Koch), quoted in Luna, "Prohibition Apocalypse," 492–93.

11. Musto, *The American Disease*, 7.

rationales—inadvertent addiction of soldiers and citizens, progressive calls for morals legislation, overt racism and fear mongering, and claims of international responsibility.

The resulting legislation was the Harrison Narcotics Act of 1914, which ostensibly placed control of narcotics in the medical profession through an orderly marketing and taxation scheme that also fulfilled America's treaty obligations. Nonetheless, federal law enforcement transformed the Act into an outright criminal ban on drugs that was eventually upheld in a series of U.S. Supreme Court cases,[12] with doctors severely restricted in their prescription of narcotics and prohibited from providing these drugs to patients who were already addicted. (In a somewhat similar fashion, federal marijuana legislation enacted in 1937 was styled as a taxation scheme but executed as a full prohibition.) The Harrison Act remained the cornerstone of American narcotics regulation until the second half of the twentieth century, enforced by the tireless drug crusader Harry Anslinger and his Federal Bureau of Narcotics. Additional anti-drug laws were enacted over the succeeding decades, increasing the punishment for drug violations and the resources for law enforcement. As a result, drug users and suppliers were slowly but surely driven underground, organized crime created a black market for narcotics, and the illegal drug business became a highly lucrative industry.

During the 1960s, however, a rift developed between those who advocated drug education and rehabilitation and those who demanded criminal law enforcement and punishment. Ultimately, the prohibition approach prevailed in government policy, partly due to the perceived threat posed by the counterculture and anti-Vietnam War movements. The result included larger law enforcement budgets, harsher penalties, and further drug criminalization, such as bans on depressants, stimulants, and any substance with a "hallucinogenic effect on the central nervous system." Moreover, a series of political and legal changes in the late 1960s and early 1970s dramatically altered drug control policy. In 1968, President Richard Nixon came to office based in part on a pledge to restore "law and order" through an all-out assault on crime, which eventually included the allegedly first declaration

12. See *United States v. Doremus*, 249 U.S. 86 (1919); *Webb v. United States*, 249 U.S. 96 (1919); *Jin Fuey Moy v. United States*, 254 U.S. 189 (1920). See also *Minnesota ex rel. Whipple v. Martinson*, 256 U.S. 41 (1921).

of a "war" on drugs—a declaration that would be repeated by succeeding federal administrations.[13] These efforts also led to the creation of a "super-agency," the Drug Enforcement Administration, with far-reaching authority over illegal drugs as well as the enforcement of a new, inclusive federal drug statute, the Comprehensive Drug Abuse Prevention and Control Act of 1970. Among the titles of this legislation was the Controlled Substance Act, the modern framework for U.S. drug regulation, which instituted a five-level approach (to be described more fully in chapter 3) predicated on each drug's putative medical value and potential for abuse. The law also established higher maximum sentences for drug crime and enhanced punishment for habitual and dangerous drug offenders. Many states adopted similarly harsh drug statutes, such as the infamous "Rockefeller Drug Laws" in New York that imposed very strict punishments on relatively low-level offenses. Nonetheless, drug crimes and punishments varied widely from state to state, something that continues to this day.

Among other things, the past three decades have been marked by provocative drug stories, rising levels of hysteria regarding drug trafficking and use, fluctuations in the popularity of certain drugs as well as the introduction of new substances, and vast increases in government resources and punishment for drug violations, broken only by occasional attempts to reduce what are often labeled the excesses of the drug war. In the 1970s, cocaine became the drug of choice in the glamorized disco scene. A few states decriminalized marijuana. The administration of President Jimmy Carter even considered decriminalizing marijuana for the federal system. But in the 1980s, President Ronald Reagan re-declared the war on drugs, premised on uncompromising criminal enforcement and adopting a succinct public slogan against drug use: *"Just Say No."* This decade also saw the rise of foreign drug cartels and a highly organized underworld for drug distribution, the escalation of violent street gangs dealing drugs in mostly urban neighborhoods, and an "epidemic" of a smokable

13. It might be noted, however, that the phrase "war on drugs" dates back to a slogan used in New York in 1921, following widespread heroin addiction among ex-soldiers of the First World War. The soldier addicts were stigmatized and often had other injuries, and therefore most of them were unemployed. Incidentally, they resorted to collecting scrap metal to support their habits, and consequently became known as junk-men, or simply "junkies"—a term which has entered the common language to refer to heroin addicts.

form of cocaine known as crack. During the mid- to late 1980s, Congress passed legislation requiring mandatory minimum sentences for drug crime, including the now-notorious five-year mandatory prison sentence for the small-time crack offender. During this same period, President Reagan issued an executive order mandating workplace drug testing for government employees and government contractors, which was followed soon thereafter by similar regulations adopted by many private sector employers.

In 1989, the Office of National Drug Control Policy was created by President George H.W. Bush to coordinate federal drug policy. During the 1990s through present day, various substances like GHB (commonly called the "date rape" drug) and MDMA (also known as "Ecstasy") became drugs of choice among certain youth groups, while methamphetamine spread throughout the country as a relatively inexpensive drug that can be easily produced in so-called meth labs. Despite massive increases in drug enforcement, interdiction, and offender imprisonment under the administrations of Presidents Bill Clinton and George W. Bush, historically popular drugs like marijuana, cocaine, and heroin continue to be widely sold and consumed by Americans. Although there have been some recent efforts to limit the scope of drug enforcement, such as the passage of medical marijuana laws in a handful of states, the federal government and, by and large, state jurisdictions continue to pursue illegal drugs with vigor. The war on drugs, it is said, is in full swing.

Common-Use Drugs: Alcohol, Tobacco, and Caffeine

The world's three most commonly used drugs are alcohol, tobacco, and caffeine. At various points in history, all three have been subject to regulation and even prohibition, but today these drugs are widely available and heavily consumed in western nations and indeed around the globe.

Caffeine

To begin with, consider the least regulated but most widely used of the common-use drugs, caffeine. This drug has been a popular stimulant since tea containing caffeine was cultivated in China in the third century BC and the coffee bean was harvested around 600 AD in Ethiopia.[14] Although coffee was banned in Egypt in the sixteenth century, for instance, the major issues involving caffeinated substances did not involve prohibition but instead international trade and taxation, best illustrated in American history by the colonists' outrage at new taxation schemes imposed by the British Crown and the resulting Boston Tea Party. Today, caffeine is available in coffee, tea, soft drinks and energy drinks, chocolate, cough and cold remedies, stay-awake tablets, and other products, subject in the United States only to minimal restrictions related to purity and labeling.

Tobacco

Until recently, tobacco and tobacco-containing products were primarily regulated by taxation. The exceptions were few and far between, such as the execution of tobacco smokers in seventeenth-century Russia and Turkey, mentioned earlier, and, in the New World, the prohibition of public smoking in certain colonial communities of Massachusetts. By and large, however, American tobacco regulation began in earnest with the control of production, eventually shifting to taxation and the generation of revenue, and finally focusing on consumption. Tobacco production was first regulated in the early eighteenth century by the establishment of a state-run warehouse system to enforce inspection. Ostensibly to control quality, the warehouse system served the interests of planters who dominated the economy. Although a federal excise tax was imposed on snuff in the wake of the American Revolution, most tobacco products remained free of taxation until the time of the Civil War, when cigars and cigarettes become a source for federal revenue. In 1921, Iowa began to tax tobacco as well, followed by most other states over the next two decades. In 1935 and 1936, Congress passed the Tobacco Inspection Act and the Tobacco Control Act, respectively, to control both the quality and quantity of tobacco.

Today, as will be seen in chapter 3, federal criminal laws related to tobacco (e.g., illegal cigarette smuggling) are enforced by the Bureau of Alcohol, Tobacco, Firearms, and Explosives within the Department of

---

14. See Paul M. Gahlinger, *Illegal Drugs: A Complete Guide to Their History, Chemistry, Use and Abuse* (New York: Penguin(Plume), 2004), 180.

Justice, while the production and taxation of tobacco products falls under the jurisdiction of the Alcohol and Tobacco Tax and Trade Bureau within the Department of the Treasury. Prior to the passage of the 2002 Homeland Security Act, both functions were carried out by a single agency. Tobacco use remains the nation's leading preventable cause of death, killing an estimated 400,000 people and costing the nation more than $150 billion in health care and lost productivity every year. Recent anti-tobacco efforts have focused on providing the Food and Drug Administration authority over this drug,[15] and federal bills have been introduced to allow the FDA to regulate virtually every aspect of tobacco production, marketing, and sales.[16] At the time of this writing, however, such legislation has not been enacted and may well be destined for failure, given the substantial political power of the tobacco lobby.

For the American public, the most obvious tobacco regulations involve the minimum age of the consumer and the permissible locations for consumption. All jurisdictions prohibit the sale of tobacco products to minors, with most states setting the minimum age at eighteen. In addition, all fifty states and the District of Columbia have clean indoor air provisions that restrict smoking in certain places, ranging from government buildings to any public structure or workplace. In turn, some, but not all, jurisdictions prohibit smoking in restaurants and bars, and the rules can even vary within a given county or metropolitan area. It is open to debate whether these recent limitations, together with slowing rates of consumption, represent the decline and fall of the cigarette in twenty-first century America after its rise at the beginning of the twentieth century, or rather, in Allan Brandt's evocative phrase, its "deadly persistence,"[17] but the impact of tobacco remains a major factor in the contemporary spectrum of drugs.

15. See "Family Smoking Prevention and Tobacco Control Act," S. 625/H.R. 1108, 110th Congress (2007). These efforts became necessary when the U.S. Supreme Court held that Congress never intended to grant the FDA the power to control nicotine delivery devices. *Food and Drug Admin. v. Brown & Williamson Tobacco Corp.*, 529 U.S. 120 (2000).

16. Allan M. Brandt, *The Cigarette Century. The Rise, Fall, and Deadly Persistence of the Product That Defined America* (New York: Basic Books, 2007).

17. Brandt, *op. cit.*

Alcohol

Although tobacco has garnered much of the recent attention about common-use drugs, alcohol may offer the most interesting American story involving regulation of a now-legal drug. The genesis of Prohibition began in the nineteenth century, driven by the so-called Temperance Movement, composed of reformers and religious leaders who sought to limit the harms associated with alcohol. Like the anti-narcotics movement, however, the advance toward a national alcohol ban was also infused with cultural and ethnic animus, attempting to limit the threat to "rural, orthodox, Protestant, agricultural, native Americans" that was allegedly posed by "the immigrant, the Catholic, the industrial worker and the secularized upper class."[18] In criminalizing the activities of these imbibing "others," the relatively dry native Protestants were fighting to secure and simultaneously venerate themselves and their way of life. As such, the criminalization of alcohol was viewed as an official governmental endorsement of their worldview, which was finally achieved through the Eighteenth Amendment to the U.S. Constitution and the enabling legislation known as the Volstead Act. Prohibition became effective in 1920, rendering illegal the manufacture, sale, or use of alcohol.

Prior to this time, beer was the most popular alcoholic beverage and men imbibed in moderation, while women and adolescents rarely drank. Prohibition encouraged a shift from beer consumption to distilled spirits, as both were equally illegal but the latter offered a more concentrated, portable substance. Some of these distillates—such as the notorious "Jake," a Jamaican ginger extract—had an alcohol content of up to eighty percent and thus a propensity to cause alcohol poisoning. Others were toxic through lead or methanol contamination from the improvised distillation process in, among other things, automobile radiators. Illness from "bathtub gin" became well known, and some hospitals were overwhelmed with cases of paralysis from "Jake leg." Moreover, drinking developed into a furtive activity; binge drinking became common; and women and adolescents, as well as men, were attracted to alcohol precisely because it was a forbidden

18. Joseph R. Gusfield, *Symbolic Crusade: Status Politics and the American Temperance Movement,* 2d ed. (Chicago: University of Illinois Press, 1986), 177.

commodity. These unintended consequences of Prohibition were only exacerbated by the economic straits facing the United States. Tax revenues from alcohol sales disappeared, government expended resources chasing bootleggers (who, in turn, paid no taxes), and at the same time many people lost the financial livelihood provided by successful bars and breweries. Needless to say, the overwhelming economic problems of the Great Depression brought more important issues to mind. After more than a dozen years of abject failure, Prohibition was finally lifted with the passage of the Twenty-first Amendment to the U.S. Constitution in 1933.

Today, alcohol is regulated by government in much the same way as tobacco products. Under fiscal pressure provided by federal prerequisites for the receipt of interstate highway funds, all states now prohibit the purchase and consumption of alcohol by those under the age of twenty-one. Both state and local jurisdictions may place further restrictions, such as the permissible times and places to purchase alcohol, the maximum alcohol content for certain beverages, and the maximum blood alcohol level for motor vehicle drivers. In some states, low-alcohol beer (e.g., 3.2 percent alcohol by weight) is available in grocery stores and gas stations but stronger beer must be purchased at state liquor stores; in other states, alcoholic beverages of any strength can be bought in stores and supermarkets. Some states maintain "blue laws" that prohibit the sale of alcohol on Sundays and most holidays; some states have one or more "dry" counties, where the sale of alcohol is prohibited—for instance, in Kentucky and Texas—and some states impose virtually no restrictions except minimum age.

Although the harms of many other widely used drugs—cocaine, heroin, methamphetamine, and marijuana, for example—are said to be the basis for prohibition and the risks of medicinal drugs the basis for prescription requirements, the harms of tobacco, alcohol, and caffeine appear to be largely ignored when compared to those of other regulated drugs. Some studies conclude that Americans are twenty-five times more likely to die from the use of tobacco and alcohol than they are from the use of illicit drugs.[19] To a certain degree this stems from the "social acceptability" of drugs like tobacco, alcohol, and caffeine and from their use among the

---

19. J. Michael McGinnis and William H. Foege, "Actual Causes of Death in the United States," *Journal of the American Medical Association* 270(18) (1993):2207–12.

middle and upper classes, as well as from the disastrous experience of Prohibition. Apparent inconsistencies in criminalization cannot be justified by the severity of physical harm or damage to society, which are much greater for alcohol and tobacco than some illegal recreational drugs, nor the physical risks from caffeine use, which are higher than those associated with some prescription drugs. These disparities are to be explored in detail in further chapters.

Prescription Pharmaceuticals and Over-the-Counter Drugs

Drug regulation is primarily a phenomenon of the twentieth century. Substances of all sorts, including opioids and cocaine, were available in the late nineteenth and early twentieth centuries at stores and by mail order without a doctor's prescription. Purveyors of drug concoctions made far-fetched assertions about their curative powers, free from government regulation on content or advertising, leading to an array of harmful consequences for the public. These harmful consequences, coupled with the problems of adulterated foods (made infamous by Upton Sinclair's *The Jungle*), prompted a progressive campaign to protect consumers that culminated in the passage of the Pure Food and Drug Act of 1906. This legislation was responsible for creating the Food and Drug Administration and, along with associated amendments, put an end to many of the most fraudulent and dangerous practices, including drug mislabeling and adulteration.

Although an important step, the Pure Food and Drug Act did not fully protect the public health. In particular, events in the late 1930s brought the issue of drug safety into sharp focus. A sulfanilamide preparation, considered a true breakthrough in medical treatment, had been developed as a systemic anti-infective, but because it proved difficult to administer the new preparation to children in capsule form, a new formulation was created by dissolving the drug in diethylene glycol, better known today as antifreeze. The formulation was tested for its ability to be administered effectively but not for its safety, and as a result, more than a hundred people lost their lives from kidney failure before the toxic nature of the solvent was recognized. While none of this was due to the sulfa drug itself, it led to the passage of the federal Food, Drug, and Cosmetic Act of 1938. This law required that all drugs had to be proven safe, including the delivery vehicles and substances used in the administration of drugs.

Still, there was no requirement for a prescription for any drug other than those defined in the 1914 Harrison Narcotics Act. In 1951, however, the Durham-Humphrey Amendment[20] to the Food, Drug, and Cosmetic Act required both proof of safety for drugs and their classification either as over-the-counter or prescription only, creating a mechanism for deeming drugs as requiring a prescription when they could not be used safely without the supervision of a physician. Over the next decades, several other developments contributed to the evolution of regulations governing drug products. These included the Kefauver-Harris Drug Amendments of 1962, which required not only that drugs be proven safe but also effective. Problems arose, however, with regard to drugs that were "grandfathered in" under the regulatory scheme, as obtaining data on safety and efficacy proved difficult after the drug was already on the market. To deal with these difficulties and appropriately implement the law, several adjustments were made by the FDA. For example, it created a series of panels composed of drugs experts (including physicians, pharmacologists, and pharmacists) responsible for evaluating over-the-counter preparations such as cough and cold medicines. The FDA also implemented a multi-phase process of approval for new prescription drugs, from preclinical testing in animals, through clinical testing in humans, to post-marketing follow-up studies. This process is now required of all new pharmaceutical drugs. Despite continuing scientific debate as well as public discussion about the speed and thoroughness in the FDA's process of drug approval, the overall requirement of testing for safety and efficacy is not challenged—at least, not for prescription drugs. There is, however, an active debate about whether this process should be extended to the next sphere of drugs: herbal remedies and food supplements.

Complementary and Alternative Medicines: Dietary Supplements

Legally known as dietary supplements, herbal drugs are part of complementary and alternative medicine (which also includes other more regulated practices

20. It might be noted that the bill's co-sponsor, Sen. Hubert Humphrey, was a pharmacist.

such as chiropractic). The path that has led to the virtually unregulated approach to herbal drugs traces back to the heyday of medicine shows and "snake-oil" salesmen around the turn of the previous century. This period was marked by unsupported, unscientific, and often outrageous claims by the producers of both foods and drugs, which provided few cures and sometimes produced illness or even death. Many things have changed in the interim, from the truth-in-labeling requirements of the 1906 Pure Food and Drug Act to the strict regulation and scientific evaluation of prescription and OTC drugs, but the herbal substances classed as dietary supplements have remained virtually free of governmental oversight to this very day.

After the passage of the Kefauver-Harris Drug Amendments in 1962, the Food and Drug Administration adopted an approach over the next two decades that any herbal product claiming a therapeutic outcome that its panels had not evaluated and approved would be considered mislabeled and subject to confiscation. Conversely, however, the FDA did not prevent the sale of herbal substances if they did not claim any value in the prevention or treatment of disease. This meant that manufacturers could simply remove the offending information from the label and market the product as a food, nutritional supplement, or food additive, which fall under very different regulatory guidelines from drugs, often leaving nothing on the label except the name of the herb. The compete lack of other information, official or otherwise, created a vacuum of knowledge for prospective consumers. For years, the FDA maintained several lists that were pertinent to herbs, including a register for those "generally regarded as safe" (GRAS). About 250 medicinal herbs appeared on this list primarily because of their additional uses as culinary spices. Another list contained the "herbs of undefined safety" and a list of 27 "unsafe herbs." Unfortunately, many herbs were listed inappropriately, and GRAS lists dedicated to herbal medicines have been more or less abandoned because no office had either the time or resources to catalog the substances.

The most recent legislation in this area is the 1994 Dietary Supplements Health and Education Act (DSHEA), an amendment to the Food, Drug and Cosmetic Act of 1938 that created the existing category of dietary supplements. DSHEA was passed in part to provide a separate regulatory framework for herbal medicines and analogous products and to increase the amount of information consumers receive on the labeling of these products. The Act has four key features: (1) it defines the term "dietary supplement" as products which include vitamins, minerals, herbs or other botanicals, amino acids, and other substances taken to supplement the diet by increasing total dietary intake; (2) it places the burden of proof for demonstrating a lack of product safety on the FDA; (3) it calls for the establishment of "Good Manufacturing Practices" (GMP) for dietary supplement products; and (4) it changes the labeling regulations to allow "structure or function" claims, those regarding an effect on the structure or function of the body that are not of a therapeutic nature. Such structure/function claims may be made only if following statement is included on the label: "*This statement has not been evaluated by the Food and Drug Administration. This product is not intended to diagnose, treat, cure, or prevent any disease.*"[21]

Obviously, there is a stark contrast in the governmental scheme for dietary supplements under DSHEA versus other drugs and substances controlled by the FDA (or subject to criminal investigation and prosecution by the DEA and other law enforcement agencies). Notably absent from regulations for dietary supplements are any requirements that manufacturers demonstrate product efficacy and safety before marketing a substance. Not only is evidence of therapeutic benefit not required, no demonstration of safety is mandated under current regulations, and government intervention occurs only after a sufficient number of adverse reactions are linked to a particular product or ingredient—in other words, only after a supplement appears to present a "significant or unreasonable risk of illness or injury" when used as recommended. Moreover, it is the FDA that must build a case against a product based on safety concerns, and it is only then that the agency can intervene. The case of ephedra—legal as a dietary supplement until 2004, when a ban was instituted and finally upheld in 2006—represents the first time that the FDA has taken such an action. However, concerns raised by other substances such as kava kava, black cohosh, and St. John's wort continue to challenge the adequacy of DSHEA to protect the public health.

---

21. 21 U.S.C. § 343(r)(6)(C). See generally I. S. Bass and A. L. Young, *Dietary Supplement Health and Education Act: A Legislative History and Analysis* (Washington D.C.: The Food and Drug Law Institute, 1996).

The expanding number of dietary supplement products (more than $20 billion in annual sales in the United States), the changing nature of the products (e.g., high potency used as a marketing feature), and the commonplace ingestion of multiple dietary supplement products, plus OTC and prescription medications ("polypharmacy"), all contribute to a very uncertain safety scenario. Furthermore, the labeling of dietary supplements is often inadequate. One study of commercial preparations of echinacea for sale in the Denver, Colorado, area in August, 2000, for example, found that 10 percent of the 59 samples studied contained no echinacea, about half did not contain the species listed on the label, and less than half met the quality standard described on the label.[22]

Since 1983, the American Association of Poison Control Centers has received some 1.6 million adverse reaction reports related to supplement products.[23] In 2005, for instance, there were more than two hundred reports related to the use of St. John's wort, including 79 hospitalizations and one death. Between 1983 and 2005 there were 257 reported deaths from supplements, and some estimate that the number of serious adverse events that are reported to the FDA is a fraction of the actual amount. Until recently, it has been voluntary for a manufacturer to inform the FDA about adverse event reports it receives from consumers. In December 2006, however, Congress enacted legislation requiring supplement manufacturers to notify the FDA whenever they receive information about a serious adverse event.

The picture in Europe is quite different. Many countries divide medicinal products derived from plants into two categories. First are the "licensed" products that require a "marketing authorization" and are regulated along the same lines as synthetic pharmaceuticals, usually requiring a prescription. A common example is St. John's wort, which is a prescription antidepressant in Germany and is subject to the same rigorous standards of efficacy, safety, and quality as any other pharmaceutical drug. Second are the unlicensed, over-the-counter products of plant origin, which

22. C.M. Gilroy, J.F. Steiner, T. Byers, H. Shapiro, W. Georgian, "Echinacea and Truth in Labeling," *Archives of Internal Medicine* 163(6)(2003):699–704.

23. Melisa W. Lai, Wendy Klein-Schwartz, George C. Rodgers, Joseph Y. Abrams, Deborah A. Haber, Alvin C. Bronstein, and Kathleen M. Wruk, "2005 Annual Report of the American Association of Poison Control Centers' National Poisoning and Exposure Database," *Clinical Toxicology* 44(2006):803–932.

are treated more like the herbal medicines and dietary supplements in the United States. The European Union recently enacted the Traditional Herbal Medicinal Products Directive (THMPD), which came into effect on April 30, 2004.[24] This directive is intended to harmonize the diverse standards for quality of products in this category across the entire EU and to require strict manufacturing standards in order for a product to be registered as a "traditional herbal medicine." Submission of data on efficacy is not compulsory, although evidence is required to document at least thirty years of medicinal use of a proposed traditional herbal medicine. A literature review on safety is also required, along with a supporting report of an herbal medicine expert. Thus the intent is to provide for different types of products derived from medicinal plants, but to impose in all cases uniform and rigorous product quality standards and content analysis.

For the first time since the passage of DSHEA in 1994, some progress on product quality has been made in the United States. On June 22, 2007, the FDA published its final rule establishing GMP standards for dietary supplements.[25] Identity, purity, strength, and composition of raw materials and finished products must be established, along with well-documented and sanitary manufacturing processes and accurate labeling. While clearly a step in the right direction, serious concerns remain. The GMPs being implemented are similar to the current standards applied to foods rather than to OTC or prescription drugs, reinforcing the lack of alignment of these products with others of therapeutic or preventative intent. And it is unclear what financial resources will be available at the FDA for inspection or enforcement. Yet the rule does respond to increasing concerns about dietary supplement products and patient safety.

Sports-Enhancement Drugs

There is a colorful history regarding the use of drugs to enhance performance in sports. Athletes in the golden era of Athens ingested hallucinogenic mushrooms and sheep's testicles (which increased testosterone) to

---

24. Medicines and Healthcare Products Regulatory Agency, online at http://www.bcma.co.uk/proposed_directive_on_traditiona.htm.

25. Online at http//:www.fda.gov/bbs/topics/NEWS/2007/NEW01657.html.

improve their performance. Roman gladiators used stimulants in preparation for their bloody games. Athletes throughout history have taken alcohol, caffeine, cocaine, opioids, and even strychnine in search of improved performance or some physical edge over their competitors. The first death related to drug taking in sports is widely cited to be that of British cyclist Arthur Linton following the Bordeaux-Paris race of 1896, attributed to an overdose of "trimethyl," said to be in vogue in the sport at the time. The report is more likely legend than truth, however—Linton is also reported to have died of strychnine (also in use in sports) and then again of typhoid fever.[26] The first testing for performance-enhancing drugs began in the late 1920s, although it was thoroughbred horses rather than humans that were being checked for such substances. For the most part, however, the regulation of performance-enhancing drugs is a relatively recent phenomenon conducted by and within the sport community rather than by the government.

Monitoring for the use of performance-enhancing drugs ("doping," as it is known) has been handled at several different stages. Each sport has its own federation that governs the sport at an international level, such as the International Federation of Athletic Associations (IAAF), and most nations have national governing bodies that control sports within that country, such as the U.S.A. Track and Field (USATF) governing body. Within each country, Olympic athletes are also governed by National Olympic Committees. Until very recently, each of these sport organizations had separate doping control regulations regarding banned drugs, testing procedures, and potential sanctions. The International Olympic Committee provided oversight for this regime, but their actual authority was limited to the Olympic Games. An athlete might train according to the regulations of her national governing body or National Olympic Committee, and then compete under different International Federation regulations at an international event. For Olympic Games, in turn, the IOC regulations would be in force.

The problems with this patchwork of regulations became obvious, and in March 2003, the World Anti-Doping Agency (WADA) was designated

26. House of Commons, Culture, Media and Sport Committee, "Drugs and Role Models in Sport: Making and Setting Examples," Seventh Report of Session 2003–04, Vol. 1. (London: The Stationery Office, 2004), 9, note 21.

as the global governing body for doping control. This consolidation has significantly reduced the inconsistencies across nations and sports, and made it possible to achieve uniformity concerning which substances are forbidden, the testing methods for these substances, and the sanctions for violations. Currently, WADA tests for several classes of drugs that, if detected, lead to sanctioning and probable disqualification from sporting competition or awards. These include stimulants, opioids, anabolic steroids, illegal drugs of abuse, peptide hormones such as erythropoietin (EPO) and growth hormone (GH), beta-2 agonists, legally available diuretics and plasma expanders that are used for weight loss or to mask the use of other banned substances, and legally available beta blockers used to steady the aim in sports such as archery and shooting. Other drugs such as antibiotics and aspirin are not thought to interfere with maintaining a "level playing field," a principal objective of performance-enhancement prohibitions, and thus are not banned.

But while WADA has exercised substantial control and the harmonization of drug use regulation has been achieved in Olympic sports, professional and non-Olympic sports present an entirely different issue. Steroid use in some sports, like professional bodybuilding, is understood to be widespread and little attempt is made to prevent it. Other sports, like American football, basketball, and baseball, have instituted drug-testing policies with differing degrees of success. The prospect of government regulation remains in the air for these sports, however, as demonstrated by President George W. Bush's call in his 2004 State of the Union address to eliminate steroids in professional athletics, and congressional hearings in early 2005 that included threats of national legislation if sufficient action were not taken by the sports leagues themselves.

Religious-Use Drugs

Evidence of the use of mind-altering substances in spiritual quests or other religious contexts dates back at least 50,000 years, and virtually all historic societies yield evidence of such use. In ancient India, the sacred texts of the Vedas contain more than 1,000 hymns devoted to *Soma*, widely believed among historians to refer to the hallucinogenic mushroom *Amanita muscaria*. Secret rites in Greece circa 300 BC attracted thousands of people to the Temple of Eleusis to drink a preparation made from ergot, a mold growing on rye and other grains now known to contain LSD. Early Christian churches used alcohol in their ceremonies, the sacramental wine representing the blood of Christ, and this practice continues in many modern churches. Numerous other religious practices employed mind-altering substances to facilitate a spiritual state, including coca and peyote. The phenomenon is so widespread that scholars have coined a term for the drugs used in a specifically religious context or otherwise to achieve a transcendent state: "entheogens," a neologism meaning "to contact the God within."

Many of these substances are illegal or at least heavily regulated in the United States, presenting a potential conflict between drug laws, often applicable to all citizens, and the religious practices of impacted groups. The tension raises questions not only of public policy, but also of civil liberties guaranteed by the First Amendment to the U.S. Constitution and in state and federal statutes designed to protect individuals engaged in religious practices. So while government is empowered to formulate policies safeguarding the public health and safety, such as restricting the use of dangerous drugs, it must also respect the religious practices of its citizens. A good example of this conflict is provided by the unique treatment of the hallucinogenic entheogen peyote, a drug used primarily by members of the Native American Church.

Peyote (*Lophophora williamsii*) is a cactus indigenous to the border region of Texas and Mexico. Archeological evidence, sculptures, and other artifacts suggest it has been used by native peoples in Central America for more than 10,000 years, and religious ingestion of peyote was described by Cortez and the first Spanish explorers in the sixteenth century. This historic practice has continued through modern times, with peyote used as a sacrament by some Native Americans in their religious ceremonies. In fact, it is considered as more than a sacrament; peyote is considered by some to be capable of placing the user in direct contact with God. As a religious practice, the ingestion of peyote and the resulting hallucinogenic experience have even melded with Christianity in certain Native American faiths. In the words of Comanche Chief Quannah Parker, "The white man goes into his church and talks about Jesus; the Indian goes into his teepee and talks to Jesus."[27] However, peyote is classified by the federal government as

27. Gahlinger, *Illegal Drugs*, 43–44. Some material in this section is drawn from Gahlinger's book.

a Schedule I controlled substance with no legitimate medical use and severe criminal restrictions on distribution, possession, and consumption.

The potential conflict between legal prohibition and religious practice was resolved, at least in part, by an exemption under federal law. Interestingly, this exemption was obtained principally through the efforts of a white anthropologist working for the Smithsonian Institution. In the late nineteenth century, James Mooney was sent to the Oklahoma Territory to research social disorganization and the high incidence of alcoholism in the Native American population. Recognizing both the value of peyote ceremonies in promoting healthful lifestyles and the increasing fervor to criminalize all drugs, he suggested that the Native American Church (NAC) incorporate for the specific purpose of protecting its religious use of peyote. Representatives of several Oklahoma tribes followed his suggestion, incorporating the NAC in 1918. Subsequent drug laws exempted Native American use of peyote, including this provision in the Code of Federal Regulations: "The listing of peyote as a controlled substance in Schedule I does not apply to the nondrug use of peyote in bona fide religious ceremonies of the Native American Church, and members of the Native American Church so using peyote are exempt from registration."[28] Federal courts have held that the exemption is available only to members of the NAC who have indigenous ancestry,[29] and a subsequent statute made this exemption explicitly race-based:

> [T]he use, possession, or transportation of peyote by an Indian for bona fide traditional ceremonial purposes in connection with the practice of a traditional Indian religion is lawful, and shall not be prohibited by the United States or any State. No Indian shall be penalized or discriminated against on the basis of such use, possession or transportation, including, but not limited to, denial of otherwise applicable benefits under public assistance programs.[30]

There are several interesting features of this policy, beginning with the notion of "nondrug" use of peyote, presumably distinguishing religious use from all other uses of the same substance. This distinction appears to be supported by the group in question, with the Native American Church insisting emphatically that peyote is *not* a drug. Indeed, its Roadmen (analogous to

28. 21 Code of Federal Regulations 1307.31. See also 21 U.S.C.§ 1996a(b)(1).
29. See, e.g., *Peyote Way Church of God, Inc. v. Thornburgh*, 922 F.2d 1210 (5th Cir. 1991).
30. 21 U.S.C. § 1996a(b)(1).

priests or ministers) insist that it is instead a sacrament, and the NAC admonishes its members to avoid all nonmedical drug use. Peyote is believed—not figuratively but *literally*—to be the body of Jesus Christ who has returned in the form of a plant. Government officials have accepted this "nondrug" religious use in administering the exemption. For instance, approximately 6,000 American soldiers with indigenous ancestry are allowed to use peyote at their own discretion as members of the NAC, even when the soldiers are on extended tours of duty. According to a Pentagon spokesman, "If they are using peyote as part of their religious practice it is a sacrament, not a drug. Just like sacramental wine is not considered a drug."[31]

Another curious feature of the federal exemption is that it appears both overly broad and overly narrow in its application only to Native Americans. Although the exemption was no doubt motivated by the need to recognize and legitimize Native American religious practice, peyote was not originally used by the native tribes north of the U.S.-Mexico border. It was only introduced into this country in the late nineteenth century from areas further south. In fact, many tribes in the United States, especially the Navajo, were initially very reluctant to permit their members to join the NAC since it was not part of their traditional culture. Perhaps the strangest implication of the exemption is that the principal founder of the NAC—the white anthropologist James Mooney—would not qualify for the exemption under current federal regulations, nor would any other non-Native American who ingested peyote as a religious sacrament. Oddly, then, a person from Maine with Micmac ancestry is permitted to use peyote, which grows at least 2,000 miles away, while a non-Native sacramental user of the substance living in Texas, who may have peyote growing on his property, would be prohibited from consumption.

For many years, peyote use by Native Americans was unique under federal statutes and regulations, as all other religious groups and churches were denied an exemption for their sacramental use of peyote or other banned substances. Consider, for example, the Peyote Way Church of God in Arizona, which subscribes to precisely the same tenets as the Native American Church and only splintered from the NAC in order to admit white members (specifically, members who had less than 25 percent Native

---

31. Gahlinger, *Illegal Drugs*, 407.

American ancestry). Despite these similarities, in 1991 an appellate tribunal held that the government has a legitimate interest in "preserving native American culture" and thus "may exempt NAC members from statutes prohibiting peyote possession without extending the exemption to Peyote Way's membership."[32] Other churches have also been denied an exemption for their religious drug use, including the Church of the Awakening, the New American Church for Peyote, the Rastafarians, and the Church of the Tree of Life. The latter church failed in its attempt to obtain an exemption by incorporation (as the NAC had done) in order to protect its members' use of bufotenin, a psychoactive hallucinogen present in the secretions of the Colorado River toad (*Bufo alvarius*) indigenous to Utah and Colorado.

U.S. Supreme Court rulings and congressional action have complicated the picture. In 1990, the Supreme Court held that a generally applicable law prohibiting drug use does not violate the Free Exercise Clause in the U.S. Constitution even if the law burdens a particular religious practice.[33] In that case, two members of the NAC were fired from their jobs at a private drug rehabilitation facility in Oregon due to their use of peyote in religious ceremonies. They were subsequently denied unemployment benefits by the state because their termination had been for work-related "misconduct"— specifically, using illegal drugs under Oregon law, which did not contain an exemption for religious use of peyote. In determining that the denial of government benefits was permissible, the Court held that the state did not have to demonstrate a "compelling governmental interest" for applying the generally applicable law—such as Oregon's categorical ban on peyote— even though it substantially burdened a religious practice. The state was not constitutionally required to recognize an exception for sacramental ingestions, and it could impinge upon religious practices through its drug prohibition as long as the burdens were merely incidental to the laws.

The ruling outraged many in Congress and eventually led to the passage of the "Religious Freedom Restoration Act of 1993" (RFRA),[34] which

---

32. *Peyote Way Church of God v. Thornburgh*, 922 F.2d at 1216. This decision has been called into question by subsequent changes to federal law in 21 U.S.C. § 1996a(b)(1) (extending exemption to all members of an Indian tribe) and the U.S. Supreme Court's decision discussed below.

33. *Employment Division v. Smith*, 494 U.S. 872 (1990).

34. 107 Stat. 1488, codified at 42 U.S.C. § 2000bb et seq.

attempted to bypass the Court's decision by requiring that even a generally applicable state or federal law must employ the least restrictive means of furthering a compelling governmental interest. In other words, lawmakers were strictly limited in the burdens they could place on religious practices, including those imposed by drug laws. In 1997, however, the Supreme Court struck down RFRA's application to state government,[35] leaving open the question as to whether this law would limit federal drug enforcement. Nearly a decade later, the Court examined this precise issue in a case involving a Brazilian-based church's use of ayahuasca (or hoasca), a substance that is a part of a long religious tradition in the Amazonian area. The União do Vegetal church (as well as other faiths such as Santo Daime) receives Christian communion by drinking an ayahuasca tea, which contains a variant of DMT (Dimethyltriptamine), a Schedule I substance. Although ayahuasca itself is not specifically listed in the schedules, it is prohibited by the United Nations Convention on Psychotropic Substances and thus effectively implemented by the Controlled Substances Act. It is also considered a Schedule I substance under the Controlled Substances Analogue Enforcement Act of 1986, which prohibits anything chemically similar to an illegal drug. In 1999, federal customs agents seized three drums of ayahuasca shipped to the United States for use by American members of the União do Vegetal. The church filed suit against federal law enforcement, successfully arguing that government interference with its members' sacramental use of ayahuasca violated the RFRA.

In 2006, the U.S. Supreme Court affirmed the rulings below in support of the church's position.[36] Among other things, the Court rebuffed the

35. *City of Boerne v. Flores*, 521 U.S. 507 (1997). According to the Court, the law exceeded the powers of Congress, interfered with the judiciary's prerogative in constitutional interpretation, and intruded upon the state governments' authority to regulate the health and welfare of its citizens.

36. *Gonzales v. O Centro Espirita Beneficiente União do Vegetal*. 546 U.S. 418 (2006). The Supreme Court refers to hoasca as "unique" to the Amazon region, but only one of the plants used to make hoasca is limited to Amazonia, while the other is widespread throughout equatorial South America and the Caribbean. In fact, both plants are now grown in Florida. Moreover, the ingredients of the tea vary among individual preparations, with up to forty different DMT-containing plants used (although all use *B. caapi*, the plant called ayahuasca in Quechua, which does not contain DMT), and countless other herbs, some of which are psychoactive. *P. viridis*, the most common DMT-containing constituent, also has many subspecies with different effects and distributions. The União do Vegetal Church only uses *B. caapi* and a specific strain of *P. viridis* in their tea, both of which they grow themselves in a nursery in Brazil.

argument that a categorical ban was necessary to protect church members and to prevent diversion of the drug to recreational users. Such claims were inconsistent with the exemption provided for the religious use of peyote by Native Americans. There was nothing that makes the former group "immune from the health risks the Government asserts accompany any use of a Schedule I substance, nor insulates the Schedule I substance the Tribes use in religious exercise from the alleged risk of diversion." Most relevant for future cases, however, was the Court's rejection of the "unique relationship" between the United States and Native American tribes as a basis for denying exemptions to other religious faiths. Moreover, the classic "slippery-slope arguments" and the generalized need for absolute drug bans will not suffice under RFRA, as the analysis must focus on the effect of a challenged law on the specific individual whose religious beliefs are being substantially burdened. The question remains, however, whether the sacramental use of banned substances by other religious groups should also be protected, an issue that will be discussed in one of the case studies posed in chapter 6.

* * * * *

These brief sketches of the status and development of drug regulation, including prohibitions, exemptions, and permissive policies, suggest some of the complexities behind the current situation involving drugs of all sorts. Beneath these stories lie competing agencies and conflicting rationales for drug regulation, rooted in inconsistent assumptions about central notions in drug theory. This is the subject of the next chapter.

3

DRUG REGULATORY AGENCIES
AND THE UNDERLYING RATIONALES
FOR DRUG POLICY

Drug theory, drug policy, and the various programs and practices concerning the use of drugs are often characterized by a kind of insular, self-enclosed, silo mentality, resulting in what seems to be an erratic patchwork of apparently inconsistent approaches and regulations. As seen in chapter 2, the current situation may be attributed to the erratic history of piecemeal policy development, sometimes tinged with racism and other problematic political motives. But before leaping to any conclusions, it is important to examine the current governmental framework for dealing with drugs, specifically, the variety of official entities that create and implement drug policy. The focus here will be on the United States; drug regulation in other countries does not necessarily have the same structure, though in many countries, much of it is equally piecemeal.

After a quick survey of the principal governmental agencies in the United States dealing with drug issues, the underlying rationales for such regulation will be considered. This review will look primarily at the various federal agencies; if state and local drug regulation entities were included, the picture would be even more complex. The central question is whether the rationales upon which the various federal agencies operate, made explicit in the federal legislation that creates and empowers these agencies, form a coherent whole. As it turns out, some of the confusion and apparent injustice in the way drugs are treated may stem from inconsistencies in the rationales of the differing regulatory agencies within which drug policies are formulated and implemented. This is not attributable to any specific agency but nevertheless characterizes the picture as a whole, compounded by the evident fact that substances do not fit into neat categories of illegal drugs, prescription drugs, over-the-counter drugs, drugs of abuse, herbal remedies, religious-use drugs, common-use drugs, or sports-enhancement drugs.

The Basic Categorization of Drugs

The broad category of pharmacologically active substances can be divided into those a society regards as requiring intervention and those that do not. Substances that require intervention may require informational intervention or regulatory intervention, that is, control. This may require regulation in production, regulation in distribution, and regulation in use. Regulation in production may entail licensing of production facilities, typically for purity and accuracy of labeling, and for ability to provide adequate quality control—the international standard "Good Manufacturing Practices." Regulation in distribution may involve governmental requirements for safe storage, with some drugs under double lock, some under single lock, some right out on the counter and immediately accessible to the general public, and some behind the counter but nevertheless available without prescription. For regulation of use, licensing permits physicians, nurses, and pharmacists to prescribe, dispense, and administer drugs. Although some substances can be sold in any retail outlet, those involving greater risk may require additional levels of licensure or registration.

Less regulated or unregulated drugs may nonetheless be restricted in specific contexts, such as competitive sports or religious ceremonies. Peyote, for example, is exempted for religious use by certain groups, although it is prohibited to others. And although they are both openly accessible, dietary supplements are less regulated than over-the-counter drugs, and they differ in labeling, manufacturing controls, and claims permitted in advertising.

Take a hypothetical substance, newly discovered in the rainforest, in a laboratory, or on the seabed floor. How does this substance get into one of these categories? To some degree, it depends on the purpose associated with the substance. If it is initially believed to have value as a medicinal drug, it will be entered into preclinical investigation, and if that shows promise and the sponsor wishes to pursue clinical investigation, then application must be made to the Food and Drug Administration for licensure for clinical investigation. In order to test the drug in humans, approval from the FDA must be obtained as an Investigational New Drug. If at any point in the investigation the substance appears to have potential for abuse, the Drug Enforcement Administration can intervene. If subsequently approved for marketing, the drug may be regulated by the FDA alone (if there is no evidence of abuse potential), by both the FDA and the DEA (if there is medicinal value but also evidence of abuse potential), or by the DEA alone (if there is abuse potential but no medicinal value).

If the drug is to be marketed as having medicinal value, a determination is made by the FDA as to whether it is to be categorized as a prescription or nonprescription (over-the-counter) drug, based on the potential health risks ascertained during clinical testing. If the drug has abuse potential as defined in the Controlled Substances Act, the DEA has the authority to schedule it in one of the five levels established under the Act—Schedule I, II, III, IV, or V—independent of its approval as either a prescription or nonprescription drug. Any party can bring a substance to the attention of the DEA; however, the FDA cannot initiate a new drug review or bring a substance to its own attention. Drugs with abuse potential may also be placed in the Schedules by Congress, as was the case in the original legislation with LSD, heroin, and marijuana. The DEA administrator cannot de-schedule any controlled substance specifically listed in the Act; this can be done only by Congress.

The Controlled Substances Act uses the term "substance" because many chemical entities that pose a risk of abuse may not be considered drugs. This allows control of substances such as certain industrial and consumer products that are also used recreationally—glues, paints and paint thinners, volatile gases, and so on. Some, but not all, of these substances are listed in the Schedule; for example, GHB is derived from a common industrial solvent, and is also a Schedule I controlled substance.

All drugs intended to be used in the treatment, cure, prevention, or diagnosis of a disease or to enhance physical or mental well-being must go through the rigorous testing overseen by the FDA. This process involves the three phases of testing and post-marketing surveillance described below. At the end of the testing, prescription drugs are considered to be relatively safe (based on a benefit-to-risk ratio) and efficacious. Some prescription drugs—such as morphine, codeine, anabolic steroids, sedatives such as

Valium, and medications containing limited quantities of certain opioids—are controlled within the schedules of the Controlled Substances Act and their use regulated by the DEA. It is illegal to use these prescription drugs outside of these regulations, but within the regulations their use is perfectly legal. For some drugs, however, mere possession triggers a criminal penalty. LSD and heroin, for instance, fall into Schedule I of the Controlled Substance Act; they have no recognized medical use and cannot be ordinarily prescribed. For other drugs, there is considerable overlap between what is illegal and what is legal. For example, the possession of morphine without a prescription for a legitimate use may be illegal, but morphine is also a prescription drug used for moderate to severe pain. Some drugs, such as codeine—are very strictly controlled (Schedule II) as sole ingredients, but they may be in the lower controlled-substance Schedule III when formulated in combination with other ingredients such as acetaminophen. They may also be available without prescription as a Schedule V controlled substance, as in the cough preparation elixir terpin hydrate and codeine. Some drugs are illegal for a user to possess or take in all nonresearch contexts (such as LSD), while others (such as OxyContin) are legal only if one holds a *bona fide* prescription. Phencyclidine (PCP) is illegal, and it is generally acknowledged to be a drug of abuse; it is not a prescription drug because it has no recognized medical use. Hydrocodone, the active ingredient in Lortab, is a prescription drug, but it is also considered an abusable drug because of its frequent street use without a prescription. Even Schedule I drugs can be legally prescribed and used under an approved research protocol—for example, MDMA, known as Ecstasy (Schedule I) has been legally used under a restricted program in Florida, as LSD theoretically could be—but such research programs are typically quite limited. In general, Schedule I controlled substances cannot be legally possessed or consumed. Drugs in Schedules II-V are subject to varying amounts of control.

Drugs sold on the open market, referred to as over-the-counter drugs (OTC), do not require a prescription and have been deemed by the FDA safe enough for use without monitoring by a health professional at the recommended dosages. Some drugs, such as ibuprofen, are OTC in smaller doses and prescription in higher doses.

Herbal remedies that are not marketed as pharmaceuticals are not tested by the FDA. In this context, they have not been deemed safe or efficacious, and are regulated only by the Dietary Supplement Health and Education Act (DSHEA). Unless the sponsor of a substance seeks FDA approval, there will be no overlap between the dietary supplements and prescription or OTC drugs. However, some substances—such as ephedra/ephedrine (Rx), and Vitamin A and Vitamin C (OTC)—are both herbal remedies and pharmaceutical drugs.

Many religious-use drugs, especially the hallucinogens, are listed as Schedule I, though there are some exceptions like alcohol or tobacco. Many performance-enhancing drugs used in sports are prescription drugs that are legal, like anabolic steroids, but are prohibited by sports associations; some are common-use drugs, like caffeine; and others are OTC pharmaceuticals or dietary supplements, like ephedra.

The Federal Regulatory Agencies

The U.S. Constitution defines the authority of the federal government by enumerating the powers it can exercise (e.g., regulating interstate commerce and granting patents) and setting limits on how it can exercise those powers (e.g., laws that prohibit the free exercise of religion or impose cruel and unusual punishments are not permitted). Thus, while the federal government may ban the use of marijuana if its use (at least indirectly) affects interstate commerce, it cannot impose the death penalty for marijuana use, because this would constitute "cruel and unusual" punishment under current jurisprudence. All federal drug regulations and prohibitions ultimately should both originate with and remain within the scope of the Constitution.

The Constitution also defines the relationship between the dual sovereigns within the United States, the federal government and the various state governments. The most important aspect of this relationship is the notion of federal supremacy, that national laws preempt conflicting state laws. Thus if Congress enacts a statute that requires drug manufacturers to label a particular drug in a specified manner, a state cannot negate this requirement. Conversely, the federal government could relieve drug manufacturers of their responsibilities under various state statutes, given that federal law always prevails over inconsistent state law. More typically, however, state laws do not conflict with, and thus exist alongside, federal laws. This explains why illegal drugs like cocaine can be prohibited under both state and federal law, and violation of drug laws can be prosecuted in either (or even both) juris-dictions. Moreover, if the federal government does not intend to occupy an entire area of law, each state is free to impose its own drug regulations and prohibitions so long as these laws do not conflict with federal law.

This arrangement can sometimes lead to counterintuitive and seem-ingly inconsistent results, as with the case of medical marijuana. Certain states authorize the sale, possession, and use of this drug with a doctor's prescription, but the federal government bans marijuana for any and all purposes. As a theoretical matter, the federal system at times encourages inconsistencies, as it allows each state to experiment and learn from each other. In the words of Justice Louis Brandeis, federalism permits each state to "serve as a laboratory" to "try novel social and economic experiments without risk to the rest of the country."[1] Whether American drug policy is an example of the "happy incidents of the federal system," as Brandeis put it, remains an open question.

Much drug policy is not a matter of state or federal legislation, however, but of the decisions made by the executive branch of government and, in particular, administrative agencies concerned with particular categories of drugs. Within the U.S. government, regulations governing the production, distribution, and use of drugs are fragmented between at least five different agencies or bureaus, including the Food and Drug Administration (FDA) within the Department of Health and Human Services; the Drug Enforce-ment Administration (DEA) and Bureau of Alcohol, Tobacco, Firearms and Explosives (ATF), both within the Department of Justice; the Alcohol and Tobacco Tax and Trade Bureau (TTB) within the Department of Treasury; and the White House Office of National Drug Control Policy (ONDCP).

The Food and Drug Administration (FDA)

Originally called the Division of Chemistry, what is now known as the Food and Drug Administration began to develop in 1906 as regulatory functions were added to the agency's scientific mission and nonregulatory research functions were later transferred elsewhere. The FDA was under the Department of Agriculture until 1940, when it was moved to the new

1. *New State Ice Co. v. Liebmann*, 285 U.S. 262, 311 (1932) (Brandeis, J., dissenting).

Federal Security Agency; it was moved again in 1953 to the Department of Health, Education, and Welfare; it was moved yet again fifteen years later to the Public Health Service within HEW; and it is now located within the Department of Health and Human Services. Although it is not a cabinet level position, the FDA commissioner is appointed by the President and confirmed by Congress.

The FDA is responsible for protecting the public health by assuring the safety, efficacy, and security of human and veterinary drugs, biological products, medical devices, the food supply, cosmetics, and products that emit radiation. Its code is the Food, Drug and Cosmetic Act of 1938, but it also enforces the provisions in dozens of other laws, including the Controlled Substances Act, the Dietary Supplement Health and Education Act (DSHEA), and the Prescription Drug User Fee Act. A primary duty of the FDA is to approve prescription drugs and OTC medications, and to maintain and enforce drug manufacturing standards.

A prescription drug begins its journey toward FDA approval as an "Investigational New Drug" shown to be safe in animals and to hold promise for human studies. In humans, the drug is then tested for adverse effects in a small number of healthy volunteers (Phase I). At this point, studies also evaluate the dosage, frequency of administration, and factors that might affect a drug's effectiveness, such as absorption, metabolism, and excretion. Next, the drug is administered to patients who have the disease or condition the drug is intended to treat (Phase II). Safety is again evaluated. The drug is then studied in hundreds or thousands of patients randomly assigned to be treated either with the test drug, a control substance, or placebo (Phase III). The results of all studies are submitted as a "New Drug Application" for review by FDA scientists and outside experts. If approval is granted, the pharmaceutical company may begin marketing the drug for treatment only for the indicated conditions. The company may also enter into an additional study (Phase IV) in which the safety of the drug is closely monitored during its initial use.[2] Phase IV investigations are normally voluntary; however, a major problem still exists with

2. Glen Hanson and Peter Venturelli, *Drugs and Society*, 6th edition (Sudbury, Mass.: Jones & Bartlett, 2001), 61–64 and appendix B, 508–10.

approved drugs that are later discovered to be associated with a low incidence of adverse effects.

This system of prescription drug regulation can be remarkably effective. However, once a drug is available for approved indications, medical practitioners may prescribe the drug for "off-label" uses, a practice that is not regulated by the FDA. For instance, Cytotec (misoprostil) is a prostaglandin approved as a gastrointestinal protectant, including the prevention of ulcers, caused by nonsteroidal anti-inflammatory drugs such as ibuprofen or aspirin. The drug also increases uterine contractions, leading some physicians to use it legally off-label to induce abortion—despite a clear warning that Cytotec is contraindicated in pregnancy, it lacks adequate testing in pregnant women, and the possibility that the drug can cause a ruptured uterus. Off-label use is often subtly encouraged by pharmaceutical companies that do not wish to spend the time and money to gain FDA approval for another application of an already-approved drug. While in general, off-label use follows peer-review publication demonstrating safety and efficacy, in some cases such practices can result in significant morbidity and even mortality.

Moreover, although the FDA is mandated to ensure that drugs are honestly, accurately, and informatively represented to the public, it does not regulate drug advertising even when it involves claims of safety and efficacy. Such regulation is within the bailiwick of the Federal Trade Commission (FTC). Nor does the FDA regulate alcoholic beverages or tobacco products, which instead fall under the control of agencies within the Department of Justice and the Department of Treasury. Moreover, it is the Drug Enforcement Administration, not the FDA, that regulates drugs of abuse and those that cause addiction.

The Drug Enforcement Administration (DEA)

Drugs that require special regulation because of their propensity for abuse and addiction are listed under the Controlled Substances Act (CSA), which is enforced by the DEA within the Department of Justice. The DEA serves as the lead agency in federal drug enforcement, with a focus on criminal organizations involved in the production and distribution of illicit drugs in the United States. Although it is typically associated with the "war on drugs" and substances like cocaine, heroin, and marijuana, the DEA is also involved in enforcing the CSA as it pertains to legally produced controlled substances.

As mentioned previously, the CSA places all controlled substances into one of five schedules based upon each substance's medicinal value, harmfulness, and potential for abuse or addiction (see table 3.1), a categorization developed in 1970. At the time the FDA is approving a new prescription drug, a determination will be made as to the likelihood that it may be abused or cause addiction. If this likelihood is high, the DEA will determine its abuse potential and place it into the appropriate schedule, thus regulating its use. Substances in schedules II–IV are prescription drugs that have gone through the clinical trials set forth by the FDA.

There is considerable debate about the categorization of drugs due to the legal consequences that flow from such decisions. For instance, the placement of certain drugs in Schedule I—the category for the most dangerous drugs with no recognized medical use—can raise significant scientific, ethical, and, of course, political and legal questions, as will be seen below with regard to the religious use of peyote and the medical use of marijuana. For example, there are some substances which provide psychoactive experiences characteristic of banned or regulated drugs, but they do not appear anywhere in the scheduling scheme and are thus wholly uncontrolled. The drugs nutmeg and datura can induce euphoric experience when consumed in sufficient quantities, and yet neither drug is subject to legal controls. It might be argued, however, that these drugs are self-regulating in some sense: the euphoria of nutmeg is followed by a splitting, multi-hour headache, while the highly toxic, potentially lethal datura produces severe nausea, vomiting, and diarrhea.

Then, too, there are debates about the scope of the Controlled Substances Act. In 2001, for instance, the U.S. Attorney General issued an interpretive ruling that would have essentially gutted Oregon's Death With Dignity Act, which permits a physician to prescribe a lethal dose of a drug to a terminally ill patient who requests it in order to end his or her life. The Attorney General claimed that using a controlled substance (usually secobarbital, a Schedule II substance with other accepted medical uses) to bring about death was not a legitimate medical practice, even when physician-assisted suicide in terminal illness is permitted by state law, and that prescribing

TABLE 3.1. Controlled Substances Schedules

Schedule	Characteristics	Dispensing Restrictions	Examples
I	1. High abuse potential 2. No accepted medical use 3. Lack of accepted safety under medical supervision	Approved Schedule I protocol required	heroin, marijuana, peyote, tetrahydro-cannabinol, LSD, mescaline, dimethyl-tryptamine, ibogaine, etc.
II	1. High abuse potential 2. Accepted medical uses 3. May lead to severe physical or psychological dependence	1. Written prescription required, only emergency dispensing permitted without prescription 2. Only required amount may be prescribed. 3. No refills allowed 4. Container must have warning label	opium, morphine, codeine, hydromorphone, meperidine, oxycodone, methadone, secobarbital, pentobarbital, amphetamine, methylphenidate, etc.
III	1. Lower abuse potential than drugs in Schedules I and II 2. Accepted medical uses 3. May lead to low to moderate physical dependence or high psychological dependence	1. 34-day supply limit 2. Written or oral prescription 3. Prescription expires in six months 4. No more than five refills 5. Container must have warning label	hydrocodone, ketamine, dronabinol, anabolic steroids, etc.
IV	1. Lower abuse potential than drugs in Schedule III 2. Accepted medical uses 3. May lead to limited physical or psychological dependence	1. Written or oral prescription required 2. 34-day supply limit 3. Prescription expires in six months 4. No more than five refills 5. Container must have warning label	barbital, phenobarbital, chloral hydrate, meprobamate, fenfluramine, diazepam, chlordiazepoxide, oxazepam, chlorazepate, flurazepam, lorazepam, pentazocine, dextropropoxyphene, etc.
V	1. Low abuse potential compared to Schedule IV 2. Accepted medical uses 3. May lead to limited physical or psychological dependence	May require prescription or may be OTC, check state law	Medications, generally for relief of coughs or diarrhea, containing limited quantities of certain opioids, like dextromethorphan, loperamide etc.

such drugs for this end was unlawful under the CSA. In 2006, however, the U.S. Supreme Court rejected the Attorney General's claim, saying that such a ruling would, among other things, "cede medical judgments to an Executive official who lacks medical expertise."[3]

The Bureau of Alcohol, Tobacco, and Firearms and Explosives (ATF) and the Alcohol and Tobacco Tax and Trade Bureau (TTB)

American history is littered with citizen grumblings over this or that tax, sometimes in relation to drugs, such as the revolutionary Boston Tea Party and the fleeting Whisky Rebellion. In 1862, Congress formed an internal revenue office within the Treasury Department that was charged with collecting taxes on, among other things, alcohol and tobacco. A decade later, federal agents smashed a distilled spirit ring involving a multimillion dollar swindle by government officials and grain dealers, but the largest challenge would come in 1920 with the onset of Prohibition. During the great booze ban, the "revenoors" (as they were called) were faced with the enforcement of a national proscription on the "manufacture, sale or transportation of intoxicating liquors for beverage purposes."[4] Given its massive tasks, the enforcement arm was elevated in 1927 to a higher institutional status, the Bureau of Prohibition, and then transferred from the Treasury Department to the Department of Justice in 1930.

When Prohibition was lifted in 1933, President Franklin Roosevelt created the Federal Alcohol Control Administration as a means of regulating the re-legalized alcohol industry, an agency that was refashioned only two years later into the Federal Alcohol Administration within the Treasury Department. At roughly the same time, the Justice Department's Prohibition-related duties were absorbed by a brand new office, the Alcohol Tax Unit, which itself merged with the Federal Alcohol Administration in 1940. The entire federal internal revenue edifice was recast in 1952 as the Internal Revenue Service, which, in turn, resulted in the renaming of the Alcohol Tax Unit as the Alcohol and Tobacco Tax Division and, a decade later, as the Alcohol, Tobacco, and Firearms Division (ATF).

3. *Gonzales v. Ore gon* 126 S.Ct. 904, 921 (2006).
4. U.S. Const. Amend XVIII.

Pursuant to the Homeland Security Act of 2003, the Department of the Treasury's ATF Division has been divided into two new organizations with separate functions. The Alcohol and Tobacco Tax and Trade Bureau (TTB) remains within the Department of the Treasury, while the law enforcement functions were transferred to the Department of Justice's Bureau of Alcohol, Tobacco, Firearms and Explosives (the new ATF). The TTB's mission is to collect excise taxes and to assure that alcohol and tobacco products are lawfully labeled, advertised, and marketed. The new ATF within the Department of Justice is empowered to conduct criminal investigations and prevent illegal and international trafficking of alcohol and tobacco products. The chronicle of federal alcohol and tobacco regulation aptly demonstrates how government control can evolve and mutate, and it is a matter of speculation how long the current agency configuration will last. One thing is currently true, though: alcohol and tobacco are not regulated as prescription drugs by the FDA.

Office of National Drug Control Policy (ONDCP)

The Anti-Drug Abuse Act of 1988 created the White House Office of National Drug Control Policy (ONDCP) in order to "establish policies, priorities, and objectives for the Nation's drug control program."[5] Specifically, its goals are reducing the production, distribution, and use of illicit drugs, as well as the crime, violence, and health consequences related to these substances. The director of ONDCP is charged with generating the annual National Drug Control Strategy report, which describes what various agencies (including those listed above) are doing with regard to illicit drugs in an attempt to coordinate efforts among federal, state, and local entities. The ONDCP director, the so-called drug czar (a title stemming from an earlier period), is responsible for evaluating anti-drug operations of federal agencies, both on the domestic and international level, as well as ensuring that such efforts support state drug enforcement activities.[6] The drug czar reports directly to the President, keeping him informed of agency

5. "About ONDCP," online at http://www.whitehousedrugpolicy.gov/about/index.html.
6. Id.

compliance with the National Drug Control Strategy and any adjustments to drug policy, personnel, and practice.

The office is sometimes described as a bully pulpit to showcase federal efforts to stem recreational drug use. Because of the many agencies involved in drug interdiction—each of which has a specific authority, personnel, and budget—the ONDCP has frequently served as an educational rather than administrative operation. Moreover, the recently created Department of Homeland Security has taken over some of the administrative-coordination functions (with the same challenges of dealing with relatively autonomous agencies). The apparent overlap in jurisdiction and purpose of these entities has led to discussion about eliminating the ONDCP altogether.

Other Drug Agencies and Allied Governmental Bodies

The foregoing agencies constitute major players in the formulation and implementation of drug policy in the United States. But to be clear, the above listing is far from all-inclusive. Other important federal officials and agencies would include the professional prosecutors and administrators in the Department of Justice, as well as the local U.S. Attorneys in charge of federal criminal cases in specific geographic districts. Likewise, the U.S. Border Patrol and the U.S. Customs Service are among the most important actors in American drug policy—at least with regard to illegal drugs like cocaine and marijuana—serving as the primary bodies for drug interdiction at international borders. Moreover, state and local agencies charged with drug-related duties remain at the forefront of government control and regulation.

It is against the historical background sketched in the previous chapter, and the structures of governmental and other forms of regulation, that many issues about drugs play out. But these are not the only forms of drug regulation. Nongovernmental regulation of drugs, as will be discussed more fully below, occurs in several arenas. In the workplace, drug use is regulated by private corporations through drug testing programs. Although drug testing occurs for a few specified drugs of abuse, such as cocaine and marijuana, a private corporation can limit the use of these drugs among its employees, at least to the extent that the testing is effective. In professional sports, Olympic sports, and some amateur and school sports, certain drugs determined to be performance-enhancing are prohibited for participants. The actual substances to be banned are determined by individual sport organizations and generally conform to those set forth by the World Anti-Doping Agency (WADA). Testing positive by a sport organization leads only to sanctions imposed by that organization, with no criminal or civil laws being violated.

Conflicting Rationales for Regulation

This has been an account of regulatory agencies within the U.S. federal government. Some drugs are regulated by government agencies and to some degree by international policy, and some—including many of the same drugs—are also regulated by nongovernmental agencies like amateur, professional, and Olympic sports organizations, religious groups, and private schools, institutions, and employers. But because government decisions dominate discussions about drug policy, it is appropriate first to discuss a variety of rationales used to justify government restrictions on drug use in all areas, as well as exemptions from these restrictions and nonintervention by government in an open market for drugs.

Ethicists and legal theorists have identified a variety of rationales for government regulation of drugs and have explored inconsistencies and incoherencies among them. Policies that variously appear to be based in one or several of these rationales—that is, in the reasons provided explicitly or implicitly to justify the policy in question—are found in all areas of drug use, from prescription drugs to illegal street drugs. These various rationales assert that drug policy, as enacted in law, can legitimately be designed, among other things, to

1. respect the free, informed choices of individuals (*autonomy*);
2. respect the free choices of individuals as long as third parties are not harmed (*autonomy, limited by the harm principle*);
3. encourage or permit good outcomes and avoid bad outcomes (*consequentialism*);
4. protect a person's own good, even if by limiting otherwise autonomous choices (*paternalism*);

5. do good to a person or persons (*beneficence*);
6. express and embody the moral judgments of individuals, groups, or society (*moralism*);
7. observe fair processes in establishing policies and implementing them in particular cases (*procedural justice*);
8. compensate those who have been specifically wronged (*compensatory justice*); and
9. allocate burdens and benefits in a fair manner (*distributive justice*).

Consider the following examples, sketched here and developed in greater detail in later chapters. First, drug policy can be designed to respect autonomy, or, second, and more plausibly, respect autonomy in accordance with the harm principle. For the latter, a government's role should be to respect and empower the individual and his or her informed, free choices, as long as those choices do not harm third parties. Under this rationale, for example, there would be no grounds for preventing a patient from taking an experimental drug at the advice or request of the medical community, even if it has substantial risk of negative effects. Likewise, there would be no basis for prohibiting Native American members of the Native American Church, fully informed about possible negative consequences for themselves, from choosing to use peyote in their religious rituals as long as third parties are not harmed. But there would also be no reason to prohibit anyone else, regardless of race or church membership, from taking religious-use drugs for symbolic or sacramental purposes. Indeed, there would be no basis for preventing any persons from taking any drugs for any reason, provided they were fully informed, acting voluntarily (and not, for example, in the grip of addiction), and did not harm other persons.

The autonomist scenario is admittedly complicated by several interrelated issues. First, it is difficult to conceive of a situation where one person's actions would not impact in some way a third party, thereby affecting the other individual's range of choices and perhaps that person's own autonomy. Second, autonomy is based, in whole or in part, on the presumption that an individual is making free, informed choices. The ability to make such decisions, therefore, requires that the individual is provided with or seeks out information pertinent to the decision being made, and that the individual possesses the skills and knowledge to evaluate the information for validity and relevance.

In the context of drugs, informed decision making about the use or avoidance of any drug—whether prescription, OTC, herbal remedy, common-use, religious, sports-enhancement, or even illegal recreational—is confounded by the overwhelming quantity and variability of "information" available. It spouts from books, magazines, public service announcements, television (from documentaries to "infomercials"), pharmacies, health food stores, physicians, patient interest groups, internet sites, blogs, and so on, but is of vastly varying reliability—ranging from personal opinion and paid testimonials to case reports and randomized double-blind placebo-controlled trials. Thus the requirement that autonomy involve *informed* and voluntary choice, while comparatively simple in principle, is difficult to ensure in practice. Of course, if a person is held fully responsible for becoming informed, the overabundance of "information" might seem less relevant— she would be held responsible for assessing the quality of information as well as using it in her decision-making, but given the complexity of drug issues in all areas this would be an utterly unrealistic expectation for most ordinary consumers: after all, how many ordinary consumers (or even professionals) fully understand the pharmacological mechanisms, including risks, benefits, and side effects, of an aspirin, a cup of tea, a shot of penicillin, or a tab of LSD?

The consequentialist scenario also raises complex problems. Drug policy could indeed be designed to encourage or permit good consequences or avoid bad ones for the people affected, including the person taking the drug him or herself. This might underwrite everything from encouraging the use of aspirin or statins to reduce the risk of heart attack to permitting doctors to coerce a patient into taking psychotropic drugs to reduce hallucinations, even if enjoyed by the patient, if that prevents bad consequences from occurring to the patient or to others. When a policy that emphasizes good consequences overrides a person's autonomous choices, it involves paternalism. Like the principle of autonomy, as limited by the harm principle, legal paternalism may also permit restrictions on free choices that harm third parties, but unlike that principle it also permits restrictions upon a person's free choices that harm only him or herself. Thus, for example, if peyote use were shown to harm users, legal paternalism might permit restricting its use even for religious purposes and even if there were no harm to third parties.

Alternatively, drug policy could be designed to express and embody the moral judgments of individuals, groups, or society. Moralism permits restrictions and prohibitions of the harmful, the obscene, the degrading, and generally the evil as understood by a majority of citizens (or at least by their political representatives). Legal moralism could suggest a variety of different drug policies depending upon the moral views of a given group. The pertinent harms would include those to individuals that are relevant in legal paternalism as well as those to third parties relevant under the principle of autonomy as limited by the harm principle. However, this rationale would also incorporate harms to the "social fabric," where society as a whole is damaged by an individual's drug use. For this reason, legal moralism can justify even greater restrictions.

As another alternative, drug policy could be designed to enhance various forms of justice-related concerns. It could take as central procedural justice, emphasizing the process by which drug policy has been established and followed, and whether it meets specific requirements like the right to notice and to be heard; these might be relevant, for instance, when a legal proceeding evaluates the administration of antipsychotic drugs to render a defendant competent to stand trial. It could take compensatory justice to be central, with the goal of correcting past or current wrongs. When an unsafe drug harms people—for instance, birth defects caused by thalidomide or heart valve problems caused by fen-phen—the law could provide a course of action whereby the injured can sue, among others, the drug's manufacturer for compensation. The American tort system generally serves this purpose.

Finally, drug policy could be designed around the principle of distributive justice to allocate burdens and benefits in a fair manner. For example, prescription drug coverage might be assured by a national health system that includes medications for those who are least able to afford them, shifting the cost burden to the government, health insurers, or employers. The policy of preventing people in sports competitions from taking steroids could also be viewed as serving distributive justice, an attempt to ensure a level playing field and thus a fair starting position, although speaking speculatively, universal access to performance enhancements in sports could also be egalitarian in practice if every player could use them.

While these and other rationales may seem to be legitimate grounds for the design and evaluation of particular drug policies, they will vary widely from one policy to another. At least initially, it seems obvious that until such variation is reduced and incompatible rationales are eliminated, only modest progress, if any, can be expected in the search for a consistent, coherent, and comprehensive drug policy or set of policies across the board.

To be sure, not all different rationales are incompatible, and even those that are difficult to reconcile theoretically may coexist in practice, for example, beneficence and autonomy. Nonetheless, there are some genuine conflicts: for instance, autonomist rationales hold that it is the individual's values that ought to be recognized as primary, at least if there is no risk of harm to others, while moralist rationales stipulate what set of values are to be primary. Policies that are rooted in substantially conflicting rationales are more likely to exhibit inconsistencies in application than others. In scrutinizing any policy, governmental or nongovernmental, it is important to recognize the various rationales that may underlie it, and consider whether apparent incompatibilities are just that, merely apparent, or are based on fully legitimate and important differences.

To illustrate, consider how some of these rationales work in theories about punishment within the criminal justice system. Retributivists generally determine punishment by looking to the nature of the criminal's autonomous act and attached mental state: a person is to be punished proportionately not only to the harm caused (or threatened) but also the wrongfulness of the act and the culpability of his or her thought processes at the time of the event. In other words, retributivists would not advocate punishing people simply because they cause harm; otherwise, individuals who attempted, conspired, or solicited another to kill, but failed or simply did not follow through would not be subject to the criminal sanction. Moreover, it is not just the act or harm itself that results in punishment. Society does not punish an errant motorist in the same way or to the same degree as a Mafia hit man; the former may not be subject to the criminal sanction at all unless the driver harbored some culpable mental state. This is not the only approach, however. Those who advocate a consequentialist approach might focus the criminal justice system on deterrence, with criminal sanctions gauged to reduce undesirable future conduct. As such, an individual offender may be punished in order to maximize the chances that both this individual (specific deterrence) and other potential offenders (general deterrence) will be warded off from such behavior in the future. These rationales, and many more, present plausible but very different options for shaping criminal justice policies.

So how does the debate play out in criminal justice? If two criminals are convicted of the same crime and they receive different punishments, are the sentences just when measured by criteria of consistency and coherence in theories and policies of punishment? If the criminal history of the offenders is different, their likelihood of recidivism is different, the impact on the victims is different, or the two are convicted in different places where the views of just deserts or deterrent effects of punishment are different for some reason, then perhaps the sentences are justifiable. But this all depends upon what underlying rationales should shape criminal justice policy. Thus, even when the theoretical bases of relevant policy considerations have been identified—autonomy, beneficence, moralism, distributive justice, and so on—the dispute has merely been framed (perhaps not even in a satisfactory way) and may still be far from resolution.

Similarly, a firmer basis is still needed to provide an adequate rationale for drug policy, both government-regulated and that within the orbit of the private sector. Not only is it necessary to determine which purpose(s) drug policy should serve, and more generally whether drug policy should serve the same purpose in all cases or may vary among specific particular situations, but a decision-maker will also need to know what constitutes serving that purpose. To illustrate, consider how many different candidates there are for what constitutes "respecting autonomy." This could mean respecting the decisions of individuals alone, not as delegated or indirectly inferred, but only as directly expressed. It might mean respecting the decisions of elected representatives as the individual's agents. Or it might mean respecting the decisions of consumers, as embodied in their market choices. Any of these variants of the principle of autonomy could undercut the basis for prescription drug laws—allowing, for example, persons to self-medicate as they wish, as was the case in the United States before the development of the federal regime and is still true in many countries. Even when buttressed by the harm principle proscribing harm to others, an autonomist rationale would allow any drug use regardless of its self-destructiveness. It would permit the use of all prescription drugs, untested supplement products, common-use and sports drugs, and illegal recreational drugs. Only where this use posed the prospect of harm to others could limits be introduced. Under autonomy-favoring principles, it would be irrelevant to ask, for example, whether alcohol, marijuana, Prozac, anabolic steroids, and crystal meth posed similar or different risks to the user; the only relevant question would be whether their use constituted harm to others. If, say, marijuana (an illegal Schedule I drug) does not in general produce aggressive, violent behavior, but alcohol (not a scheduled controlled substance and perfectly legal) often does, the current legal policies concerning these drugs would have to be revised.

But these are not the only plausible interpretations of the autonomy principle. Respecting autonomy might mean respecting the un- or under-informed decisions of individuals where they had an opportunity to be informed—if, for example, information about the dangers of specific drugs or their adulterants were available in public libraries, clinics, and on the internet. Thus, under one interpretation, a person might be said to be acting autonomously in deliberating, choosing, and purchasing a product containing *Echinacea purpurea* (purple cone flower, commonly "echinacea"), although the lack of regulatory oversight under DSHEA may mean that the bottle marked echinacea contains only trace amounts of plant material and, therefore, virtually no therapeutically active ingredient, with the rest of the contents consisting of filler and byproducts, or worse, undisclosed contaminants and adulterants[7]: she *chose* to buy the drug. Under this view of autonomy, it might also be said that a person acts autonomously in deliberating, choosing, and purchasing a bottle of echinacea—the person has the opportunity to be informed of these matters, whether or not she took advantage of it. In contrast, under another interpretation autonomous choice could also be understood just as choice that actually is adequately informed; unlike the previous understanding of autonomy, this one would rule out the echinacea purchase she made.

Then again, autonomous choice can also be understood as a decision not coerced by either external or internal forces. Such a view of autonomy

---

7. Gilroy et al., "Echinacea and Truth in Labeling," 699–704.

would require attention to the role that addiction plays in drug use—from prescription pharmaceuticals to common-use drugs to illegal ones—since addiction itself may compromise autonomous choice. Can the addict autonomously choose to continue to use a specific drug, especially if he exhibits no interest in trying to quit and no discomfort about his use of the drug? Many "addicted" smokers appear to be perfectly content with their habit, while others say they struggle desperately to quit. Are they all autonomous choosers, or only the ones who do not want to quit (i.e., who are happy with their addiction), or who do want to quit but cannot (i.e., who reject their addiction although they are unable to break it), or both, or neither? (Chapter 4 will consider the central issues about addiction.)

Finally, "respecting autonomy" might mean respecting primarily those decisions that implicate aspects of personal identity or matters of conscience. Such an interpretation of the principle of autonomy might protect, for example, the choice to use (or not use) psychotropic drugs such as Prozac or other drugs that affect one's sense of self, social drinking that enhances one's sense of social acceptance, or religious-use drugs like peyote or sacramental wine. Arguably, it might also protect the use of sports-enhancement drugs that allow one to be known as a record-breaking home run hitter or a legendary sprinter or a renowned English Channel swimmer, if extraordinary performance in these feats is understood as central to an individual's identity and does not harm others. Under this reading of the principle of autonomy, use of self-image altering or performance-enhancing drugs, or for that matter drugs inducing a spiritual experience—for example, the hallucinogens used by many traditional religious groups—are to be protected or favored rather than prohibited under appropriate drug policies.

There are further issues here about the conflict between consequentialist and deontological arguments in debates about drug policy. Robert MacCoun and Peter Reuter's perceptive analysis in *Drug War Heresies*,[8] for instance, examines the differing types of argumentation employed in policy disputes over the question of whether drugs should be legalized.

8. Robert J. MacCoun and Peter Reuter, *Drug War Heresies. Learning from Other Vices, Times, and Places* (Cambridge: Cambridge University Press, 2001), 55–71.

They point out that although philosophical positions are not always made explicit in these debates—when, for example, some partisans point to the bad consequences of drug use while others condemn drug use on moral grounds—these distinctions contribute to the shaping of policy. These differences are important, and they will be at work in the rationales employed by various government agencies involved in drug regulation.

Incompatibilities in Rationales for Drug Regulation within the Government Framework and Elsewhere

The five different federal agencies for drug regulation and control sketched above, the FDA, the DEA, the TTB, the ATF, and the ONDCP, are all large and complex government bodies, each of which has a distinctive mission within the overall orbit of management and regulation of drugs. (Of course, these are only the major federal-level drug regulatory agencies; also part of the overall scene are the various forms of state and private control, including actions by private employers, religious groups, educational institutions, social clubs, and sports associations.) But does this elaborate architecture of regulation contribute to justice in drug policy? The question here is whether the underlying rationales for the existence and operations of each of these federal agencies are consistent with each other and whether they form a coherent whole.

The Apparent Incompatibility of Rationales among Federal Agencies

It would be a Herculean and, in the end, frustrating task to try to sort out all the complexities and nuances of underlying rationales for each of the aforementioned federal drug-related agencies. After all, a full depiction of the underlying rationale for an agency cannot be simply read off from its mission statement or the applicable statutes and other legal mandates. Yet even a quick glimpse can point to apparent conflicts in rationales that are to be explained, at least in part, by looking at still deeper conceptual issues, those to be examined in the two chapters that follow.

Consider, for instance, the difference of focus and potential conflict between the FDA and the ONDCP. These two agencies normally occupy quite different silos of thought about drugs, the former concerned primarily with medicinal drugs and the latter with illegal drugs. But both are concerned with drugs, seen across the board, and thus their underlying rationales could be expected to be at least consistent and sufficiently compatible to form part of a coherent whole.

The FDA's purpose and mandate is to approve and regulate medicinal drugs in a way that assures the end-user—the patient—that they are safe and effective. It approves drugs for use by medical practitioners, based on evidence of safety and efficacy, and enforces manufacturing standards. In this sense, it is an enabling agency. Although any such characterization must necessarily be somewhat simplistic, it is also fair to say that the FDA's underlying rationale is broadly autonomist, within the constraints of the harm principle—to enhance the capacity of the patient, as mediated by the physician, to choose what drugs to use by providing full and accurate information. This information also allows the patient to choose to avoid certain prescription drugs, whether because she has an adverse reaction to them, because she does not wish to risk certain side effects, or for other personal, religious, or ideological reasons. After all, the FDA and the prescription-legend regulation it administers arose in part as a response to an earlier historical period in which unscrupulous drug salesmen touted "miracle cures" that at best had little or no worth, and at worst could be harmful to naïve purchasers. Thus, in effect, the FDA's restrictions in establishing the prescription legend and in imposing manufacturing standards enhances the patient's capacity to choose safe and effective drugs.

But the FDA's rationale is not wholly autonomist; it is also partly paternalist, in the sense that the patient's range of choices is limited to those that are safe and efficacious within identified bounds. To be sure, its approach has evolved, from highly paternalist a few decades ago to a much more autonomist approach in the present, with new doctrines of informed consent placing the patient in a more autonomous position and the physician in a more "autonomy-supporting" role. Under the prescription legend, the patient's choice is mediated through the prescriber—the physician, dentist, nurse practitioner, physician assistant, or other licensed prescriber as determined by the states—the party who understands and interprets the information about the potential risks and benefits of a drug, and who determines whether it is medically appropriate for the condition to be treated.

Within these bounds, however, the patient is entitled to decide whether to use a drug and thus what counts as safe enough for him or her.

It is important to note that the term "safe" means that the drug is safe for use within the context of its labeling (which includes the detailed information printed as a "package insert" that is placed in every prescription drug package). All drugs have potential toxicities. Thus the term "safe" must be interpreted within the context of the risk-to-benefit ratio. For example, a drug that can induce remissions in 40 percent of patients with a specific, aggressive cancer might be considered safe if the cancer would be expected to be rapidly lethal in 75 percent of patients—even if the drug might cause lethal toxicity in 10 percent of the patients receiving it. Conversely, a drug that lessens symptoms of the common cold (which normally resolves with or without symptomatic therapy in about a week) would not be considered safe for use if it caused any significant toxicity.

Needless to say, the FDA has a difficult charge: it must guarantee that drugs are safe and efficacious, but it must also provide mechanisms to ensure that needed drugs are marketed as quickly as possible to prevent and treat diseases. As such, the agency is continually pressured by opposing interests. Some want drugs to reach the market more quickly—particularly intense pressures came from AIDS activists, for example, during the early development of antiretroviral drugs for HIV—while others want more stringent testing completed before the drugs are approved for marketing, as reflected in consternation over the weight-loss drug fen-phen. As a part of the Department of Health and Human Services, the FDA must address the demands of the executive branch of the federal government, and at the same time must satisfy Congress that it is operating efficiently in order to get the necessary funding. The public often fears the risks of new drugs that are being introduced in haste, putting pressure on the FDA to require that experimental drugs be studied more thoroughly before approval for human use. On the other hand, individuals often perceive potential benefits for themselves or loved ones and want drugs approved more rapidly.

When social and medical exigencies occur, like the fear of mutated bird influenza that came into public consciousness in 2006, members of Congress typically insist that the FDA expedite drug development (e.g., influenza vaccine manufacturing methods). When adverse reactions occur, such as the 2005 disclosure of the association of the anti-inflammatory arthritis drug rofecoxib (Vioxx) with cardiovascular toxicity, society (and Congress) call for more careful premarketing studies of new drugs. This may be seen as a tension between autonomist and paternalist conceptions of the FDA's appropriate role.

Such conflicts in underlying rationales for federal drug regulation are played out on many fronts. In the past decade, the United States has seen the approval of direct-to-consumer advertising of prescription drugs. Advocates of this practice argue that patients should have a right to discuss new drugs with their prescribers. Detractors note that the average visit with a primary care physician is less than ten minutes long and few clinicians will spend part of that valuable time trying to convince their patients that different, less expensive medications are more appropriate. Some argue that direct-to-consumer advertising inappropriately creates a demand for drug treatment of ordinary human conditions, whether it is sadness, baldness, transient anxiety, or attention-demanding behavior in children. Lay patients are often incapable of judging accurately the validity of such advertising and physicians may have trouble resisting their demands.

The arguments on both sides have merit. In countries with single payer or nationalized health systems, duplicative ("me too") drugs rarely are approved. In contrast, in a largely free enterprise health care system such as that in the United States, licensure cannot be denied if a drug meets the criteria for approval, even if it is inferior to already available agents. Here, the role of private actors may be critical. While the FDA must approve a "safe and effective" medication regardless of how it compares with other similar compounds, insurance carriers need not pay for its use. These private firms (or in the case of Medicare and Medicaid, governmental institutions) are an important factor in the FDA's balancing act, given the financial considerations implicated by drug approval.

An autonomist system within which the consumer—in this case the patient—has the right to choose the product to use assumes that the consumer is knowledgeable about the item and its alternatives. Is that a reasonable assumption in an area as complicated as pharmacological activity and toxicity? The purpose of advertising is to make a consumer *desire* a product. Is that a good idea in the case of prescription medications? One might contend that such advertising allows the patient to inform the clinician of an appropriate medication that the clinician would not have otherwise considered. Conversely, one might argue that direct-to-consumer advertising causes health care costs to escalate because more expensive medications are prescribed, though they provide little or no advantage. Indeed, the tensions here—between commercial free speech on the one hand and potentially misleading (and thereby harmful) advertising on the other hand, especially when it is directed to a vulnerable population like people who are ill (or believe they are ill)—is an excellent example of fundamental tensions within the U.S. legal system.

Autonomist, paternalist, consequentialist, and other rationales for drug regulation all appeal to the notion of safety. Yet the notion of drug safety itself is decidedly complex. Some drugs licensed by the FDA are not "safe" in any usual sense—certain chemotherapy agents used in treating cancer, for example—although they may offer a reduced risk of death compared to allowing the disease to go untreated. Other drugs are safe when used correctly, but potentially lethal if misused, such as insulin. Some drugs, specifically antibiotics, are restricted to prescription status because if misused—that is, if overused or inappropriately used—they can constitute harm not only to the patient but also to others by allowing antibiotic-resistant organisms to develop. And some drugs, like opioids used in pain management, are not "safe" according to understandings prevalent in other spheres of drug issues. But under the prescription legend system administered by the FDA, it is still up to the patient, at least in theory and under contemporary understandings of informed consent, to decide whether to accept or decline a given drug based on information the physician provides about its risks and benefits. While it would indeed be simplistic to claim that the underlying rationale of the FDA is wholly "autonomist-within-limits-of-the-harm-principle-and-with-paternalist-elements," it more closely approaches this than others of the potential rationales just outlined. The central emphasis is to empower the patient to make reasonable choices, mediated by the physician, about what drugs to use within a generally safe range.

Contrast the underlying rationale of the FDA with that, say, of two regulatory agencies involved with common-use drugs, the ATF and the TTB. The latter entities are concerned with collecting revenue from taxation of these products: the ATF seeks to reduce illegal trafficking of alcohol and tobacco, often to avoid payment of taxes, and the TTB's mandate is to collect taxes and to ensure appropriate labeling, advertising, and marketing.

While the underlying rationales of these agencies are not wholly distinct from that of the FDA—for instance, the TTB does regulate labeling and advertising of alcohol and tobacco in the interests of providing the public with reliable information—the ATF and TTB are intended more to facilitate revenue collection than to enhance consumer choice or protect user well-being, like the FDA.

Ironically, however, death and disease caused by tobacco and alcohol products far exceed that caused by both prescription drugs and illegal drugs—not only because these common-use drugs can be so destructive, but because they are so widely used. Yet under the current scheme of agency oversight and enforcement, these drugs are virtually unregulated when it comes to the health and safety of the user and his or her fully informed choice. Information about risks and benefits is not systematically provided, nor are these products "prescription legend" in the sense that their use requires supervision by a knowledgeable professional, such as a physician. Nor are potential harms to others, such as second-hand smoke or drunk driving, part of the purview of the ATF and TTB. Even the public health initiatives reminding consumers of the implications of their choices—like the requirement of black-bordered "scare" labeling of such products, "Surgeon General's Warning: Cigarettes May Be Harmful To Your Health"—actually come from a different agency, the Department of Health and Human Services.

If anything, then, the rationales for the ATF and the TTB seem to be consequentialist only in the sense of augmenting the public coffers (presumably for the benefit of all), rather than a concern about the consequences of using a potentially dangerous drug where individual choice may be compromised by addiction. Thus the underlying basis for the ATF and TTB does not seem to be user-directed or "autonomist" in the sense of maximizing prospective users' capacities to make an *informed* choice about whether to use these drugs or not. Attempts to put the regulation of tobacco products under the authority of the FDA have been repeatedly and successfully undermined by the tobacco industry, which may underscore the difference in underlying rationales among these agencies: the industry accepts regulation by the ATF and TTB, but seeks to avoid regulation by the FDA, which operates under a very different mandate and conception of what is involved in drug management and control.

Now consider the underlying rationales for the DEA, an agency within the Justice Department, and the ONDCP, an office within the White House.

In contrast to the FDA's partial autonomist justification and the tax-oriented consequentialism of the ATF and TTB, the DEA and the ONDCP direct their principal efforts toward the eradication (or at least heavy regulation) of drugs seen to have abuse potential. The underlying rationale of these agencies can be described as paternalist in character, in the sense that their objective is to protect prospective users from drugs that are harmful or addictive. It is also consequentialist in that it serves to protect society from crime and other costs associated with drug use. But the rationales of these agencies are quite different from the user-directed efforts of the FDA or the largely revenue–protecting operations of the TTB and ATF; rather, the DEA and ONDCP aim to deny or restrict access to certain drugs altogether. The DEA does not require that adequate information about relative risks and benefits of a drug be made available to users; its mechanisms for drug control are designed to block abuse or use of specific drugs altogether. In turn, the ONDCP focuses almost exclusively on the risks of illegal drugs, attempting to reduce the abuse of drugs by educating the public about their dangers.

The DEA's primary legal code, the Controlled Substances Act (CSA), includes some prescription drugs (e.g., opioids), some sports-enhancement drugs (e.g., anabolic steroids), as well as some religious-use drugs, but it does not cover alcohol or tobacco. The CSA's Schedules place all regulated drugs into one of the five categories depending upon each substance's medicinal value, harmfulness, and potential for abuse or addiction. Here, the goal is to protect users from harm, rather than to facilitate their well-informed choices, and also to indirectly benefit society as a whole by removing the threat of substances associated with crime and social harm in general. Specific restrictions, like limitations on the amount of a drug that may be prescribed by a physician (Schedules II-IV), are intended to control abuse and "leakage" to other parties than the specific patient in question. The underlying rationale for the DEA, as for the ONDCP as well, is thus essentially consequentialist, rather than autonomist, insofar as the efforts of both are best understood as intended to benefit society as a whole by eliminating or reducing usage of harmful or addictive drugs.

Consequentialist rationales refer to predicted outcomes of specific policies and practices. In the service of prediction, the collection and assessment of data is central. Such a role is played by the Drug Abuse Warning Network (DAWN), a program of the federal Substance Abuse and Mental Health Services Administration (SAMHSA) within the Department of Health and

Human Services. DAWN is a voluntary national data collection system that gathers information on substance abuse resulting in visits to hospital emergency rooms in the United States. Hospitals participating in the DAWN system include nonfederal, short-stay, general hospitals that have twenty-four-hour emergency departments plus a sample of hospitals in twenty-one major metropolitan areas. The system also collects data on drug-related deaths from a nonrandom sample of medical examiners. Such data are published annually in separate reports titled *DAWN Medical Examiner Data*.

The data collected by the DAWN system represent one of the most widely utilized national indicators of drug abuse. These data are frequently used by researchers and policymakers to determine the nature and extent of medical consequences of drug use nationally and in the participating metropolitan areas. Although often relied upon to monitor patterns and trends of drug abuse, DAWN data are assembled from voluntary reports by substance abusers and thus are not validated. Most commonly, substance abusers take multiple substances concurrently but report only one or two, frequently the "drug du jour" or substance that is most discussed and sought by abusers in that location at a given time. Furthermore, DAWN data represent information only on individuals who enter an emergency room because of their drug use. Therefore, the information reflects only the most serious cases of drug abuse. Consequences of drug use that are less severe are not represented in the data.

Recognizing numerous flaws in DAWN, SAMHSA launched a redesign of the system in 2003. Changes involved hospital samples, target populations, geographical boundaries, criteria for defining DAWN cases, content data, methods for finding cases, and methods to ensure quality. Nonetheless, the system is still limited by its very nature as a voluntary reporting system using less than reliable sources for the data, namely, substance abusers themselves. The DEA regularly uses DAWN data as its "evidence" of the drugs being abused, thus leading to questions as to whether DEA-sponsored policy may be flawed as a result.

This sketch of the various federal agencies involved in drug regulation may seem to overemphasize differences when there is a great deal of commonality among them. For example, all these agencies are dedicated, in their various ways, to controlling dangerous drugs, to preventing harm to users and to society, and to curbing addiction. Yet the contrasts among them are striking. If the DEA were to adopt the more autonomist rationale that appears to underlie the workings of the FDA, it would work to ensure that prospective users of drugs—including all the controlled substances over which it has jurisdiction—had access to full, reliable information about a drug's risks and benefits. This information might be complex enough to require interpretation by a trained professional, for example, a physician or pharmacist, but the choice to use the drug would remain in the hands of the prospective consumer. Access to a drug might be obtained only through a trained professional where overuse or misuse would constitute a potential harm to others—similar to medical oversight of antibiotics to prevent the development of resistant organisms, for example—but policies would be user-oriented in a way that they do not seem to be under the current approach. On the other hand, if the FDA were to function more like the DEA, at least as it functions with Schedule I controlled substances, it would simply bar drugs said to be dangerous or addictive with little or no reference to any purported benefits.

To be sure, the scheduling system does recognize that some drugs that are dangerous or addictive also have medicinal uses. It is also true that the FDA's primary purpose is to approve (and in theory, the DEA is not to forbid) the use of dangerous drugs as long as the benefits outweigh the harms. But while the FDA controls approval of drugs, the DEA has significant authority in their assignment to the controlled-substance Schedules and thus can affect access to these drugs. Whether the functions of the FDA and the DEA can be construed as compatible is a controversial issue. Nonetheless, the clear emphasis of the DEA in practice is to limit or prevent access to those substances that it sees as harmful. This is a largely consequentialist rather than autonomist view, in that the DEA is focused much more clearly on the good of society than on enhancing patient and clinician choice, and it has substantial power to eliminate or restrict drugs that are considered a threat to the social fabric.[9]

Apparent Inconsistencies in Drug Classification

It might be plausible to hold that differing underlying rationales for agencies that engage in drug management and control are appropriate because

---

9. These contrasts among autonomist, paternalist, and consequentialist elements in drug theory and policy have been discussed in detail in Douglas Husak's *Drugs and Rights* and in MacCoun and Reuter's *Drug War Heresies*, especially in analyses of arguments for and against drug legalization.

the types of drugs they regulate are different. Thus the basic principle of justice—*treat like cases alike*—would not be violated. For instance, it might be said, medicinal drugs used to treat medical ailments (prescription drugs) are different from lower-risk drugs that patients are able to use on their own (over-the-counter drugs), and these, in turn, differ from dietary supplements and herbal remedies. They also differ from drugs like alcohol, nicotine, and caffeine (common-use drugs), entheogens such as peyote and ayahuasca (religious-use drugs), and steroids and other muscle-building or endurance-promoting drugs (sports-enhancement drugs). In general, it might thus be argued, medical-use drugs, are different from addictive, health-damaging, and crime-producing illegal recreational-use drugs like cocaine and heroin. Because the types of drugs themselves differ, this argument continues, different rationales for regulating them are appropriate. The organizational rationales of the various agencies, both governmental and nongovernmental, simply attempt to track the types of drugs they are dedicated to controlling. Different rationales are adapted to the differing kinds of drugs with which they deal.

But this argument—that differences in rationales track differences in drugs—would only be plausible if differing types of drugs were classified consistently according to an intelligible, well-reasoned schema. As seen previously, however, much of the current drug classification and assignment to various agencies is the product of erratic historical events, in which drugs were classified one way or another for reasons having more to do with public perceptions and political pressures—even ethnocentric and racist ones—than with the properties of the drugs themselves. This is true for drugs in each of the major silos under consideration. Consider the following:

Prescription Drugs. Most prescription drugs are "medicinal," that is, intended to cure, prevent, or ameliorate the medical condition of a patient. But some are not, and the distinction itself is contentious. Prescription-legend drugs are those that carry enough risks that they require the supervision of a physician or other licensed prescriber for safe use. Some are dangerous even if intended as curative, such as cancer chemotherapy. Some are medicinal in the sense of enhancing function by compensating for biological deficiencies that are not, however, illnesses in the usual sense—methylphenidate (Ritalin and others), for instance, or sildenafil (Viagra)—though, of course, these distinctions are easily challenged. Insulin used in the treatment of diabetes compensates for a biological deficiency; attention deficit hyperactivity disorder (ADHD), treated with Ritalin, is classified as a medical illness. Active agents can be used both "medically" and as "enhancement," for example, to increase to normal range the height of short-stature children, or to tall range the height of normal-stature children. Botox (botulinum toxin) can be used to treat wrinkles (often though not always a vanity issue), but also to treat spastic torticollis, a painful spasm of the neck muscles, a disabling medical condition.

The argument that medical-use drugs are categorically different from recreational-use drugs is particularly problematic.[10] Among the controlled substances that constitute prescription drugs, sodium oxybate (Xyrem), a Schedule III controlled substance approved for use in narcolepsy, is chemically identical to GHB, gamma-hydroxybutyrate (the "date-rape drug"), a Schedule I substance that is illegal. Dronabinol (Marinol) is synthetic tetrahydrocannabinol, the major active ingredient in marijuana, and is commercially available as a Schedule III controlled substance, medically indicated for nausea and also for appetite stimulation in AIDS. Furthermore, the schedules themselves may be inconsistent in their treatment of specific drugs. Hydrocodone in combination with other drugs such as acetaminophen is a Schedule III controlled substance—while very close chemical analogs, such as oxycodone in combination with acetaminophen, are Schedule II controlled substances. It is questionable whether there can be any scientific or clinical basis for this scheduling distinction.

Over-the-Counter Drugs. Over-the-counter drugs are identified as medicinal drugs that are safe enough for a patient to use without the supervision of a physician. But some OTC drugs are identical to prescription-legend drugs except in dosage. For example, pseudoephedrine 30 mg tablets are OTC but some higher strengths are prescription, thus raising the question of whether this drug is safe for use without the supervision of a physician. While the drug may be safe at a lower dose—according to the label—there is no mechanism preventing the patient from taking a higher dose, other than the label's dosing instructions. At the same time, three nonsteroidal anti-inflammatory

10. See Douglas N. Husak's lucid discussion of difficulties with attempts to draw this distinction in *Legalize This! The Case for Decriminalizing Drugs* (London and New York: Verso, 2002).

drugs (NSAIDS)—ibuprofen, ketoprofen, and naproxen sodium—are OTC, while well over a dozen other NSAIDS with very similar properties and toxicities are only available by prescription. Of approximately two dozen NSAIDS on the market, three are available OTC but the others are not.

Dietary Supplements. Herbal medicines and other dietary supplements, sometimes called "complementary and alternative medicines" or CAM, are widely assumed to be innocuous substances safe for a person to use in self-medication or health maintenance. But most are not well studied and some are potentially toxic. Contrary to widespread popular belief, "natural" does not equal "harmless." There is still scant evidence of safety and efficacy for most of these drugs, to say nothing about continuing problems with product quality and content. Some are merely ineffective. Echinacea, one of the most commonly used dietary supplements, is not only not reliably purveyed—what is on the label often does not match what is in the bottle—but has been found of no value in preventing or reducing the severity or length of colds or flu, and has no known medical benefit. Another dietary supplement, ephedra, was widely used for weight loss and has well-known medical value, but it also has been associated with a number of adverse events, including fatalities.

Common-Use Drugs. Caffeine taken as coffee or tea is not classified as a drug; caffeine taken as NoDoz is classified as an OTC drug. The common-use drugs alcohol and tobacco are classified separately from other drugs, although they have addictive properties and abuse potential that would suggest classification as controlled substances. In turn, tobacco and caffeine also have enhancement properties—increased alertness, for instance—that might indicate a class similarity with sports-enhancement drugs. If, on the other hand, ubiquitousness of use is the criterion for classification of "common-use drugs," then other drugs also widely used might be included in this category—marijuana, for example, or perhaps even sugar or chocolate, or in some cultures, coca, betel nut, and khat.

Religious-Use Drugs. This classification is problematic in the sense that it does not identify what counts as use, and whether it is properties of the drugs themselves or the conditions of use that give rise to religious experience or important symbolism. The wine that is central to Roman Catholic mass is ingested in such small quantities that it cannot produce physiological euphoria. In traditional Judaism, in contrast, inebriation with alcohol is expected on the feast of Purim, the celebration of the saving of the Jewish people in ancient

Persia. The highly toxic drug strychnine is used together with serpent-handling in certain Holiness Churches in the Appalachian region of the United States, a deliberate risking of death as a demonstration of faith. Is there any univocal sense in which both practices count as the religious *use* of drugs?

Performance-Enhancing Drugs. Substances in this class are generally prescription drugs, such as anabolic steroids, as well as some drugs of abuse (e.g., cocaine or marijuana), that have been deemed to enhance athletic performance or said to be detrimental to the "spirit" of sport. These are the same drugs controlled by federal agencies (i.e., the FDA and DEA), but in this context they are privately regulated within the sport as well as publicly regulated by the government. Their use within the sport carries no violation of criminal or civil law, and as such, their use carries no penalty other than that imposed by the sport.

Illegal Drugs. This classification appears to reflect a variety of background political events, not simply properties of the drugs' ingestion, such as physiological harm to the user or other individuals. Some illicit drugs—for instance, peyote and marijuana—are not addictive and do not produce aggressive or otherwise harmful behavior in themselves (though, as will be seen in chapter 5, harm may be associated with the illegal behavior engaged in to obtain the drug). Some drugs that are addictive and harmful to the user are also not illegal—tobacco, for example—and even some drugs that are addictive, harmful to the user, *and* may generate aggressive or violent behavior are not illegal—alcohol, for instance.

Thus the argument that differences in regulatory rationales are designed to track differences in drugs is not supported by pharmacology or actual practice. Such an argument might be plausible if differing types of drugs were classified consistently according to an intelligible, well-reasoned, consistent, and coherent schema. Yet much of the current drug classification and thus assignment to a particular agency appears to be the product of politically motivated historical events, rather than by the properties of the drugs themselves or their effects in users.

* * *

Clearly, the autonomist/paternalist/consequentialist contrast, as well as that with beneficence, moralism, and various forms of justice-related concerns, is useful in explaining some of the differences among the various federal agencies that regulate drugs and the policies they employ. Were this analysis to be extended, it would no doubt also be useful in characterizing contrasts between governmental and various nongovernmental entities, too. Incompatible rationales are clearly a major part of the problem, and inconsistent classifications of drugs also play a substantial role in the lack of coherence in overall drug policy. But a large source of this trouble lies at a deeper conceptual level, to be examined in the next two chapters. All these agencies, both governmental and nongovernmental, are alike in their dedication to controlling dangerous drugs, to preventing harm to users and to society, and to curbing addiction. These are noble aims. But conceptual inconsistencies—fissures within more fundamental notions like "addiction" and "harm"—may jeopardize the pursuit of these goals in very real ways.

4

CORE CONCEPTUAL PROBLEMS: ADDICTION

Addiction is perhaps the most feared aspect of drugs, and the potential for addiction is a primary force behind efforts to restrict or prohibit certain drugs. Unlike other risks associated with "dangerous" drugs, addiction is not simply a matter of adverse physiological outcomes but also a question of behavior. What constitutes addiction, however, varies widely, and the subject remains a contentious issue charged with both social and moral concerns.

As discussed in more detail in chapter 5, every decision to use a drug, whether for medical purposes, recreation, or some other reason, carries inherent risks. The potential harm may have little to do with the drug's legal status, and it may be independent of whether the user is suffering from addiction. Opioids can cause death due to respiratory depression; it does not matter whether the drug is used on the street or in the operating room. Hallucinogens may result in death if, for example, someone believes she can fly and jumps out a window. Cocaine can cause death due to cardiac arrhythmias or stroke. The risk of addiction is simply another hazard of drug use, associated with a limited number of drugs. But although it is greatly overestimated by both health professionals and the general public, virtually all agree that addiction can have catastrophic consequences. In medical applications, the decision to employ any pharmacological substance is assumed to be based on a determination that the potential benefits outweigh the potential risks. In recreational settings, however, users typically lack sufficient information to make such decisions, and the user's perceived benefits as well as the user's perception of the risks involved often outweigh the objective risks.

Two inherent risks associated with numerous pharmacologically active substances are the development of pharmacological (physiological) dependence and the development of addiction. Unfortunately, these terms have become highly value-laden and often are used incorrectly. This chapter addresses conceptual tensions at the root of the concept of addiction, tensions revealed by examining how the concept is defined in different fields.

Addiction in History

Fundamentally, addiction is considered a loss of self-control. The word comes from the Latin *ad dicere*, to be appointed or spoken for, in the way that a slave is bound to a master. The derivation of addiction is also exemplified by reference to Addictus, a Roman debtor whose capacity for spending borrowed money far exceeded his ability to repay.[1]

Documented observations of addiction date back to 3,500 BC, when Egyptian hieroglyphics depicted opium habituation and warned of the adverse effects of dependence. Not until the nineteenth century, however, was addiction generally perceived in the United States as requiring more than social disapproval. Unrelated events on three different continents caused a shift in public perception of addiction as neither a personal shortcoming nor an illness, but as a threat to the entire society. The first of these, and arguably the mildest, was Thomas De Quincey's 1821 account of his own chronic opium addiction, *Confessions of an English Opium Eater*. Before the appearance of De Quincey's lurid memoir, opium dependence was viewed no differently from other habits, such as the consumption of tobacco and alcohol. It was seen as quaint, perhaps even gentlemanly in moderation, but evoked disgust when present in the lower classes and especially when it was taken to excess—like the difference between evening cocktails and beer-hall drunkenness. De Quincey's story changed that perception rather abruptly. Opium became publicly reviled; its use became more discreet but certainly not extinct.

1. William Smith, D.C.L., LL.D.: *A Dictionary of Greek and Roman Antiquities* (London: John Murray, 1875) (3) 406. Addictus is the name central character in a play of that name by Plautius Rufus, also called Titus Maccius Plautus (254 BC); see http://www.ancientlibrary.com/smith-bio/2740.html.

In China, opium use had been well known for thousands of years. By the 1830s, however, the drug had become associated with high levels of crime and corruption, leading the Chinese government to ban opium use and importation. Subsequent disputes between Chinese officials and British opium importers resulted in the Opium Wars (1839–42 and 1856–60), both of which ended in crushing defeats for China and its acquiescence to continued opium importation. By the turn of the century, an estimated half of the adult Chinese male population was addicted to the drug. The government of China was humiliated militarily, economically, and socially by the effects of opium on its population, and these events served as a major impetus for global narcotic regulations.

In America, opium in various forms—principally the aqueous extract known as "black drop" and the camphorated, alcoholic tincture known as laudanum—was typically considered a common and relatively benign medication. Indeed, it was cheaper and considered less harmful than alcohol. That perception changed, however, with widespread morphine addiction among soldiers who served in the Civil War, with this "soldier's disease" resulting to some extent from the liberal use of morphine in battlefield treatment of injuries. Addiction became known as a debilitating habit that promoted irresponsibility and laziness that was in sharp opposition to the prevailing Protestant work ethic.

The Harrison Narcotics Act of 1914, the first national drug law in the United States pertaining to opioids, was enacted in part to position the United States as an international leader in combating opioid abuse, but it also had the effect of protecting the American public from the toxicity of opium derivatives, particularly with regard to personal harm and overdose. The law was framed as a taxation statute to permit the orderly marketing and dispensing of drugs, with drug control vested with the Treasury Department. Still, an underlying motivation for this legislation was the fear of addiction as a loss of social control; the addict was seen as beholden to a drug rather than to social mores or to the law. This position was forwarded by leading government officials, such as Harry J. Anslinger, the anti-drug crusader and the first Commissioner of the U.S. Bureau of Narcotics, who led federal drug enforcement efforts for three decades.

But the view that addiction was a moral weakness—a seductive but depraved activity like gambling, prostitution, and other culturally disapproved behaviors—did not go uncontested. In particular, a different conception arose within the medico-scientific communities: that addiction is a disease. The shift away from a solely behavioral model to the disease model has steadily gained ground in some circles and is now accepted in medicine, although the popular view remains ambivalent. At the same time, however, the term "addiction" has to some degree lost favor in clinical circles, partly because of the latent moralism carried by the word itself and partly because it is an imprecise and potentially pejorative term.

Since 1969, the World Health Organization (WHO) and the psychiatric literature have favored use of the term "dependence," which is sometimes subdivided into two categories: (1) physical dependence, defined in part by the presence of withdrawal symptoms if the drug is rapidly discontinued, and (2) psychological dependence, defined by "craving." But this use, as is to be explored, is not consistent across all spheres of concern with drugs. For some, "dependence" amounts to essentially the same thing as "addiction"; in others, however, it does not. Use of the term "dependence" in this compartmentalized, "siloed" way, to be discussed below, has greatly confounded the concept of addiction.

The Stigma of Addiction

"Addiction" is a term with pronounced negative connotations. Declaring that the relationship between a user and a substance is an "addiction" typically indicates both that the substance is being misused and that the relationship is shameful or unhealthy. An addict is by the very use of this term typically labeled as dangerous and self-destructive. Yet not all observers hold that addiction is undesirable or that the terms "addict" and "addiction" are pejorative. These terms can be used as objective, denotative terms, just as "obesity" can be used descriptively without the negative connotations. But for the most part, addicts and their addictions are cast in an array of negative roles, from the pitiful prisoner of uncontrollable foreign desires to dangerous individuals ready to do anything to satisfy their appetites. Different notions of addiction abound, but they are almost uniformly negative, usually differing only in how culpable the addicts are thought to be for their own addictions. This permits policymakers to assume that insofar as the potential or reality of addiction can be identified in a relationship with a drug, regulation or prohibition is thus warranted. Yet the way addiction is defined affects how the addict as a moral agent is viewed and influences policies regarding all forms of addiction and addictive substances. For this reason, the concept of addiction must be carefully examined.

Drug and Nondrug Addiction

Addiction most often involves the use of a chemical substance, affecting the addict's body and behavior, often characterized by a strong, even over-powering desire to obtain drugs and a decreasing ability to control this desire.[2] A variety of euphemisms are also used to describe this relationship or to refer to the drugs involved, such as "habituation" and "habit forming," for example, but these are usually quite imprecise and both clinically and legally meaningless.

Addiction is also said to occur with many sorts of activities and prac-tices, like gambling, sex, or exercise. The idea that there can be distinct conditions of physical and psychological addiction remains controversial. For example, consider the occasional marijuana user who consumes the drug to steady himself and improve his occupational performance (a case to be discussed in chapter 6). In some sense, he is drawn to drug use by the nature of his work, but it is unlikely that he is physically addicted. A high-pressure executive may use Prozac or another antidepressant medication periodically to enable her to perform adequately in a position of authority, but it would seem odd to say that she is addicted to the drug. Yet it is not uncommon for both professionals and lay people to speak quite seriously about addictions to such things as television, exercise, or sex. In fact, addic-tions to sex and gambling are well-known and significant psychopatholo-gies, but neither addiction involves a substance. Gambling addiction, for instance, can be classified as a robust addiction to a nonchemical object.[3]

In terms of neurobiology, addiction—at least in its end-stage—can involve changes in the normal dopamine reward systems in the brain and

2. Peter W. Kalivas and Nora D. Volkow, "The Neural Basis of Addiction: A Pathology of Motivation and Choice," *American Journal of Psychiatry* 162 (2005): 1403–13.

3. Jon Elster and Ole-Jørgen Skog, eds., *Getting Hooked: Rationality and Addiction* (Cambridge: Cambridge University Press, 1999).

cellular adaptations in the prefrontal cortex that promote compulsive behavior by decreasing the value of natural rewards, diminishing cognitive control, and strengthening the response to stimuli associated with the drug or behavior which is the focus of the addiction.[4] Recent scientific advances show that there are neurobiological similarities in drug and nondrug addictions. Even when these "addictions" are admitted in jest, they connote some unease or unhealthiness. Studies in the addictionology literature have found that 9 percent of the entire population will be addicted to something at some point in their lives.[5] Whether or not the objects of addiction are drugs, the addictions usually are thought to be harmful and preferably avoided.

Whether addiction is considered intrinsically wrong, even "evil," or whether addiction is seen as morally neutral but to be avoided because of the self- or other-regarding harms it produces, the idea of addiction as "bad" is ubiquitous and influential. There may be exceptions, such as addition to exercise, work, or caffeine. In general, however, the promise of overcoming addiction provides both motivation for the founding of various treatment and prevention organizations and the urgency of their endeavors, ranging from private organizations such as Alcoholics Anonymous to a succession of government-sponsored campaigns by lawmakers and law enforcers.

Preventing Addiction

In addition to spurring movements to eradicate already existing addictions, the stigma of addiction also cultivates an aversion to activities that might create further addiction. A paradigmatic case of this can be found in pain medicine. Fear of inappropriate use of opioids in pain management medicine has become sufficiently commonplace to have spawned the term "opiophobia." Though this condition is defined as the "irrational and undocumented fear that appropriate use of opioids causes addiction,"[6] it still motivates many health professionals to underprescribe these

---

4. Kalivas and Volkow, "The Neural Basis of Addiction," 1403.

5. David A. Fishbain, "Chronic Opioid Treatment, Addiction and Pseudo-Addiction in Patients with Chronic Pain," *Psychiatric Times* 20(2) (February 2003), online at http://www.psychiatrictimes.com/p030225.html.>

6. J. P. Morgan. "American Opiophobia: Customary Underutilization of Opioid Analgesics," *Advances in Alcohol and Substance Abuse* 5(1–2)(1985):163–73.

medications despite their full indication for pain control, largely out of concern that these drugs might spark an addiction.

Thus the stigma of addiction has been a two-edged sword. On one hand, the stigma has prompted the formation of organizations like Narcotics Anonymous (NA) to help individuals overcome destructive behavior patterns involving what is assumed to be addiction to illicit drugs. On the other hand, this stigma proves detrimental when clinicians' fear of producing addiction results in patients not receiving needed pain treatment in medical settings.

Addiction: Differing Concepts

So what, precisely, is meant by "addiction"? Many discussions of addiction, including accounts of the causes of addiction, reasons for preventing addiction, and treatment of addiction, are based on no more than an intuitive idea that is taken as uncontroversial despite the considerable consequences of the definition. Loose, unclear notions of addiction are not the only source of ambiguity and confusion. Even when people speak of addiction with a clear definition in mind, their terminology may conflict with that of another definition circulating in a different sphere of thought about addiction, in another silo, so to speak. Even when people who have thought carefully about addiction in their fields of expertise come together to discuss prescription pharmaceuticals or illegal drugs, for instance, they may speak past each other, arguing about what constitutes the essence of addiction when, in fact, the dispute stems at least in part from a lack of definitional and hence conceptual agreement.

This section is descriptive, illustrating the current muddle by providing something of a map of the territory that details and connects the various formal definitions and diagnostic criteria that are recurring themes in the general topic of addiction. It also is constructive and thinly normative, premised on the idea that this map can work to diminish at least some of the confusion and incoherence in the discussion of addiction generally and perhaps in policies designed to combat addiction, both by highlighting areas that need to be made consistent with one another and by enabling dialogue between the various communities through mutually understandable and usable terminology.

This discussion begins by presenting two influential but incompatible accounts of "addiction" that are employed by multiple academic, medical, legal, and therapeutic communities—one primarily in the pain medicine and general medical communities, and the other more frequently in the mental-health and substance-abuse communities—as well as the related but distinct concepts of dependence and tolerance. The concepts of "pseudoaddiction" and "iatrogenic addiction" are described and differentiated from "addiction" and "tolerance" per se. The two accounts discussed here are by no means the only definitions of addiction that have been proposed—consider, for example, the definitions formulated by organizations like the World Health Organization[7] and the National Institute on Drug Abuse,[8] as well as those offered by individual practitioners and scholars like Jerome Jaffe[9] and Aviel Goodman.[10] The two examined here, however, are among the most broadly accepted.

The AAPM/APS/ASAM Consensus Definition

In 1988, an international group of professional societies sought to formulate definitions of addiction and several other phenomena related to substance abuse. Specifically, the group used a four-stage Delphi survey of substance abuse experts to help achieve greater clarity and uniformity in terminology associated with alcohol and other drug-related problems. As reported by R. C. Rinaldi of the American Medical Association (AMA) and his colleagues, the result was a list of fifty substance-abuse terms, along with the most agreed upon definition for each term. Addiction was defined as the compulsive use of a substance resulting in physical, psychological, or social harm to the user *and* continued use despite that harm.[11]

7. World Health Organization Technical Report Series 116(9)(1957), section 8.

8. Alan I. Leshner, "The Essence of Drug Addiction" (Washington D.C.: The National Institute on Drug Abuse, 1997), online at http://www.nida.nih.gov/published_articles/essence.html.

9. Jerome H. Jaffe, "Drug Addiction and Drug Abuse," in Louis S. Goodman and Alfred Gilman, eds., *The Pharmacological Basis of Therapeutics*, 6th ed. (New York: Macmillan, 1980).

10. Aviel Goodman, "Addiction: Definition and Implications." *British Journal of Addiction* 85 (1990): 1403–08.

11. R. C. Rinaldi, E.M. Steindler, B.B. Wilford, D. Goodwin, "Clarification and Standardization of Substance Abuse Terminology," *Journal of the American Medical Association* 259(4)(1988): 555–57.

Some years later, the addiction medicine and pain management communities sought to develop a definitional agreement that expanded upon the 1988 work, particularly in light of subsequent research about the biological and genetic aspects of addiction. In 2001, three leading organizations—the American Academy of Pain Medicine (AAPM), American Pain Society (APS), and American Society of Addiction Medicine (ASAM)—established a Liaison Committee on Pain and Addiction that developed and published consensus definitions of "addiction," "physical dependence" and "tolerance" to apply to opioids. In addition, ASAM has adopted a public policy statement that includes a definition of alcoholism, another substance use (addiction) disorder.[12] Today, the 2001 AAPM/APS/ASAM consensus definition (hereafter "consensus definition") of addiction is generally used in pain management and other general medical situations. Some practitioners may still use alternative definitions, especially those of the *Diagnostic and Statistical Manual of Mental Disorders* (DSM), in the course of actually dealing with patients, families, courts, or other parties. The consensus definition is intended primarily to define addiction rather than to provide detailed, quantitative diagnostic criteria as does the DSM. The consensus definition does contain some nonquantitative criteria for addiction, however, and is used by some clinicians as a diagnostic guide.

The consensus definition states:

> Addiction is a primary, chronic, neurobiologic disease with genetic, psychosocial, and environmental factors influencing its development and manifestations. It is characterized by behaviors that include one or more of the following: impaired control over drug use, compulsive use, continued use despite harm, and craving.[13]

A number of important points should be considered. While the 1988 AMA definition (reported by Rinaldi et al.) lists continued use of the substance despite harm as a *necessary* criterion for addiction, the 2001 consensus definition includes "continued use despite harm" as one behavior indicative

---

12. The ASAM definition of alcoholism is accessible at http://www.asam.org.

13. Howard A. Heit, "Addiction, Physical Dependence, and Tolerance: Precise Definitions to Help Clinicians Evaluate and Treat Chronic Pain Patients," *Journal of Pain & Palliative Care Pharmacotherapy* 17(1)(2003): 15–29.

of addiction—but only one among others. "Use despite harm" is neither a necessary nor a sufficient condition for addiction. In other words, it appears that an individual might be suffering from addiction without harm to himself or to others under the consensus definition.

The consensus definition also identifies addiction as a *disease*. To conceive of addiction as a disease is usually thought to diminish the stigma of addiction by reclassifying it from a moral failing to a medical condition, and if an addiction might not involve harm at all, the stigma may be reduced further by making the condition appear less extrinsically or intrinsically bad.

Moreover, the consensus description of addiction as a *disease* is consistent with an increasingly common viewpoint in science and medicine, although it is not accepted or implicit in all contemporary definitions. As used here, the term should connote its technical medical definition as an identifiable constellation of symptoms for which some underlying neurobiological causes are known, which makes the notion of addiction as a disease even more robust than it might initially seem. Not only are instances of addiction assumed to be identifiable by their outward behavioral manifestations, but some of the causes for these behaviors are thought to be understood as a matter of altered brain function as well.

An important question, then, is whether drug addiction is truly a disease rather than the result of a behavior or conscious decision. A disease is commonly defined as an abnormal function characterized by a set of symptoms and for which a consistent pathophysiology is known. As the understanding of biological bases for drug addiction increases, the appropriateness of classifying it as a disease is further supported.[14] Certainly, the concept of addiction as a moral failing is still prominent in many segments of society. Yet it appears that the rapidly growing understanding of the neurobiology of drug addiction may well provide additional evidence that drug addiction is not a function of choice alone. Instead, addiction is a developing process characterized by succeeding stages through which the addict advances: a first stage of acute drug effects, in which dopamine release produces intense rewarding effects; a second stage of transition to

14. Nora D. Volkow, T-K Li. "Drug Addiction: The Neurobiology of Behaviour Gone Awry," *Nature Reviews/Neuroscience* 5(12)(2004): 963–70.

addiction, that is, from recreational use to true addiction; and a third stage, characterized by enduring cellular changes and equally enduring vulnerability to relapse, even after years of being "clean," known as end-stage addiction.[15] Neuroimaging studies have been used for over a decade to support this view.[16] As this type of evidence increases, methods to prevent and treat drug addiction will likely be identified, and public policy could change to reflect these new findings.

To be sure, some theorists have opposed the conception of addiction as a disease, a disorder, or as being nonvolitional altogether. Among others, Herbert Fingarette,[17] Stanton Peele,[18] Thomas Szasz,[19] and Jeffrey Schaler[20] have variously argued that such understandings are incorrect—"addiction is a choice," to use the title of Schaler's 2001 book. However, with the exponential growth of science, especially genetics and central nervous system visualization, including fMRI (functional magnetic resonance imaging) and PET (positron emission tomography) scans, which have demonstrated valid physiological risk factors and predispositions, there is increasing support for the concept of addiction as a disease.

The research also shows that addiction is a multifactorial problem with huge amount of inter-individual variability. This makes it particularly difficult to extrapolate from any one sample to the entire population. Furthermore, it

15. Kalivas and Volkow, "The Neural Basis of Addiction," 1408.

16. Nora D. Volkow, Hampton Gillespie, Nizar Mullani, Lawrence Tancredi, Cathel Grant, Allan Valentine, Leo Hollister, "Brain Glucose Metabolism in Chronic Marijuana Users at Baseline and During Marijuana Intoxication," *Psychiatry Research: Neuroimaging* 67(1) (1996): 29–38.

17. Herbert Fingarette, *Heavy Drinking: The Myth of Alcoholism as a Disease* (Berkeley: University of California Press, 1989); Herbert Fingarette, "Addiction and Criminal Responsibility," *Yale Law Journal* 84(3)(1975):413–34; Herbert Fingarette, "The Perils of Powell: In Search of a Factual Foundation for the Disease Concept of Alcoholism," *Harvard Law Review* 83(4)(1970): 793–812.

18. Stanton Peele, *Diseasing of America: How We Allowed Recovery Zealots and the Treatment Industry to Convince Us We Are Out of Control* (New York: Jossey-Bass, 1999); Stanton Peele, *The Meaning of Addiction: An Unconventional View* (New York: Jossey-Bass, 1998).

19. Thomas Szasz, *Ceremonial Chemistry: The Ritual Persecution of Drugs, Addicts, and Pushers,* rev. ed. (Syracuse: Syracuse University Press, 2003); Thomas Szasz, *Our Right To Drugs: The Case for a Free Market* (Syracuse: Syracuse University Press, 1996); Thomas Szasz, "Bad Habits Are Not Diseases: A Refutation of the Claim that Alcoholism Is a Disease," *Lancet* (2)(7767)(1972): 83–84.

20. Jeffrey A. Schaler, *Addiction Is a Choice* (New York: Open Court, 2001).

is now recognized that many illnesses have both biological and environmental components, the latter of which may be within the control of the patients. A common example is Type 2 diabetes. Persons who are genetically predisposed to this common disease often can prevent its onset or manage its occurrence through diet and exercise. So although addiction may have a volitional component in many cases, there also can be a biological, genetic basis. Thus, these two often seemingly incompatible causalities are not mutually exclusive.

Dependence

Of particular importance, the 2001 consensus statement, like the 1988 AMA publication, distinguishes between *addiction* and *physical dependence*.[21] Physical dependence is defined as:

> a state of adaptation that is manifested by a drug class specific withdrawal syndrome that can be produced by abrupt cessation, rapid dose reduction, decreasing blood level of the drug, and/or administration of an antagonist.[22]

Addiction and physical dependence are separate conditions that may co-exist but must be differentiated due to their distinct causes, management, and prognoses for long term adverse outcomes.

In comparison to the disease model of addiction, dependence is "state of adaptation," primarily a physiological/pharmacological rather than psychological state. For example, after a week of taking regularly scheduled opioid analgesia, most patients will become physically dependent on the drug. But once the medication is no longer needed, the drug can usually be tapered and stopped in five to ten days.[23]

Dependence is characterized by an abstinence syndrome (withdrawal effect) when the substance is stopped too rapidly or an antagonist is administered.

21. American Academy of Pain Medicine, American Pain Society, and American Society of Addiction Medicine, "Definitions Related to the Use of Opioids for the Treatment of Pain," *Wisconsin Medical Journal* 100(5)(2001):28–29; see also Seddon R. Savage, David E. Joranson, Edward C.Covington, Sydney H. Schnoll, Howard A. Heit, A.M. Gilson, "Definitions Related to the Medical Use of Opioids: Evolution towards Universal Agreement," *Journal of Pain and Symptom Management* 26(1)(2003): 655–67.

22. Heit, "Addiction, Physical Dependence, and Tolerance," 18.

23. B. D. Hare and A.G. Lipman, "Medication Use and Misuse in Chronic Pain Management," *Problems in Anesthesia* 4(4)(1990): 561–689.

Dependence commonly causes drug-seeking behavior similar to that often manifested by addicts, because using the drug again eases the withdrawal symptoms. In contrast, a true addict will drug-seek for more complicated psychological, social, or environmental reasons. Addicts need not be dependent, as seen in weekend-binge users (commonly referred to in addiction medicine as "chippers") who consume their drugs of abuse only for a day or two each week and therefore do not become physically dependent. But based on their drug of choice, many addicts and all people who are physically dependent will experience withdrawal symptoms if they do not consume the drug or an analogue once the previous dose has worn off. Typically, all but addicts who use drugs intermittently become physically dependent on the drugs.

So unlike addiction, physical dependence is understood as a purely physiological-pharmacological phenomenon, making it less plausible to apply the concept to anything other than chemical substances. While an individual might sensibly speak of being "addicted" to work, it would be difficult to define him or her as being "physically dependent" on work unless, of course, the work involves an altered chemical state or change in brain function.

Tolerance

In turn, "tolerance" is a state of adaptation in which exposure to a drug induces changes that result in a diminution over time in one or more of the drug's effects.[24] As a purely pharmacological phenomenon, tolerance is neither necessary nor sufficient for addiction, although it is a phenomenon that may be expected in many (but not all) cases of addiction. Tolerance can manifest itself either when the effects of a consistent amount of the substance gradually decrease—for example, an individual consumes a six-pack of beer every evening and finds that he or she no longer experiences the intoxicating effects of the alcohol—or when the amounts of medication need to be increased continually in order to maintain the desired effect. Different types of tolerance can develop with different biological bases depending on the pharmacological profiles of the substances involved.

24. Heit, "Addiction, Physical Dependence, and Tolerance," 18.

Addiction to illegal drugs is neither the only context involving the continued use of a drug over time nor the only context in which tolerance may develop. Diabetics, asthmatics, individuals with high blood pressure, people with hypothyroidism, and transplant recipients all may require continual drug use for some time period or even for the remainder of their lives. Although their dosage requirements might well increase over time, these are not considered to be cases of addiction. The need for increased doses can usually be explained by physiological or pathological changes. In whatever context, this increased dose requirement (tolerance) is likely to result in more frequent "drug seeking behavior" in the sense of requiring greater amounts of the drug, but such behavior is not in and of itself sufficient to indicate an addiction. For this reason, it cannot be assumed that only addicts develop tolerance or that tolerance, by itself, is indicative of addiction.

True Addiction and Its Causes

Thus, under the 2001 consensus definition that is typically used in pain medicine and other medical contexts, true addiction has a more complex etiology than—and is not the same condition as—physical dependence or tolerance. According to this definition, addiction involves genetic, psychosocial, and environmental factors. While the inclusion of psychosocial factors in the definition is hardly surprising, the genetic and environmental factors deserve further consideration.

Genetic Factors

In some animal models, there is a clear correlation between genetically determined biology and the way they react to particular addictive substances. For instance, researchers have isolated genes in specifically bred mice that correlate with three sorts of behavior.[25] Mice with one genetic profile consistently avoid both alcohol and nicotine, often to the point of starving to death rather than ingesting food or water containing these

25. Erin L. Meyer, Louise C. Gahring, Scott W. Rogers, "Nicotine Preconditioning Antagonizes Activity-Dependent Caspace Proteolysis of a Glutamate Receptor," *Journal of Biological Chemistry* 277 (2002): 10869–75.

substances. Mice with a second genetic profile sometimes but not always opt for drug-laced food, thus appearing almost indifferent to the substances despite the ensuing physiological effects. A third genetic profile correlates with mice that ravenously seek out alcohol and nicotine, fighting with their cohorts for a greater share and sometimes overindulging to the point of premature death. Recent clinical data in humans confirms that genetic variations between people profoundly influence the risk of alcohol and nicotine dependence.[26]

These studies seem to indicate that the resulting behavior is at least partially explained in terms of genetics, given that the complex environmental, social, and psychological pressures that might lead humans to seek out addictive substances like alcohol or nicotine are presumably absent in the mouse populations. Most researchers and clinicians now accept the concept of the intergenerational transmission of addiction, as mounting epidemiological and etiological evidence suggests that such disorders run in certain families. Like other diseases of lifestyle (e.g., diabetes), a family history must be recognized as a risk factor for substance addiction. Although more research is needed to understand the complex interactions of genetic vulnerabilities with family and community environmental risk, as well as protective processes to prevent this intergenerational transmission, there have been sufficient twin, adoption, and family studies to show that addictions have a substantial genetic and biological basis.

Studying the genetic contribution to addiction in a specific area, that of alcohol, for example, researchers have proposed a distinction between Type I and II alcohol addiction. Type I—the conventional variety—accounts for about 75 percent of alcoholics, and normally occurs after the age of 25. Type I involves a low degree of spontaneous alcohol-seeking behavior and alcohol-related fighting, a low degree of novelty-seeking and a high degree of harm avoidance, and involves psychological dependence, together with guilt and fear about alcoholism. Type II has the stronger genetic predisposition to addiction. Type II alcoholics, whose condition is sometimes

26. Sibylle G. Schwab, Petra E. Franke, Barbara Hoefgen, Vera Guttenthaler, Dirk Lichtermann, Matyas Trixler, Michael Knapp, Wolfgang Maier, and Dieter Wildenauer, "Association of DNA polymorphisms in the synaptic vesicular amine transporter gene (SLC18A2) with alcohol and nicotine dependence," *Neuropsychopharmacology* 30(12)(2005): 2263–68.

called "early onset alcoholism" or "male limited alcoholism," are about twelve times more likely to develop addictions than the general population. The onset of Type II typically occurs before age 25, involves a high degree of spontaneous alcohol-seeking behavior and fighting together with a high degree of thrill seeking and a low degree of harm avoidance; feelings of guilt and fear about alcohol dependence are infrequent. Given the markers of Type II alcoholism, the highest risk children have either mothers who are addicts or alcoholics, or fathers who developed alcohol abuse younger than age fifteen. Moreover, children living with their biological parent(s) seem doubly at risk to become addicts—by both genetics ("nature") and by family influence ("nurture").

Ongoing research seeks to uncover the genetic risk factors transmitted from parent to child that contribute to substance abuse. While genetic, biological, cognitive, and temperament traits may all be correlated with later substance abuse, a genetic factor has been determined to be a clear marker in the case of alcoholism.[27] Specifically, major genetic vulnerability factors appear to be related to prefrontal cognitive dysfunction leading to an over-stressed and overly active thrill-seeking child or adult, such as autonomic hyper-reactivity, subclinical high behavioral activity level, or hyperactivity. Major risk factors for substance abuse related to this prefrontal cognitive dysfunction include an inability to predict consequences of one's actions and to cognitively override or control ingrained behavioral habits or impulses to actions that would lead to negative consequences. Recent research suggests that the prefrontal cognitive areas of the brain normally develop as late as twenty-five years of age. In drug abusing or genetically at-risk youth, this judgment area of the brain can be even more delayed in development, leading to poor decisions about drug use and behaviors. This prefrontal

27. Ann P. Streissguth, "Recent Advances in Fetal Alcohol Syndrome and Alcohol Use in Pregnancy," In *Alcohol in Health and Disease*, Agarwal and Seitz, eds. (New York: Marcel Dekker, 2001), 303–24; Ralph E. Tarter, Ada C. Mezzich, "Ontogeny of Substance Abuse: Perspectives and Findings." In *Vulnerability to Drug Abuse*, Meyer D. Glantz and Roy W. Pickens, eds. (New York: American Psychiatric Association, 1992), 149–77; Ralph E. Tarter, H. Moss, M.Vanyukov, "Behavior Genetic Perspective of Alcoholism Etiology," in *Alcohol and Alcoholism*, Vol. 1. *Genetic Factors in Alcoholism*. H. Begleiter and B. Kissin, eds. (New York: Oxford University Press, 1995); Mark A. Schuckit, "Longitudinal Study of Children of Alcoholics." In *Recent Developments in Alcoholism*, Vol. 9: *Children of Alcoholics*, Galanter and Begleiter, eds. (New York: Plenum Press, 1991), 5–19.

cognitive dysfunction, which may also result from substance abuse and may require over two years for recovery, is also related to verbal deficits in children of Type II alcoholics. These verbal deficits can lead to dislike of school and school failure, which is often linked to later substance abuse.

Additional biological or genetic risk factors for substance abuse, especially of alcohol, include genetically inherited differences in liver metabolism of alcohol. In certain Native American and Asian populations as well as some Jewish families, there are atypical liver enzymes that contribute to high acetaldehyde buildup.[28] This can lead to avoidance of alcohol due to the adverse effects of acetaldehyde or, conversely, to overuse due to a liking for the euphoric, reinforcing effects of alcohol. Genetically inherited or biologically created neurotransmitter chemical imbalances in the brain also contribute to later substance abuse disorders because of self-medication for specific deficits. Possible examples of these imbalances linked with substance abuse include dopamine, which affects pleasure and is believed to relate to stimulant misuse, serotonin in alcohol dependency, and endorphins in opioid dependency antisocial personality, conduct disorders, and depression in women.[29] Because of the numerous characteristics associated with vulnerability, many genes located on several chromosomes may be involved. The complexity of this genetic basis confounds discovery of the biological mechanism of gene expression in addiction to alcohol or other substances.

Environmental Factors

Evidence suggests that access to an addictive substance in an environment that condones or encourages use can influence the origins and continuation of an addiction. For instance, studies of American soldiers whose heroin use had been remarkable and chronic while serving in the Vietnam

---

28. Deborah Hasim, Efrat Aharonovich, Xinhua Liu, Ziona Mamman, Karen Matseoane, Lucinda G. Carr, Ting-Kai Li, "Alchohol Dependence Symptoms and Alcohol Dehydrogenase 2 polymorphism: Israeli Ashkenazis, Sephardics, and Recent Russian Immigrants," *Alchoholism: Clinical and Experimental Research* 26(9)(2002).

29. Joanne E. Turnbull, Edith Gornberg, "Impact of Depressive Symptomatology on Alcohol Problem in Women," *Alcoholism: Clinical and Experimental Research* 12(3)(1988): 374–81.

War found that, in most cases, heroin consumption entirely subsided when they returned home.[30] Controlling for environmental factors, some studies found that those soldiers who could not abstain after returning home (i.e., when the environmental factors were removed) may have been more genetically predisposed to addiction.

Psychosocial Factors

The relationship between an individual's genetics, socioeconomic environment, and psychology cannot be easily disaggregated.[31] Biological and neurobiological factors create a vulnerability that interacts with temperament traits[32] and environmental risk and protective factors.[33] A child with high genetic risk factors *and* a high-risk environment is at increased risk of developing a substance addiction, while family risk and protective processes are prominent environmental precursors interacting with biological vulnerabilities. Hence, it is true that neither "nature" nor "nurture" completely controls one's drug addiction destiny. For instance, some youth have parents, extended family members, mentors, and friends who help them to learn to manage their biological vulnerabilities to substance use or abuse through alternative methods. Some youth are resilient and seek positive mentors or role models to help them to resist their tendency to addictions. Others,

30. See Waldorf, Dan, and Patrick Biernacki, "Natural Recovery from Heroin Addiction: A Review of Incidence Literature," online at http://www.drugtext.org/library/articles/narehead.ntm.

31. For instance, some epidemiological studies suggest significant co-morbidities in drug addicts, particularly with regards to drug abuse and affective disorders, anxiety disorder, and conduct disorders. Ronald C. Kessler, S. Aguilar-Gaxiola, L. Andrade, R. Bijl, G. Borges, J. J. Caraveo-Anduaga, D. J. DeWit, B. Kolody, K. R. Merikangas, B. E. Molnar, W. A. Vega, E.E. Walters, H-U. Wittchen, "Cross-National Comparisons of Co-morbidities Between Substance Use Disorders and Mental Disorders." In *Handbook of Drug Abuse Prevention: Theory, Science, and Practice.* Z. Sloboda, W. Bukoski, eds. (New York: Kluwer Academic/Plenum Publishers, 2003), 447–72.

32. Ralph E. Tarter, Susan B. Laird, M. Kabene, Oscar Bukstein, Yifrah Kaminer, "Drug Abuse Severity in Adolescents is Associated with Magnitude of Deviation in Temperament Traits," *British Journal of Addiction* 85(1990): 1501–04.

33. Karol L. Kumpfer, "Special Populations: Etiology and Prevention of Vulnerability to Chemical Dependency in Children of Substance Abusers." In *Youth at High Risk for Substance Abuse*, B.S. Brown, A.R. Mills, eds. (Rockville, Md.: National Institute on Drug Abuse) 1987, 1–71.

however, do not have these advantages of biology, character, and environment. Even then, there is no guarantee that they will become drug addicts. While there is increasing understanding of the neurobiology of addiction as a developing process characterized by succeeding stages through which the addict advances, the relationship between this process and genetic, environmental, and psychosocial factors is still imperfectly understood.

DSM-Derived Definitions

In contrast to the 2001 consensus definition of addiction is the approach taken by the American Psychiatric Association's *Diagnostic and Statistical Manual of Mental Disorders, or DSM*,[34] which is considered by many to be the bible of mental health diagnoses. Specifically, the *DSM* describes a pair of distinct but related "substance use disorders" that have become ubiquitous concepts within the mental health and substance-abuse communities. The two descriptions involve both terminological and ideological differences from the consensus definition commonly used within pain medicine and many other medical communities. These descriptions are diagnostic criteria rather than definitions per se, but they are often understood and used as definitions in public and even professional contexts.

The two conditions in the *DSM* are called "substance abuse" and "substance dependence," both of which fall under a more general category of "addiction." Substance abuse and substance dependence are termed "maladaptive behaviors" in the *DSM*, although it holds that substance dependence is the more serious condition. It thus appears to many readers that "dependence" as used in the *DSM* can be considered a surrogate for "addiction."

Substance abuse is defined in the *DSM* as follows:

A. A maladaptive pattern of use leading to clinically significant impairment or distress, as manifested by one (or more) of the following, occurring within a 12-month period:

34. The current edition of the *DSM* is known as the "*DSM-IV-TR*," indicating that it is the fourth edition with text revision. This revised edition was published in July 2000 in light of the fact that the next major revision of the DSM will not appear until 2010 or later (at least 16 years after *DSM-IV*). The primary goal was to maintain the currency of the

1. Recurrent substance use resulting in a failure to fulfill major role obligations at work, school, or home (e.g., repeated absences or poor work performance related to substance use; substance-related absences, suspensions, or expulsions from school; neglect of children or household);

2. Recurrent substance use in situations in which it is physically hazardous (e.g., driving an automobile or operating a machine when impaired by substance use);

3. Recurrent substance-related legal problems (e.g., arrests for substance-related disorderly conduct); [and/or]

4. Continued substance use despite having persistent or recurrent social or interpersonal problems caused or exacerbated by the effects of the substance (e.g., arguments with spouse about consequences of intoxication, physical fights).

B. The symptoms have never met the criteria for Substance Dependence for this class of substance.

In turn, *DSM* lists for *substance dependence*:

A maladaptive pattern of use, leading to clinically significant impairment or distress, as manifested by three (or more) of the following, occurring at any time in the same 12-month period:

1. Tolerance, as defined by either of the following:
   a. need for markedly increased amounts of the substance to achieve intoxication or desired effect;
   b. markedly diminished effect with continued use of the same amount of substance;

2. Withdrawal, as manifested by either of the following:
   a. the characteristic withdrawal syndrome for the substance;
   b. the same (or closely related) substance is taken to relieve or avoid withdrawal symptoms;

3. The substance is often taken in larger amounts or over a longer period of time than was intended;

DSM-IV text, with most of the major changes confined to the descriptive text coupled with a handful of corrections to criteria sets identified in the original fourth edition. In addition, some of the diagnostic codes were changed to reflect updates to the ICD-9-CM coding system adopted by the U.S. government.

4. A persistent desire or unsuccessful efforts to cut down or control the substance use;

5. A great deal of time is spent in activities necessary to obtain the substance (e.g., visiting multiple doctors or driving long distances), use the substance (e.g., chain smoking), or recover from its effects;

6. Important social, occupational, or recreational activities are given up or reduced because of substance use;

7. The substance use is continued despite knowledge of having a persistent or recurrent physical or psychological problem that is likely to have been caused or exacerbated by the substance (e.g., current cocaine use despite recognition of cocaine induced depression, or continued drinking despite recognition that an ulcer was made worse by alcohol consumption).

Perhaps the first and most obvious disconnect between this DSM account and the 2001 consensus definition is terminological. Both involve the specific concept of dependence, although the concepts are alike in name alone. In the field of pain medicine, which typically uses the consensus definition, "dependence" is regarded as a relatively easily managed physiological-pharmacological phenomenon distinct from addiction. In contrast, many addiction specialists and others who use the DSM as a reference consider "substance dependence" as the serious, necessarily harmful, and most acute form of addiction-related substance use.

Second, the difference between the two definitions is pronounced in considering whether harm is a necessary component of addiction. The consensus definition lists "continued use despite harm," but does not make this a necessary condition of addiction—that is, this definition does not require that there be continued use despite harm in order for the patient to be considered addicted. In contrast, the DSM mentions specific kinds of harms including "persistent or recurrent social or interpersonal problems" and "failure to fulfill major role obligations" as possible criteria of substance abuse, and a "persistent or recurrent physical or psychological problem that is likely to have been caused or exacerbated by the substance" as a possible criterion of substance dependence. Listed examples include depression induced by cocaine use or an ulcer made worse by alcohol consumption. Neither the 2001 consensus definition nor the DSM criteria clarify the nature of the harm needed to provide evidence of addiction, but one offers a much looser, open-ended account than the other. These differing positions will result in discrepant conclusions as to whether a seemingly clear case should be deemed addiction.

The Cases of Carl and Harry

As an example, consider a person—call him Carl—who has an intense relationship with coffee. Carl's mind is often filled with thoughts of obtaining or enjoying coffee; he drinks numerous cups a day, often drinking coffee even when he intends not to, and feeling a strong craving for coffee if he goes without it for even a few hours. Among other things, Carl will take paths that travel past Starbucks even if it is out of his way. As such, Carl certainly exhibits symptoms of tolerance as well as physical and psychological dependence. He often drinks coffee for the effects of the caffeine, to stay awake and remain alert at the odd hours he has to work. Over time, Carl has developed tolerance to caffeine requiring more and more of it to obtain these desired effects. He wishes he did not drink so much coffee, especially when he has the coffee "jitters," and from time to time he tries to cut down. However, his efforts to limit the amount of coffee he drinks never last very long. Moreover, Carl not only craves coffee when away from it for any significant amount of time but also experiences withdrawal symptoms manifested by grogginess and headaches. Whether or not Carl's affinity to coffee is partly genetic, it is certainly affected by his social makeup, perhaps caused by his desire to seem sophisticated and "fit in" with his coffee-drinking peers; and it is clearly influenced by a work environment that fosters a coffee culture. Indeed, there is a coffee pot in the office mailroom, and his work requires long hours in which a stimulant like caffeine can be helpful.

But assume that Carl's coffee drinking does him no significant harm. On occasion, he might suffer from a morning caffeine-withdrawal headache or mild sleep deprivation, and at times he gets the jitters or seems a little jumpy to his co-workers. But as with most users of caffeine, neither his blood pressure nor any other physiological functions are impaired. The evidence is that, except for certain individuals, coffee is not harmful even when as much as five cups per day are consumed. On the other hand, some evidence does show that chronic caffeine consumption elevates diastolic blood pressure in some sensitive individuals.[35] Chronically elevated blood pressure is a risk factor for heart attack and stroke. One study suggests that caffeine may be harmful to patients who are predisposed to cardiac pathology,[36] and another indicates that those who carry a genetic predisposition to metabolize caffeine slowly are at heightened risk of nonlethal heart attack at younger ages.[37] But Carl does not have any such conditions. Caffeine-associated seizures have been reported but are rare and associated with excessive doses of the stimulant.[38] On the contrary, Carl may even be helped, rather than harmed, by his coffee drinking. Although a causal link has yet to established, there are some suggestions of health advantages from caffeine consumption. For example, habitual coffee consumption is associated with a substantially lower risk of alcoholic liver disease and Type 2 diabetes and, although it may raise the risk of leukemia, may offer a protective effect against certain types of cancer, including colon, rectal, and liver cancer.[39] So in general, current evidence suggests that Carl's coffee habit is not harmful to him and may even provide health benefits. And, of course, coffee is known as a cognitive enhancer. As for Carl, he is healthy and relatively successful, enjoying modest personal triumphs in his work and private life, keeping his appointments, maintaining his relationships, and generally acting as a responsible citizen. In other words, Carl's relationship with coffee, however intense, is not significantly harmful.

35. Neal L. Benowitz, Peyton Jacob III, Haim Mayan, and Charles Denaro, "Sympathomimetic Effects of Paraxanthine and Caffeine in Humans," *Clinical Pharmacology and Therapeutics* 58(1995):684–91. Also see http://medweb.rcm.upr.edu/publications/sidney_kaye/toxicology-of-caffeine.htm.

36. Semerl J. Selb, K. Selb: "Coffee and alcohol consumption as triggering factors for sudden cardiac death: case-crossover study," *Croatian Medical Journal* 45(6)(Dec. 2004): 775–80; Comment in: *Croatian Medical* Journal 46(1)(Feb. 2005): 148–49.

37. Marilyn C. Cornelis, Ahmed El-Sohemy, Edmond K. Kabagambe, Hannia Campos, "Coffee, CYP1A2 Genotype, and Risk of Myocardial Infarction," *Journal of the American Medical* Association 295(2006): 1135–41.

38. Leonardo Bonilha and Li M. Li, "Heavy Coffee Drinking and Epilepsy," *Seizure* 13(4)(June 2004): 284–85.

39. See, for example, Rob M. van Dam, Frank B. Hu, "Coffee Consumption and Risk of Type 2 Diabetes: A Systematic Review," *Journal of the American Medical Association* 294(1)(2005): 97–104; also, Lenore Arab, speaking at the American Society for Nutrition's "controversy session" on coffee at the 2007 meetings of the Experimental Biology Association, reported online at http://www.eurekalert.org/pub_releases/2007-04/foas-nsc042207.php

Given the centrality of addiction to an exploration of drug theory, policy, and practice concerning drugs, it is important to recognize how differently the two major accounts described above would identify Carl's situation. According to the 2001 consensus definition, Carl's relationship to coffee is clearly one of addiction. It is influenced by psychosocial and environmental factors, if not by genetic ones. It includes three of the four behaviors that the definition identifies as characterizing addiction: impaired control over drug use, compulsive use, and craving. The only criterion it does not satisfy is continued use despite harm. Were Carl to have a predisposition to cardiac illness, be subject to mild stimulant-induced seizures, carry a genetic predisposition to metabolize caffeine slowly, or have an anxiety disorder that would be exacerbated by caffeine, this criterion might be satisfied too. The fact that coffee does him no real harm is not enough to disqualify Carl's relationship with coffee from being a "disease," an addiction under the consensus statement definition, as continued use despite harm is only one of four characteristic behaviors. Only one of these characteristics must be met to indicate addiction and Carl satisfies *three* of them. According to the consensus definition, then, Carl is a coffee addict.

But this same case will be classified differently according to the DSM. Carl's condition satisfies at least four and perhaps five of the criteria for substance dependence (the more serious of the conditions), including tolerance, withdrawal, greater than intended use, persistent unsuccessful desire to control use, and perhaps time spent in obtaining and using, although it meets none of the conditions required for a case of substance abuse (the less serious condition). Yet Carl's coffee drinking cannot qualify as either substance abuse or substance dependence under the *DSM* criteria because it involves only minimal if any harm. Regardless of the fact that Carl's condition may satisfy subsidiary *DSM* criteria, it is not "maladaptive" in any sense of the word, and the *DSM* will not classify it as abuse or dependence unless it involves "clinically significant impairment or distress." Because Carl's intense enthusiasm for coffee is not impairing his life's projects, harming his body, or harming others, it cannot be deemed abuse or dependence under the *DSM*. Thus, with respect to Carl, the two accounts yield strikingly different conclusions. Using the consensus definition Carl is a coffee "addict." Using the *DSM* definition he is not, although he still meets some of the specific criteria for dependence.

Thus the conclusion of one definition classifies Carl as an addict, while the other seems to fit with the intuition that the average person would not call Carl an addict and few if any clinicians would describe him that way. Yet some scientific usage would identify Carl as "dependent." For example, a 1983 cross-sectional survey of 4,757 Australians reported that average caffeine consumption was 240 mg/day, equivalent to approximately five 150 mL (five ounce) cups of medium strength coffee, and that one-third of the population that ingested this level or more "may be considered to be physically dependent on caffeine."[40]

Now consider someone—call him Harry—with what the average person might view as a serious addiction. Harry is a thirty-six-year-old white-collar professional who has been using cocaine for the past two years. For whatever reason, Harry simply finds the effects of cocaine far more enjoyable than any other drug with which he has experimented. He makes no attempt to hide his use and is quite vocal regarding the "benefits" of consuming cocaine, which, he observes, include the "rush" of pleasure when it is snorted, as well as the feeling of warmth and well-being that follow. He also enjoys the condition of heightened activity during the euphoric high that is associated with cocaine. Preferring to keep his professional position during the week, Harry uses the drug only on the weekends, spending Friday evening obtaining the drug from one of his dealers and then snorting lines over the course of the next day and a half, followed by a period of recovery on Sunday when he sleeps off the effects of his weekend high. Harry has been known to drive his car under the influence of cocaine, but has not been involved in any accidents. Although he was once an avid weekend golfer and gardener, Harry now spends his entire weekend on this iterative process of obtaining, using, and recovering from the drug (i.e., coming down from the exhaustion that develops from both the drug effects and his accelerated activity when he was high). He seems to have settled on a finite amount of cocaine to consume each weekend. He is not compulsive nor does he crave the drug during the work week, and he has suffered no withdrawal symptoms, although he has yet to go without his weekend fix for two years running. Harry has

40. Megan J. Shirlow, "Patterns of Caffeine Consumption," *Human Nutrition-Applied Nutrition* 37(4)(1983):307–13.

not been hospitalized for an overdose or any cocaine-related problem. His income supports his habit and he does not steal or engage in other criminal activity to obtain the drug. Although Harry's overt support for and use of the drug have cost him some relationships, others among his family and friends continue to stand behind him. By and large, he has a new set of friends with whom he socializes on the weekends, many of whom also use illicit substances. Although his girlfriend since graduate school dumped Harry, saying that she refuses to date a "cokehead" any longer, he is now dating someone who does not object. Harry shakes off negative interpersonal consequences: "If people really care about me," he says, "they will accept me for who I am." While he is aware of the potential dangers from his weekend activities and that cocaine carries stiff punishment for possession and use, he has so far avoided trouble with the law.

This case also illustrates counterintuitive results under both the 2001 consensus definition and the *DSM*. Although Harry's cocaine use has been consistent for years, accompanied by weekly drug-seeking behavior that is followed by a pattern of consumption and recovery, there is no evidence of craving for the drug, or of compulsive use of the drug, or of impaired control over his use of the drug. He remains "clean" five days a week. Moreover, it is debatable whether Harry has suffered any cognizable harm from cocaine. True, social relationships have ended due to his drug use, but he has a new group of friends. It would be difficult to categorize this as the type of harm understood under the consensus definition, given that cocaine has caused no bodily, economic, or other tangible injury to Harry. So under the consensus definition, because he does not exhibit impaired control over drug use, compulsive use, or craving, Harry's cocaine use would be unlikely to qualify as an addiction. And although the consensus definition is not stated in neurobiological terms, it is clear that Harry's cocaine use has not passed through the three stages of cellular change culminating in "end stage" addiction.

In contrast, while his cocaine consumption meets the criteria for "substance abuse" as defined under the DSM, it does not meet the criteria for the more serious category of "substance dependence." Harry's drug use has produced interpersonal problems only in the sense that one girlfriend left him, but he has replaced one set of friends with another and maintains many of his original relationships, including those with his family and those with his co-workers during the week when he is not using. He does use the drug in physically hazardous circumstances by driving under the influence of cocaine. As such, he meets at least one of the factors for substance abuse, but only one such criterion need be met under the *DSM* criteria. However, Harry would not meet the standard for the more serious category of "substance dependence." There is no evidence of tolerance, withdrawal, taking cocaine in larger amounts or for a longer period of time than he intended, or an unsuccessful desire to cut back or control his drug use. Although he is clearly exhausted on Sunday evenings after his weekends of heightened activity associated with use, he not only has no desire to cease cocaine use; on the contrary, he openly celebrates it. He does not take the drug for a long enough period (just two days a week) to experience pharmacological withdrawal. Moreover, Harry consumes a consistent amount of cocaine, his weekend "dime bag," and as of yet, he has suffered no physical or psychological problems from his drug use. So although Harry meets two of the listed criteria—he spends a great deal of time obtaining, using, and recovering from drug use, and he has given up all other activities on the weekends—he is not dependent on cocaine under this definition, which requires an individual to meet three or more criteria.

The cases of Carl and Harry expose real tensions between the two principal accounts of addiction used in various spheres of drug theory, policy, and practice, reaching surprising and evidently inconsistent results. Under the consensus definition typically used in pain medicine and in other medical contexts, Carl the coffee drinker is suffering from an "addiction"; under the *DSM*, although not engaging in maladaptive behavior, Carl is nonetheless "substance dependent," the more serious condition, and does not meet the weaker criteria for "substance abuse." At the same time, Harry the cocaine user has neither an "addiction" according to the consensus definition nor "substance dependence" according to the *DSM* definition. His drug use would qualify only as the less serious condition of "substance abuse" under the *DSM* definition. Not only do the two definitions, the primarily medical one and the primarily psychological one, disagree about what to call Carl, but both define Carl as having a more serious disorder than Harry.

Thus, when examining the conceptual foundations of drug theory, on which policy constructions and matters of practice are based, there seems to be a fissure in the accounts of addiction that are used in differing spheres of talk about drugs—evidence suggesting a "silo" mentality.

Definitions and Diagnoses

Of course, it could be argued that this confusion is only apparent, and that although the consensus definition and the *DSM* approach use different terminology and appear to yield different conclusions, this is because they have different purposes. The consensus definition, on this view, it is not designed explicitly for diagnostic purposes. It is intended above all as a global definition of addiction, while the *DSM* provides the criteria for diagnosis.

This view holds that there is an important distinction between a definition and a diagnosis. No general account of addiction can be derived from the *DSM*, and no diagnosis can be determined using the consensus definition of addiction. Hence, on this view, there is no real problem here, and to say that Carl is an addict and Harry is not an addict is to misunderstand how these "definitions" actually function.

According to this line of argument, one of the primary purposes of the *DSM* is to diagnose whether a mental health problem exists. In general, a mental health problem is basically defined by the level of impairment in one's life, evident in areas such as work, school, interpersonal relationships, recreational activities, and so on. That is, the definition of whether someone is mentally healthy or not is primarily based on how well that individual fits into a society or culture. Someone may present physiological dependence to a drug but not be diagnosed as having a mental health disorder such as the *DSM*'s understanding of dependence or abuse if there is no evidence of mental health impairment—that is, if the person is fully functional in the society.

The *DSM* also provides a nomenclature for classifying and studying the various diagnoses. For example, if it is found that certain types of alcoholics who meet particular criteria for *DSM*-defined dependence are more refractory, perhaps there is a different phenotype, and perhaps they will respond better to a different type of treatment than those who meet a different subset of criteria. Thus, there is both necessity and value in detailed criteria used in making diagnoses. Someone may have high blood pressure, for instance, but does she indeed have hypertension? High blood pressure, while having a medical definition, does not have to be a problem, and it may simply arise as a result of being nervous regarding your appointment with a physician. But hypertension, which is a specific diagnosis, can indeed have serious consequences and may need to be treated if certain types of criteria are met. Furthermore, the level and type of treatment needed will depend upon *which* criteria are met. Any knowledge of the most appropriate treatment strategy is due to past research and experience on the severity and refractoriness of conditions that meet some criteria but not others. It is impossible to just diagnose Carl and Harry on the basis of simple definitions; diagnostic criteria must be part of it as well.

Such differences in purposes of definitions do not only exist within the mental health field. Criteria for diagnoses, whether they are physical or mental health related, will always be more detailed than the definition of the actual disorder. For example, the American Heart Association defines hypertension as "a blood pressure greater than or equal to 140 mm Hg systolic pressure or greater than or equal to 90 mm Hg diastolic pressure." However, the actual diagnosis of hypertension includes these elevated blood pressures "on at least at least three controlled readings, two occasions from measurements taken on three separate days are required. Secondary causes are then ruled out to make a determination of primary hypertension."[41] Similarly, the National Institute of Mental Health defines schizophrenia as "one of several brain diseases whose symptoms may include loss of personality, agitation, catatonia, confusion, psychosis, unusual behavior and withdrawal"—but the diagnosis of schizophrenia expands this definition to include numerous and specific criteria. In turn, the American Diabetes Association defines diabetes as a "disease in which the body does not produce or properly use insulin," while a diagnosis of diabetes requires much more expanded criteria for each of Type 1 and Type 2 diabetes.

Thus, on this argument, the two "definitions" are not incompatible after all. Since the consensus definition is not intended as a definition of a diagnosable mental health disorder of addiction, it really should not be compared with the *DSM* diagnostic criteria to determine whether Carl and Harry have addictions, and the finding above—that Carl is an addict and Harry is not—is simply a mistake, illustrating what happens when definitions are erroneously applied and definitions and criteria are conflated.

41. http://www.americanheart.org/presenter.jhtml?identifier=4623, accessed May 7, 2007.

What does happen when definitions are erroneously applied? The case of Carl assumes, for example, that there is no harm in his life as a result of his love for coffee. The first consideration in making a DSM diagnosis of dependence or abuse is whether there is "a maladaptive pattern of use leading to *significant impairment or distress*." Only if such impairment or distress is present does one go forward with exploring the possibility of a diagnosis of abuse or dependence. But as the case assumed, Carl's coffee drinking does him no significant harm; if so, it would appear that the possibility of a diagnosis of either abuse or dependence has already been ruled out, and thus, Carl would not be diagnosed as having caffeine dependence—he could not be a coffee addict. On this argument, Carl could be recognized as having a physiological dependence but not a diagnosis of a mental health disorder, since there is no significant impairment. But if he has no impairment, he has no mental health disorder, and if he has no mental health disorder, he has no true addiction.

This idea of significant impairment is important. At the very minimum it is interpreted as the presence of some kind of harm, whether physical, psychological, or social. Because of this, it may seem difficult to imagine a scenario where there would be disagreement between the concept of significant clinical impairment as noted by the *DSM* and the concept of continued use despite harm as described by the consensus definition. Yet while Carl is described as not suffering physical harm—he is not among those few persons susceptible to caffeine-induced stroke, for instance—a good deal of his life is governed by coffee, and he clearly views it as a harm. That is why he wants to cut down.

The conclusions in the case of Harry are also misleading in this view. Harry's cocaine use is described as not really causing any problems in his functioning. If this is the case, then he does not have a diagnosis of addiction since he does not have significant impairment. Does he meet the criterion of recurrent use in hazardous situations? All that is described is that "he has been known to drive while under the influence of cocaine." This alone, it can be argued, will not meet the criterion for impairment: many people who drink alcohol have been known to drive while under the influence, but this does not mean they meet the criterion for recurrent use in hazardous situations, and thus do not meet this criterion for a *DSM* diagnosis of alcohol abuse. Or are drivers who routinely drink and drive actually addicts, albeit comparatively well-controlled ones?

A specialist in addiction might argue, however, that the answer to whether Harry (and actually Carl, too) has a diagnosis of an addiction is that there is not enough information to make a meaningful determination—in *either* Carl's or Harry's case. Diagnoses are made with a great deal of attention to influences that are cognitive, emotional, situational, cultural, and so on. The following queries are illustrative of the type of information that would have to be gathered to determine whether Harry has an addiction:

Where does Harry meet his dealer on a Friday? In a back alley? In a dangerous location? Is his dealer armed? Is Harry armed? Why does it take all evening? Why is his use so important that he is willing to engage in illegal behaviors? Does he drive when he is actually impaired or just under the influence? Is he alone in the vehicle on these occasions? Does he have minors in the car? Small children? If he is so vocal regarding the benefits of using, how is it that his employer doesn't know? Does he have to hide his weekend activities from his colleagues and boss? If not, what has been their reaction? Does he miss golfing and gardening? Is he happy with the way he spends his weekends? How much is he using? How much is he spending? How has the cost affected his financial situation? Would he encourage his nieces and nephews to use? What does he think would happen if he missed a weekend? Why is it so important to him that he never misses a weekend of use? What does he mean by his family and friends "standing behind him"? Do his new friends have legal problems? What is the extent of their illicit drug use? What do they do together? Do they only use together or do they engage in other activities during the weekdays? And can we answer the same questions about Harry's current girlfriend? Does he grieve the loss of his former girlfriend? What kinds of things is he doing to "avoid trouble with the law"? What does he mean by "they will accept me for who I am"? Does he meet criteria for other mental health diagnoses such as a personality disorder? Are there inconsistencies in his report? Is there a deliberate attempt to misrepresent his situation? How good is his reality testing? Is there collateral information available?

This is the way addictionologists would approach the case of Harry—and to some extent Carl's case as well, at least if he were to be suspected of addiction at all. But it is not clear that these questions are always the right ones to ask. Do these questions about back alleys and armed dealers and how the cost affects Harry's financial situation actually identify *addiction*, or do they merely reflect the social circumstances of drug use in a society in which Harry's drug of choice is illegal and expensive, but Carl's drug of choice is not? If so, this rebuttal holds, they would do more to diagnose the conditions of a society than the presence or absence of genuine addiction.

By rejoinder, it can be argued that many of these questions are about compulsion, a central, even identifying feature of addiction. But it seems that Carl's compulsion may be stronger than Harry's. After all, Harry quits use every week, but Carl is never even able to cut down.

These tensions between the silo of pain medicine and those of some more traditional elements of addictionology, between the consensus definition and the *DSM* approach, are real; we have seen them fought out even within our own discussions. Miscommunication among practitioners and others dealing with drug use, abuse, and addiction is confounded by the fact that the consensus definition is just that—a definition per se, without measurable diagnostic criteria, while the *DSM* statement is a list of criteria intended to operationalize the definition of addiction in order to permit reliable diagnosis. They are both valuable documents and play central roles in their fields, and they are closely related. But they are not fully consistent. And while the intent of these two documents differ, they are in practice often confused by clinicians, lawyers, corrections personnel, and many others. In clinical practice and in many other contexts, these are often misused. Indeed, there are members of the addictionology community who favor changing the *DSM* wording of "substance dependence" back to "addiction."

Is the apparent conflict between the consensus definitions of addiction and dependence and the *DSM* diagnostic criteria for substance abuse disorders just a turf battle, or something deeper? More illustrations could be provided of surprising and conflicting verdicts about what counts as addiction and what does not, all pointing out that even intelligent, dedicated, and informed individuals who think persistently and carefully about addiction in their respective disciplinary spheres can nonetheless generate definitions that produce conclusions that are mutually inconsistent. A likely cause of this troubling result is the influence of the disparate fields within which the phenomenon is examined and the lack of effective communication among persons from the different fields that focus on addiction issues. While clarification of the different roles of definition and diagnosis may clear up some of the confusion, it is clear that there remains a fissure at the root of the concept of addiction, in that it is understood in one way by some professionals, in quite another way by others. In practice, this fissure is rarely explicitly recognized, though it distorts many discussions. The consensus definition represents a major achievement insofar as it was the first effort of two quite different silos—pain medicine and addiction medicine—to try to reach a common definition, and the *DSM* is also a major achievement is that it represents an ongoing effort to present a comprehensive view of psychiatric research. But they still find themselves on differing sides of this fissure.

Common Confusions: Pseudoaddiction and Iatrogenic Addiction

Addiction and related states must be differentiated to understand their clinical and societal implications for the states. These phenomena typically involve opioids and are frequently mentioned in the pain management literature. However, they should be considered in nearly every context in which addiction is addressed. Yet still other concepts related to addiction also cause confusion, especially those of pseudoaddiction and iatrogenic addiction.

Pseudoaddiction

In 1989, partly to mitigate the stigma often associated with the use of opioids for pain, two pain management physicians, David Weissman and David Haddox, defined a treatment-induced syndrome that they termed "pseudoaddiction," in what is now considered a classical paper in the pain management literature.[42] This syndrome appears much like, and is easily mistaken for, adverse drug-seeking behavior often seen in genuine addiction. But its cause is not the complex physical, psychological, and environmental factors associated with an addiction disorder.

Pseudoaddiction results from health professionals providing too little pain medication and thus causing their patients to seek more medication.

---

42. David E. Weissman, J. David Haddox. Opioid Pseudoaddiction—An Iatrogenic Syndrome. *Pain* 36(1989): 363–66.

A physician might prescribe a month's supply for a patient with a severe chronic pain syndrome, for instance, ninety tablets of an opioid analgesic to be taken three times a day. The patient might be instructed that the dose is not to exceed six tablets per day, which the physician regards as the upper limit rather than the basic dose. The physician also tells the patient that this medication may not be refilled for a month. A prescriber who is uneasy about the possibility of contributing to substance abuse in a patient would be particularly likely to do this. The patient, whose pain is real and responsive to the six-tablet daily dose but is not fully controlled at a regimen of three tablets per day, takes six tablets (two tablets three times) per day for fifteen days. Thus the total of ninety tablets is consumed, leaving the patient with no medication for two weeks before the physician will represcribe the drug. Many patients quickly learn that they must manipulate the system to obtain a sufficient amount of medication to meet their needs. For instance, they may go to numerous prescribers ("doctor shopping") and numerous pharmacies ("pharmacy shopping"), much like true addicts. They also may devise tales about how their tablets or prescription vials were lost, or they may engage in illegal behavior to obtain more drugs. Although these patients seek more medication to manage their pain, not to get "high," their efforts are seen as adverse drug-seeking behavior, especially by "opiophobic" physicians, pharmacists, and nurses. The signs and symptoms of such pseudoaddiction, however, typically subside when the pain is controlled.

Thus, pseudoaddiction is a pattern of drug-seeking behavior that can be mistaken for addiction—under either the consensus definition or the *DSM* diagnostic criteria. For pain specialists, the term is most commonly used in reference to drug-seeking behavior of patients receiving inadequate amounts of analgesic medication. The authors of the original paper describing pseudoaddiction, Weissman and Haddox, emphasized that it is a treatment-induced or iatrogenic (doctor-caused) syndrome.

The concept described as pseudoaddiction may also be extended to types of drug-seeking behavior for conditions other than pain management and use not involving opioids. Consider the following examples. First, an adolescent student, Amy, uses albuterol, a short-acting asthma medication (bronchodilator), to control episodes of asthma. Not long ago, however, Amy was not permitted to carry the medication under her school's zero-tolerance anti-drug policy. Therefore, she engaged in characteristic drug-seeking behavior, including exchanging favors or objects for medicine, sneaking medicine, contravening school policy (always with the risk of expulsion), and compulsive use as defined by an obsession with seeking or using the substance in a repetitive manner.[43] While Amy's school finally changed its policy, Amy was at risk for several years.

Or consider Marv, a construction assistant who was diagnosed with Attention-Deficit/Hyperactivity Disorder (ADHD) in childhood and treated with methylphenidate (Ritalin). He has been successful despite lingering symptoms of ADHD and used Ritalin for five years since graduating from high school. Now he has been promoted to painter, a job that demands concentration and persistent attention to detail. Although Marv loves his new job, he has difficulty concentrating. He does not have health insurance and is reluctant to return to the use of Ritalin due to its side effects. However, friends tell him that marijuana is effective in improving focus and diminishing distraction. He smokes marijuana daily before and at work, with the result that he is able to "get into the zone" and focus on his painting. His work is considered exemplary, and he is praised and again promoted. Marv finds himself continually seeking and using marijuana because he believes he cannot function well without it, as verified by the times he has been without the drug, although he denies addiction and says he can easily go without using marijuana—he just cannot work effectively.

Iatrogenic Addiction

The family of drugs known as opioids (i.e., derivatives and analogs of opium, prototypically morphine) is often associated by clinicians and patients with addiction. This provides an occasion for the question of

43. Based on the case of Philip Gonzalez, a California fifth grader who died of an asthma attack after the school district failed to inform parents of an unwritten school policy that would have allowed students to carry inhalers, although other medications were to be stored in the school office. Philip's inhaler was also kept in the school office, where he could not reach it in time. Philip's mother was awarded $9 million in damages, an amount later reduced to $2.225 million. *Gonzales v. Hanford Elementary School District,* Nos. F033659, FO34555, (Super.Ct. Nos. 0031 & 1109) (2002).

whether the relevant "addiction" is pseudoaddiction, true addiction, or something else, and whether it can be produced by physician-ordered medical treatment. Popular lore and claims involving public figures abound with allegations concerning iatrogenic addiction. Elvis Presley, for example, asserted that his multiple addictions were caused by medical treatment. During the seven-month period between March and September 2003, talk-show host Rush Limbaugh filled prescriptions for 1,733 hydrocodone tablets, 90 OxyContin tablets, 50 Xanax tablets, and 40 time-release morphine tablets. Describing his addiction as iatrogenic but continued voluntarily, he explained:

> You know I have always tried to be honest with you and open about my life. So I need to tell you today that part of what you have heard and read is correct. I am addicted to prescription pain medication.
>
> I first started taking prescription painkillers some years ago when my doctor prescribed them to treat post-surgical pain following spinal surgery. Unfortunately, the surgery was unsuccessful and I continued to have severe pain in my lower back and also in my neck due to herniated discs. I am still experiencing that pain. Rather than opt for additional surgery for these conditions, I chose to treat the pain with prescribed medication. This medication turned out to be highly addictive.
>
> Over the past several years I have tried to break my dependence on pain pills and, in fact, twice checked myself into medical facilities in an attempt to do so. I have recently agreed with my physician about the next steps.
>
> Immediately following this broadcast, I am checking myself into a treatment center for the next 30 days to once and for all break the hold this highly addictive medication has on me. The show will continue during this time, of course, with an array of guest hosts you have come to know and respect.
>
> I am not making any excuses.[44]

The data on the prevalence of opioid addiction acquired in the course of medical treatment are difficult to interpret. There is some evidence to support the belief held by many pain clinicians and addictionologists that addiction is relatively rare among patients (1) with legitimate medical

44. Limbaugh statement, http://transcripts.cnn.com/TRANSCRIPTS/0310/10/bn.03.html.

conditions, (2) who respond appropriately to opioid therapy, and (3) who do not have a recent history of substance abuse or any of several psychiatric disorders that may predispose them to substance abuse, such as bipolar, personality, and severe affective disorders. Several published surveys suggest a low incidence of iatrogenic addiction in patients treated with opioids for pain, perhaps less than one percent.[45] Although these surveys are retrospective and probably underestimate the true frequency of iatrogenic opioid addiction, they nonetheless support the contention that the actual incidence is far lower than many governmental agencies, health professionals, and counselors contend.

Failure to distinguish among addiction, pseudoaddiction, physical dependence, and tolerance is probably a major reason for the over-exaggeration of the incidence of opioid addiction. While uncommon when opioids are used appropriately, iatrogenic addiction is what professionals fear when they are said to have "opiophobia"—despite the fact that what is perceived as addiction may be a medically acceptable condition that has its origins in the prescribed treatment regimen. Addiction in a very small number of predisposed patients may be unavoidable and an acceptable risk if the benefit of the medication outweighs the risk of the condition. But in the end, it is very rare.

Although some instances of iatrogenic addiction qualify as addictions in a robust sense with unique origins, their frequency is massively overestimated when cases of both pseudoaddiction and physical dependence are mischaracterized as iatrogenic addiction. Such issues might also arise with the use of sports-enhancement drugs, and while drugs recommended by athletic trainers or coaches for performance enhancement are rarely addictive, potentially addictive opioids are sometimes used by athletes for pain control. One such scenario involves the use of painkillers after an injury, potentiated by alcohol (as apparently occurred in the much-publicized case of Brett Favre, the Green Bay Packers quarterback, who was required by the

45. Jane Porter, Hershel Jick, "Addiction Rare in Patients Treated with Narcotics"(letter), *New England Journal of Medicine* 302(2)(1980):123; Samuel Perry. George S. Heidrich, "Management of Pain during Debridement: A Survey of U.S. Pain Units," *Pain* 13(3)(1982): 267–80; Jose Medina, Seymour J. Diamond, "Drug Dependency in Patients with Chronic Headache," *Headache* 17(1)(1977): 12–14.

NFL to enter substance-abuse treatment).[46] Similar issues about "iatrogenic" addiction might arise with religious shamans using drugs in sacramental or ritual ways. And despite accounts of the "soldier's disease" of the Civil War era, verifiable cases of iatrogenic addiction based solely on a medical treatment regimen are uncommon in patients without a history of substance abuse or psychiatric disorders that predispose to substance abuse.

This conclusion was first established and illustrated by a 1980 report of a study from the Boston Collaborative Drugs Surveillance Program,[47] which examined nearly 12,000 patients receiving opioids for as long as two years for a wide range of disorders. In this large survey sample, only four patients were found to have clearly developed a treatment-induced addiction. Because this was a retrospective survey, it may have underestimated the true prevalence of treatment-induced (iatrogenic) addiction. However, this report and other publications suggest that iatrogenic addiction occurs less frequently than many clinicians and society as a whole commonly believe.

An interpretation of all reports of addiction may be confounded by the definition of addiction in play. Although the above-cited report predated the formulation of either the AAPM/APS/ASAM consensus definition or the current edition of the DSM, the result of that survey continues to be widely cited, even without attention to the question of whether the number of patients who developed treatment-induced addiction would be higher, lower, or about the same using one account of addiction rather than another.

Despite the apparently low prevalence of iatrogenic addiction, it is still perceived as a very real threat, due in part to the confusing nature of pseudoaddiction and the ease with which it can be mistaken for an addiction that has begun in the context of treatment. Pseudoaddiction might also be a manifestation of patients' physical dependence on or tolerance to the drugs used in their treatment. Whatever its genesis, pseudoaddiction is characterized primarily as drug-seeking behavior engaged in by a patient to alleviate or control the pain he suffers, whether it is the original pain for

---

46. Tony Kornheiser. "Favre Chews the Scenery, and I'm Eating it Up," *Washington Post,* Tuesday, January 31, 2006, E02.

47. Porter and Jick, "Addiction Rare in Patients Treated with Narcotics," 123.

which the drugs were prescribed or the pain of withdrawal symptoms due to physical dependence. Because the drugs are sought to alleviate this pain, the drug-seeking behavior tends to subside with the pain itself.

In pseudoaddiction the drug user has a simple and achievable aim, to alleviate pain. Even the most ingenious drug-seeking behavior by patients is an effort to achieve pain control that their clinicians failed to provide, often due to underprescription of analgesics in the first place.

Tolerance, as outlined earlier in this chapter, is a state in which an increasing amount of a substance is needed to maintain the effect. Patients' demands for increasing doses of medication can stem from addiction, pseudoaddiction, or tolerance. In most such cases, the clinician who is being asked to increase the dose has to consider adverse drug-seeking behavior as a motivation for the demands. Similar behavior can stem from clinicians failing to increase the dose of pain medication in response to increased illness, which is an instance of a larger phenomenon that has been described as "pseudotolerance."[48] Pseudotolerance has been described as a phenomenon that may occur when greater amounts of a drug are needed to maintain the desired clinical effect due to some other cause than tolerance to analgesia per se. The increased need might come as a direct response to an increase in the pathology being treated or the onset of a new ailment (e.g., cancer metastases) rather than the patient developing physical tolerance to the analgesic effects of the drug. Like pseudoaddiction, behavior in response to this condition might mimic an addict's drug-seeking behavior, but it is neither addiction nor tolerance. To complicate matters further, pseudotolerance might also result from excessive activity, noncompliance, drug interactions, drug diversion, and even (rarely) addiction itself. But with the obvious exception of true addiction, each of the other listed causes of pseudotolerance may be thought of as some kind of faux tolerance.

To distinguish addiction—under either the consensus definition or the *DSM*—from pseudoaddiction and pseudotolerance, it is necessary to look to the different causes of observable behavior rather than the external manifestations. It is equally possible for a specific chemical substance to be involved in both true addiction and pseudoaddiction when administered

48. Marco Pappagallo, "The Concept of Pseudotolerance," *Journal of Pharmaceutical Care in Pain & Symptom Control* 6(2)(1998): 95–8.

by a clinician. Moreover, there is no reason to exclude the (admittedly rare) possibility that the substances could be involved in mere pseudoaddiction when the drug is self-administered or administered by some authority figure other than a clinician. These possibilities could be particularly important in contexts such as religious drug use promoted within a spiritual tradition or administered by a religious shaman, or sports-enhancement drugs recommended or administered by an athletic trainer.

Because so many symptoms overlap in cases of physical dependence, tolerance, pseudoaddiction, and pseudotolerance, they can often be difficult to identify in any given case, as for example in ongoing and increasing use of nasal decongestant sprays such as oxymetazoline (the over-the-counter nasal decongestant Afrin). Increasing use often results from attempts to manage the rebound congestion that occurs following frequent dosing, a common phenomenon despite product labeling that explicitly warns of this risk. Compulsive or increasing use of such a nasal spray may look like addiction, pseudoaddiction, or a self-medicating quasi-iatrogenic addiction, when in all likelihood, it is the result of rebound congestion. Such distinctions may not be easy and excessive use of a substance may result from a combination of factors. These practical difficulties should not prevent pseudoaddiction and iatrogenic addiction from being kept conceptually distinct from one another as well as from the concept of addiction.

*   *   *

This chapter has involved a tour through the complexities of the concept of addiction and the related concepts of substance abuse, substance dependence, tolerance, pseudoaddiction, iatrogenic addiction, and more. It also considers the difference between definition and diagnosis. But most public rhetoric fails to differentiate all these very different phenomena. Professional discourse about drug use and misuse within the various spheres within which pharmacotherapy and drug abuse occur, and within which both governmental and nongovernmental drug policy are developed and analyzed, also often conflate these terms. Well-informed, careful, rigorous attention to drug theory, drug policy, and drug practice has consuming importance in contemporary discussions of drugs, but these discussions often are beset by confusion over addiction, perhaps the most central of the core issues about drugs.

The full range of theories of the causes and nature of addiction, whether appealing to genetics, disease, psychosocial causes, or all three, do not always distinguish sufficiently carefully among dependence, tolerance, pseudoaddiction, pseudotolerance, abuse, and true addiction. Drug policy intended to avoid or prevent addiction or to mitigate the harms of addiction may rest on an uneven foundation, where it is not clear how addiction is defined and perceived. Addiction and the personal and social harms associated with it are central concerns of drug theory and drug policy affecting prescription drugs; over-the-counter drugs; dietary supplements; common-use drugs like alcohol, tobacco, and caffeine; religious-use drugs; sports-enhancement drugs; and illegal recreational drugs. Many of the practical dilemmas examined in the following chapter are difficult in part because inconsistent assumptions about or incoherent accounts of addiction lie at their core.

5

CORE CONCEPTUAL PROBLEMS: HARM (AND BENEFIT)

Discussions about drug use, like discussions about drug addiction, routinely involve claims about harm. Indeed, it would be difficult to exaggerate the harm caused both by the misuse—and abuse—of drugs and by society's response. In 2002, the National Survey on Drug Use and Health estimated that each month more than six million Americans used prescription drugs for nonmedical uses. The White House estimates that in 2000, Americans spent $36 billion on cocaine, $11 billion on marijuana, $10 billion on heroin, $5.4 billion on methamphetamine, and $2.4 billion on other illegal substances.[1] A majority of inmates in federal prisons and more than a fifth of those in state prisons are incarcerated for drug-related crimes,[2] and a substantial percentage of government budgets are dedicated to controlling the use of illicit drugs. Tobacco use alone is estimated to account for over $75 billion in direct medical costs.[3] And in the words of a representative of the U.N. Office on Drugs and Crime (UNODC), "The size of the world's illicit drug industry is…equivalent to 0.9 percent of the world's GDP, or higher than the GDP of 88 percent of the countries in the world."[4]

1. Office of National Drug Control Policy, The White House, *ONDCP Drug Policy Information Clearinghouse Fact Sheet* (2003):1–8, online at http://www.whitehousedrug-policy.gov/pdf/drug_datasum.pdf.

2. *Sourcebook of Criminal Justice Statistics* 519(2003), tbl.6.56, online at http://www.albany.edu/sourcebook/pdf/t656.pdf; *Sourcebook of Criminal Justice Statistics Online* at http://www.albany.edu/sourcebook/pdf/t600012002.pdf.

3. National Institute on Drug Abuse, *InfoFacts: Cigarettes and Other Nicotine Products*, online at http://www.drugabuse.gov/Infofacts/Tobacco.html. See also http://www.cdc.gov/MMWR/preview/mmwrhtml/mm5235a4.htm.

4. Online at http://www.csdp.org/news/news/reut_un05_062905.htm.

The costs and harms of drug use are not to be estimated only in financial terms, but also in human tragedy. More than 100,000 people die annually from pharmaceutical mishaps.[5] Another 440,000 die from causes related to tobacco, which is associated with some 150 different diseases.[6] Alcohol is involved in an estimated 85,000 deaths, including road accidents and other causes; added to these are an estimated 17,000 deaths from illegal drug use.[7] In theory, policy, and practical measures about drugs, the possibility of harm must always be regarded as a central concept.

The ever-present risk of harm is reflected in a cardinal idea in clinical pharmacology, attributed to Paracelsus, that every drug has the potential to do harm. At the same time, of course, drug use can provide benefits. Medicinal drugs, including both older drugs known for decades or centuries and modern compounds synthesized in the current heyday of scientific pharmaceutical development, provide enormous benefits in treating illness, ameliorating pain, and repairing bodily functions. Over-the-counter drugs allow people to self-medicate for minor conditions, control symptoms, and reduce pain for many kinds of difficulties—from sleeplessness to sunburn to stomach ailments—that might otherwise cause more substantial trouble. And some herbal remedies, supplements, and vitamins are thought to improve health. The seemingly obvious notion that the use of drugs can convey very substantial benefits is sometimes overlooked in contemporary discussions. The War on Drugs with its "just say no" mantra has painted drugs as bad or evil with a broad brush, but benefits must also be considered in any full appraisal of drug use. Although the complement of "every drug has the potential to do harm," namely that "every drug has the potential to do good," may not be true—consider Sarin, a drug so toxic that it has no known benefits other than killing one's enemy—the role of both harm *and benefit* in the use of drugs will be part of any thoroughgoing inquiry.

5. Gary Null, Carolyn Dean, Martin Feldman, Debora Rasio, and Dorothy Smith, *Death by Medicine, Life Extension* (March 2004); online at http://www.lef.org/magazine/mag2004/mar2004_awsi_death_02.htm.

6. National Institute on Drug Abuse, *InfoFacts: Cigarettes and Other Nicotine Products*, online at http://www.drugabuse.gov/Infofacts/Tobacco.html.

7. Ali H. Mokdad; James S. Marks; Donna F. Stroup; Julie L. Gerberding, "Actual Causes of Death in the United States, 2000, *Journal of the American Medical Association* 291(10)(2004): 1238–45.

When an across-the-board view is taken, it becomes apparent that the various silos of drug theory and policy employ different conceptions of harm and benefit as well as different priorities in assessing them. Much of current theory and policy about drugs reinforces the misleading assumption that legal drugs primarily yield benefits, while illegal drugs almost exclusively cause harms (which may in part explain their classification). Although there is some truth to this assumption, it is grossly oversimplified and cloaks an underlying conceptual problem in any discussion of drugs. This chapter exposes some of the differences in the ways the various silos approach the issue of harm and benefit, in the hope that it will encourage theorists, policymakers, and practitioners in each area to reexamine how they employ these different conceptions, and ultimately lead to more consistent and coherent thinking about drugs.

Drugs as Causes of Harm: Primitive and Modern Views

Since the earliest periods of human history for which there is archeological evidence, certain drugs have been known to cause harm and others to provide benefits. In more recent centuries, this awareness has undergone a seemingly minor but quite significant conceptual change. Contemporary scientific understanding now clearly recognizes that it is the *use* of drugs, not the drugs themselves, that causes harm or brings benefits. This distinction might seem trivial to modern ears, but it is in fact quite important in understanding certain ambiguities and equivocations in the ways in which harm is understood in drug theory and policy.

The primitive view of drugs (still evident in many cultures and policies) is that a drug itself has the ability to act on people apart from consumption, a view understandably held by those without a scientific understanding of physical properties and effects on human physiology. For instance, traditional sorcery relied on claims about the innate powers of certain substances to act at a distance: drugs could be worn in an amulet, offered to a deity, or laid on the doorstep of an enemy to work their magic. Many cultures viewed drugs themselves as moral agents worthy of blame, much as ancient Greek and medieval Christian cultures are said to have assigned moral responsibility to inanimate objects and animals. Even today, for example, members of the Native American Church believe that peyote can have a powerful and beneficial influence when worn in an amulet, or prayed to on behalf of others who are not present.

The modern scientific view, in contrast, recognizes that drugs produce their effects by biochemical action on the body. In order to have a physiological effect (beyond that due to suggestion, psychological anticipation, or the placebo effect), drugs must be ingested, inhaled, injected, or otherwise absorbed. In short, they must be *used*. The drug itself is neither harmful nor beneficial. Consequently, as a matter of ethical analysis, it is misleading to say that a drug is "bad" or "evil"; it is drug *use* that should be subject to evaluation. As Paracelsus, the "father of scientific medicine," observed half a millennium ago, every substance can be innocuous in very small doses or toxic in sufficiently large amounts. It is as true for water as it is for heroin.

Some drugs contain virtually no pharmacologically active ingredients and are purposely processed this way. For example, preparations of homeopathic drugs such as *Arnica montana, medorrhinum*, and *Lobelia inflata* are so diluted that they consist of virtually nothing but water, lactose, or alcohol. The dilution is intentional—homeopathic theory holds that the effective properties of a drug are transferred to the water or other substance, even though the drug itself has been diluted by factors of a hundred or more. But in general, any drug with active ingredients can be innocuous or toxic depending on dose.

This distinction has subtle but potentially enormous implications for the control of drugs: the ostensible purpose of control should focus not on the drug itself, but on drug use. However simplistic this distinction may seem, the two are often conflated, at least in the public mind. For example, prescription drugs are often seen as *good* or *good for you* and illegal drugs as *bad* or *bad for you*. But prescription drugs are not simply good. Any "miracle drug" can be troublesome if misused, as when an antibiotic is not taken for a sufficient length of time and thus allows resistant bacteria to develop, or when AIDS drugs are not taken on a rigorous schedule. The 2.1 million injuries each year that result from adverse drug events[8] are in some large measure due to misuse—including overuse, irregular use, inappropriate use, mistaken use due to confusion with another drug, or use not indicated for the patient's condition (as in prescription errors, dispensing errors, and patient non-adherence). Nor are illegal drugs simply bad. For example, cocaine has appropriate applications

---

8. Martin S. Manno, "Preventing Adverse Drug Events," *Nursing* 36(3)(March 2006): 56–61.

in medicine; so do virtually all the narcotics, hallucinogens, stimulants, and depressants that are restricted under the federal Schedules I and II. What is problematic with illegal drugs is the way they are used.

In the past, the failure to distinguish adequately between drug use and the drug itself has led to unintended consequences. Consider, for instance, the temperance movement. Its ultimate objective, Prohibition, was instituted to root out "demon rum," as if the rum itself were the cause of social problems. Only by getting rid of this dangerous drug altogether could society be saved from ruin. At least in its rhetoric, the temperance movement made the primitive assumption that alcohol is in itself bad and thus must be banned altogether, rather than that certain kinds of alcohol use were bad, such as heavy drinking to the point of aggressive drunkenness. Indeed, society has come to understand that drinking alcohol in moderate quantities not only does not have all the harmful effects alleged during the temperance movement, but in some forms it appears to have beneficial health effects (e.g., improved cardiovascular health from moderate red wine consumption). While alcohol clearly can be misused—consider the estimated 10 million alcoholics in the United States alone—it is not bad in itself.

There is some danger that the same primitive assumption is at work today when drug control focuses on supply interdiction to the exclusion of behavior modification. Indeed, it might be argued that the global lack of success in the control of drugs is due in part to a widespread misunderstanding of how drugs cause harm. Drugs are not poisons like environmental pollution, although the analogy—even the equivocation—is often made. We speak of "drug-ridden countries" or "drug-infested" neighborhoods as if they existed on toxic waste sites. This language is misleading when the focus should be on the widespread drug use, or on the production and distribution of drugs. (Like everyone else, we will often speak this way throughout this book, but we recognize that referring to the effects of drugs is a loose and careless way of referring to the effects of drug use.)

The Connection between Drug Use and Drugs

Of course, more can be made of this distinction than should be. After all, isn't saying "drugs don't cause harm, people using drugs causes harm" similar to the slogan "guns don't kill people, people kill people"? If one believes the latter mantra is misleading about firearms, the former may be even more misleading for drugs. The distinction between drug use and drugs is often ignored because the association between the presence of a drug and drug use typically seems so tight—so tight that the "primitive" assumption about the causal effect of drugs at times is justified as a practical matter. To take another example, while the calories in that slice of cake on the table have no effect at all on your waistline as long as the cake stays on the table, proximity, appetite, and temptation being what they are, the presence of the cake is likely to add to your girth. That is just to say that the relationship between the cake's presence and its consumption or "use" is very tight. The same assumption is made with respect to drugs: if they are present, they will be used.

But even with this example, some mechanism of connection must explain why the presence of the cake leads to its consumption. Even if the connection between an item and use of the item is tight, this does not eliminate the need for an explanation of the tightness of that relation. Many theories of the relationship between drugs and drug use simply presuppose such a mechanism of connection, but often without full articulation of what it is. At issue here is an understanding of what is involved in "proximity, appetite, and temptation." In the case of drug use, a full explanation often requires reference to psychological theories that point to background influences and social factors from early childhood onward, or to disease theories of addiction or neuroscience and genetic models that point to brain- and biology-based accounts. The question is as relevant in OTC, sports, and prescription drugs as it is in illegal drugs, even if the mechanisms of connection may turn out to be different.

To develop a coherent account of drug theory, policy, and practice across the board, it is essential to be alert to these (usually unstated) assumptions, since they are likely to differ from one discipline or silo to another. Consider, for example, the phenomenon of "noncompliance" associated with prescription drugs, now often referred to as "non-adherence." Patients are prescribed but do not "use" a regimen of drugs for conditions a physician has diagnosed; that is, the patients do not fill the prescription, do not take the pills if filled, or instead take them erratically and not in accord with the pharmacologically optimum schedule. The drugs are available, so why do they *not* lead to use? Most accounts of non-adherence to a treatment regimen focus only upon choice and make characteristically voluntar-ist assumptions—that is, they see noncompliance as rooted primarily in a largely conscious decision, a refusal, made by the patient. But alterna-tive explanations could be advanced as well, including rationales rooted in patient psychology, disease-model explanations, or neuroscience and genetic explanations based perhaps in failed brain chemistry or heritable traits of rebelliousness.

Or take the forms of "self-medication" associated with complementary and alternative drugs. These herbal remedies, vitamins, plant prepara-tions, and so on, are occasionally recommended by physicians in a medical context, but far more often they are identified and selected by the users themselves, who form their own conceptions of the health benefits of these preparations. Why do some people load up on St. John's wort and ma-huang when at the health food store and others walk right past them? Is it counterculture or anti-establishment inclinations that best explain the widespread use of these drugs? Or gullibility, self-deprecation, social pres-sure, one's early experience as a child, unreasoning optimism about the likely effects of the drug, or what? While a conscious choice is certainly involved—some choose to, others do not—a voluntarist explanation does not seem adequate to tell the whole story, but how that narrative is filled in may be central for an understanding of the connection between drugs and their use. More important, it may be essential to understanding how to mitigate or eliminate the harms caused by drug use.

What about over-the-counter drugs? Here the connection between drugs and drug use is likely to be explained, in large part, in terms of adver-tising—OTC drug manufacturers, it will be said, *persuade* consumers to use their products. But when we turn to common-use drugs like alcohol, tobacco, and caffeine, claims about social pressures and social expectations, not to mention addiction, are likely to be added to the mix. The same may be true for drug use in religious practice: devotees use drugs typically to explore and express their faith, but also because doing so is part of the normal, expected practices of the group.

Does the best explanation involve social pressure, neurobiology, volun-tary choice, or what? Think about sports. Here, the availability of drugs is said to lead to drug use because of ambition, competition, and the drive to be a winner. Although this account recognizes social pressure, it is this athlete's *choice* to try to be the best, and to take drugs to accomplish that aim. Is such an explanation consistent with explanations for drug use in other areas, for example, the self-medication associated with alternative medicines or the reasons for the social use of alcohol and tobacco? Is the drive to be "the best" the same, whether in sports or the workplace or social situations?

The sphere of illegal drugs offers the biggest array of explanations for the connection between drugs and their use—that is, explanations that do not focus only upon voluntary choice—ranging from poor upbringing and bad parenting styles to the neurochemical grip of addiction. To be sure, it would be naïve to assume that all cases of movement from drug availability to drug use are to be explained in the same way. But the point is that public policies (as distinct from scientific theories) are typically rooted in a single, not-well-articulated conjecture about this relationship. That assumption often appeals to the irresistible urges involved in addiction—but as became evident in the previous chapter, what counts as addiction may be understood in very different ways. Sometimes the assumption is so poorly articulated that it is simply left to the public imagination. Consider reports about the growing use of heroin among teenagers, often said to start with teens' use of their parents' prescriptions for OxyContin. Because OxyContin is a legal prescription drug, so the argument goes, teens think it is not as bad as heroin. The narcotics officer on a recent specific case observed that "young people often move from OxyContin to heroin within two weeks, mainly because heroin costs less and, some say, gives them a more-intense high."[9] But these reasons—more intense high and lower cost—cloak the absence of an underlying explanation in the first place: if drugs are available to teens (as they clearly are), why do teens actually use drugs, and why do they use the particular types of drugs they do?

After all, not everyone eats cake when it is in front of them, including diabetics, (successful) dieters, and people without a sweet tooth. The "tight" relation between the cake on the table and the consumption of the cake requires much more thorough analysis. Uncovering the hidden assumptions is part of the work a coherent theory of drugs must do—and

---

9. Justin Hill, "Teen Use of Heroin Growing in Utah," *Salt Lake Tribune*, July 5, 2005, A1.

it must do it for all areas of drug use, across the board, even if there turn out to be relevant differences among various areas of drug use.

The Primitive View in Drug Theory and Drug Policy

So should drug theory and drug control policies be based on the "primitive" assumption that drugs cause harm, together with the assumption that the presence of the drug is tightly connected to use of the drug, so that getting rid of the drugs themselves is the obvious policy strategy? Or should drug policy adopt the modern, scientific assumption that drug *use* causes harm, so that it is behavioral regulation that is more appropriate where the focus is on the mechanisms that leads to use? While a practical policy may recognize both, it still must answer a question of central emphasis: Should drugs themselves be indicted or human behavior changed?

This is not an easy question to answer. It cannot simply be assumed that the "primitive" assumption is inappropriate in all spheres of drug use, across the board. In some venues drugs are understood as bad (or good) independently of the way they are used. For example, Olympic anti-doping policy might be said to classify performance-enhancers such as steroids as "bad"—that is, prohibited outright—without reference to how they might be used, whether overused, underused, or whatever. Indeed, it may be that no relationship with these drugs at all could be justifiable in athletics, meaning that *any* use, possession, or contact with such drugs may be grounds for dismissal from competition. Indeed, if athletes test free of steroids but steroids are found in their bag, they can still be disqualified from competition. Similarly, possession of cocaine is a crime, even if intent to use or distribute cannot be demonstrated (to be sure, proof of intent to distribute can result in penalties for a more serious offense). In turn, some religious groups' prohibitions of drugs like alcohol, nicotine, and caffeine appear to treat these drugs as bad in themselves, irrespective of the way in which they might be used: there is no good use as distinct from misuse.

At the opposite end of the spectrum, some drugs, such as aspirin, seem to be publicly regarded as only good. But virtually no drugs offer only benefits, and virtually all drugs can be misused, even those classed as over-the-counter, available for purchase by anyone without specific permission or prescription, that is, classed as "safe for medically unsupervised use." That virtually all drugs can be misused does not hold just for prescription drugs and illicit drugs, but also for herbal medicines and dietary supplements, which are subject to almost no controls. The possibility of aspirin causing gastric bleeding, for instance, Reyes' Syndrome in inappropriately treated children, or even overdose reinforces the notion that it is drug *use*, not the drug itself, that is "bad" or "good" even if it is widely viewed as good. Furthermore, nearly every drug falls in both the "good" and the "bad" categories. OxyContin, like other prescription pharmaceuticals, is highly effective and beneficial when used correctly in medical pain management, but on the street, where it is typically overused, it can produce devastating harms.

Perhaps adopting the primitive view, several international treaties appear to be aimed at ridding the world of specific drugs altogether—through, for example, prohibitions on coca and poppy growing. These treaties underwrite interdiction on a global scale. In contrast, the contemporary scientific view might seem to suggest that, in at least some cases, it is human behavior rather than the substance itself that must be regulated, with equally far-reaching implications for drug policy. Neither eradicating drugs nor changing human behavior presents an easy task, but they can differ in deep theoretical ways, which are often confused and conflated in both theory and policy.

While considering the role played by different conceptions of harm in the formulation of drug theory and policy, it is important to keep in mind what it is that causes the harms (and benefits) that in turn generate concern, as well as what explanatory mechanisms are at play, sometimes below the surface. While avoiding this confusion may not itself be a sufficient condition for formulating coherent and consistent drug policy, it is a necessary condition.

The Nature of Harm

Harm is a central concern for both drug theory and drug policy. The prevention of harm is a primary justification for the policies leading to the various controls on drug use. This makes perfect sense: How could anyone disagree that harm should be prevented? Yet it is the intuitive appeal of harm prevention that leads to trouble. As will become evident, claims that certain policies will prevent harm are among the least scrutinized in the discussion of drugs, and for that reason the most likely to lead the various disciplines or silos to talk past one another.

Harm to Self

At first glance, it seems a simple matter to determine whether to use a certain drug. People just weigh benefits and harms, and as long as they believe the benefits outweigh any harm and third parties will not be harmed, then they should use the drug. For example, if Ann is deciding whether to take an aspirin, she might weigh the benefit of being able to concentrate without her current headache against the harmful effect the aspirin may have on her stomach. If the headache is bad enough, then Ann should take the aspirin, but she is not morally blameworthy if she concludes it is not worth the risk of an upset stomach, even if others would have come to a different conclusion. As long as third parties are unaffected, such decisions should be left to each person; it is "none of our business," as it were, whether Ann takes the aspirin. In the parlance of ethical theory, as long as the resulting harm will be only "harm to self," many theorists hold, the decision of whether to use a drug typically is left to the person using the drug.

Harm to Others

There are circumstances, however, in which society seems justified in preventing someone from using a drug (or perhaps even in forcing someone to use a drug), usually when a third party will be harmed. For example, if we are deciding whether Bob can be prevented from smoking cigarettes at the office, benefits and harms are not weighed only from Bob's perspective and the decision is not simply left to him. Instead, whether Bob's smoking will cause harm to others in the form of second-hand smoke is thought to be determinative of whether such a restriction is justified. If someone else will be harmed by Bob's drug use, then it becomes "their business." In the vernacular of ethical theory, if drug use will cause "harm to others," then the decision is not simply left to the drug user, and society is justified in prohibiting or regulating the drug use. For this reason, it is harm to others that is often the primary focus of discussions about drug policy.

The principle that decisions should be left to each individual unless "harm to others" will result is commonly referred to as the Harm Principle, the classic formulation of which is credited to John Stuart Mill.[10] The Harm Principle does not tell society when it should step in to restrict or regulate behavior, but it does provide what seems to be a fairly straightforward mechanism for determining when society would be justified if it decided to do so. While this picture is simple and has intuitive appeal, as with so many things, the devil is in the details. Difficult questions lurk just below the surface.

For instance, what counts as harm? What Connie considers harmful, Dan may find beneficial. Consider the effects brought on by the use of LSD, which has essentially no biological toxicity but carries a risk of psychosis. Connie may find the hallucinations and state of depersonalization that comes with the psychosis harmful, but this may be precisely what Dan is looking for. Or consider Evan's decision about whether to use morphine in his final illness. He sees the decision as involving a tradeoff between pain and obtundation—between continued suffering from his terminal cancer and the continuing possibility of emotional contact with his family and loved ones. Though Evan's choice may have consequences for his family, his physicians, and others, this is often considered to be a primarily self-affecting choice appropriately left to him alone.

As these examples show, questions about whether a person is harmed can look much like questions about whether a person is in pain. If Evan says he is in pain, then it would be odd to insist he is not. The views of others about Evan's pain are rarely, if ever, taken to trump his own report of the matter. Does harm work the same way? Is whether someone is harmed merely a subjective matter? As long as third parties are not negatively affected, there does not seem to be anything wrong with concluding that different people just consider different things to be harmful and leaving it at that.

Yet "leaving it at that" is not an option when third parties are (or are likely to be) harmed. If people's own opinions about when they are harmed by others were determinative, then nearly *any* regulation on drug use could be justified. After all, there appear to be few situations in which a choice to use (or not to use) a drug will not harm, or at least potentially harm,

---

10. John Stuart Mill, *On Liberty* [1859] (Indianapolis: Hackett, 1981).

a third party. For example, Evan's choice of obtunding doses of morphine in his last days may rob his family of contact that is emotionally urgent for them; or conversely, Evan's choice to forgo morphine may also have difficult emotional consequences for them, as they watch him endure unbearable suffering on his deathbed. Even much more trivial choices about drugs may harm others. While Ann might be willing to take the aspirin to get rid of her headache even though it is likely to upset her stomach, what about her poor spouse who now will not enjoy spicy Mexican food for dinner because of Ann's decision? Is *this* enough to make Ann's decision about whether to take the aspirin her "spouse's business"? With harm defined this broadly—to include the loss of minor benefits as well as major interests—it is difficult to imagine any pure harm-to-self cases. As long as someone who loves us finds our decision to use or not to use a drug to be self-destructive, isn't that person harmed? While Fran, suffering from schizophrenia, may be perfectly willing to give up her career to avoid having to take her antipsychotic medication with its well-known side effects, this decision is likely to harm members of her family, even if the harm is just distress over the loss of her career. Again, does *this* qualify as harm to others sufficient to justify intervention, in this case intervention to force someone to use a drug?

While it may seem obvious that not every decision involving drug use that harms third parties thereby becomes "their business," it is important to try to understand why. How much harm to others is required before intervention is justified? The question is more pressing than it may seem. If motorcycle helmet and seatbelt laws are justified because, as it is often argued, offenders are likely to impact medical insurance costs when they are injured, then wouldn't consistency demand that nearly every decision regarding drug use be "everyone's business"? Just how remote or slight must a potential harm be before it ceases to qualify as harm to others?

The problem of narrowing the scope of harms relevant to justifying intervention is not dependent upon an assumption that a number of people are slightly impacted. Consider Gloria, who finds drunkenness offensive and also finds herself sitting near drunken patrons at a comedy club. There is a sense in which Gloria is harmed by the presence of the drunken patrons, much as one might be harmed by standing near someone who has not bathed. But is this harm at all? And if so, is it the kind of harm to others that would justify banning all alcohol sales at the comedy club?

Gloria's case highlights the insurmountable practical problem with simply defining harm subjectively and considering any harm to others to justify intervention. If harm is defined subjectively and Gloria need only announce she is harmed by the other patrons' drug use—much as Evan need only announce that he is in pain—to gain a moral stake in their drug use, then policies that appeal to the Harm Principle appear hopelessly restrictive. What if other patrons, or especially the comedian, do not believe it is at all harmful for some patrons to be drunk? After all, they are not *hurting anyone* merely by being drunk. Well, that is just the issue, isn't it? What harms are relevant to applying the Harm Principle and when are they sufficiently severe and immediate to justify intervention?

Philosophers have defined "harm" as something that has an adverse effect on a person's interests.[11] Some constructions of this view may seem to invite an objective appraisal of harms, implying that the degree to which one or more of a person's interests have been harmed can be measured from the outside, so to speak. If what counts as harm is an objective matter, then theorists would have a way to weed out certain harms and thereby reduce to a more intuitive level the instances in which intervention is justified. However, defining harm objectively is not a simple matter. One person might claim to be harmed by an occasion of public drunkenness, while another shrugs it off as a mere nuisance, if negative at all. How would one go about determining which person is (objectively) correct in such a dispute? Also, while defining harm objectively perhaps works well for certain types of harm, such as physical harm, which can be anatomically verified, it does not work as well for other types of harm, such as psychological harm, which is more difficult to assess. Yet the latter types of harm often are most important.

To avoid such problems with defining harm objectively, one simply could accept a subjective definition of harm, but argue that not just any harm (so defined) can justify intervention. On this view, the offense Gloria takes to public drunkenness would still be considered a harm—as seems intuitively appropriate—but this harm might be too slight to constitute harm to others and thereby too slight to make it any of "Gloria's business"

---

11. Joel Feinberg, *Harm to Others* and *Harm to Self: The Moral Limits of the Criminal Law.* Vols. 1, 3. (New York and Oxford: Oxford University Press, 1984 and 1986, respectively).

whether others are drunk in public (but otherwise causing no problems for anyone, including themselves). While such modifications remove the simplicity from the picture, they seem necessary for theories that appeal to subjective notions of harm.

Yet employing an objective definition of harm or limiting which subjective harms constitute harm to others is precisely what generates controversy, as these modifications allow theorists to smuggle their favored moral theory into applications of the Harm Principle. Often, what one considers to qualify as harm to others depends upon the moral views one already holds. For example, the same people who would not consider Gloria's offense to public drunkenness sufficient to justify a restriction on drinking alcohol in comedy clubs might consider the baseball fans' offense at finding out their heroes might be compromising the "integrity of the game" sufficient to justify restrictions on steroid use in baseball.

Or is perhaps a better comparison that between Gloria's offense and the offense Hal might feel in observing the bulked-up condition of some sports players? Hal finds bodily modifications like tattooing and piercing aesthetically unattractive, but recognizes these are not genuine offenses or harms to himself. However, when he sees a lineman who has bulked up to 320 pounds or a whole football team of artificially exaggerated human beings, he is deeply, genuinely disturbed. Bodybuilders are in between, in Hal's view, since they merely pose, but prizefighters and football players attempt to crush each other, and he finds the spectacle of over-sized human beings in socially sanctioned pseudocombat just too much to take.

Inge, meanwhile, is offended by smokers like Bob. It is not just that she fears the effects of second-hand smoke or remembers her earlier life as a smoker, long before she quit. In fact, she recognizes that the potential physical harm to her from Bob's smoking is very remote, perhaps even too remote to justify restricting his smoking at work. For Inge, it is the mere fact of smoking—that it should be so widespread, so heavily promoted, conducted so openly—which is truly offensive, enough that she is harmed by this knowledge of what is going on around her all the time. And Jill and Kevin, recalling Aldous Huxley's exploration of "the doors of perception" and the "turn on, tune in, drop out" controversy surrounding Timothy Leary in the 1960s, are outraged by the very idea of the "religious" use of drugs. For them, religion is a serious matter to be taken earnestly, not something to be corrupted by what they see as a doper's misconception of paradise.

What these examples, and many others like them, illustrate is that the line between harm and mere offense can be hard to draw. Yet drawing this line is crucial for any theory that holds society may intervene to prevent harms to others, but not to prevent mere offense. The prevention of offense, this view holds, erodes too greatly the protections of liberty that a society ought to maintain, and the ideological disagreements that would occur in a society that tried to legislate offense would be too severe to allow reasonable policy to be developed (also a harm).

Thus, when determining which kinds of harms can justify control over drug use, it is important to avoid relying upon unexamined moral assumptions that happen to be shared by those in a particular sphere of drug discussion—what kinds of harms count, what severity of harm counts, how likely the potential harm must be, whether mere offense counts, and so on. The point is not that everyone must agree about these issues. Rather, it is to emphasize the importance of recognizing when disagreement between and among theorists and practitioners is based upon unshared assumptions, and thus in the end may not be principled disagreement at all. It is one thing to say, for example, that secondhand smoke does not harm third parties by appealing to empirical studies of the effects of second-hand smoke, but quite another to say that the harm itself is too great, or on the contrary too remote, to justify the regulations by appealing (often implicitly) to theoretical assumptions about the nature of harm and the scope of the Harm Principle. Fruitful dialogues between those who disagree require that the parties at least understand the kind of disagreement at issue.

Harm to Society

While unexamined appeals to harm to others risk begging important questions, appeals to another type of harm often lead to even more confusion. The most contentious debates over when harm justifies intervention often involve a third category: harm to society. Even if Gloria is not sufficiently (or at all) harmed by public drunkenness, there may be a sense in which *society itself* nonetheless is harmed. Many philosophers argue that society is a distinct entity and not just the aggregate of its members. If so, then perhaps society can have distinct interests that permit it to suffer harm. While these are contentious claims, many people at least appear to accept them, and if they are correct, shouldn't government be permitted to protect society from such harm, just as it does for innocent third parties?

Harm to society is often couched in terms of moral shortcomings, which are said to damage the "moral fabric" of society, but they need not be. Consider, for example, claims about the effects of drug use in a subgroup in society. In sports, there are at least three distinct claims at issue regarding drugs: (1) that enhancement drugs harm the physical health of the athletes who take them, (2) that they put other athletes at an unfair disadvantage, and (3) that they harm the integrity of the sport itself. For one or more of these reasons, anabolic steroids—which are available by prescription or over the Internet, or in some health food products—are absolutely prohibited for athletes in certain forms of competition, like the Olympic Games, or in certain other venues, such as professional football. But these claims about the harms caused by drug use in sports need to be disentangled and examined independently, each with a clear account of what constitutes a harm of that sort, and what the relationships are between these claims.

Ironically, in the context of sports drugs, the greater the benefit is to the user (in achieving athletic goals anyway), the greater the alleged harm is to the sport itself, or as it is often put, the "integrity of the sport." But what is it to say that the use of enhancement drugs by players harms the game or the integrity of the sport? After all, inanimate objects cannot be harmed, at least not in any usual sense. Inanimate objects do not have interests; a rock is not "harmed" when it is broken in half, even though its structure is changed. But what about entities like "the game of baseball"—can they be harmed? One of the three central rationales above for the exclusion of performance-enhancing drugs from sports rests on the notion that this serves to protect the game itself, as distinct from protecting the players and their health.

To be sure, human institutions—baseball among them—really can be harmed, but what is tricky here is to identify precisely what do and do not count as harms to human institutions as opposed to the humans themselves. Is the sport harmed when undisclosed drug use destroys the public's trust in athletes, and thus undercuts the loyalty fans have toward the sport itself? Or is a player's use of anabolic steroids to boost his performance a type of cheating analogous to using a spitball or a corked bat—a violation of the express provisions of the game? Of course, rules can be set in various ways. Major league baseball permits only wooden bats, but college baseball allows aluminum ones. Would using an aluminum bat in a major league game be harming the game of baseball and compromising the integrity of the sport, or would it merely constitute violating its rules? The challenge here is to articulate exactly why using performance-enhancing drugs in athletic competition might be harming the sport, beyond merely being a violation of its rules. It appears inconsistent to hold that some activity harms the game or harms the integrity of the sport but also recognize that the activity represents nothing more than an infraction of the game's rules. If it is a mere rule violation, then the alleged harm to the sport cannot justify the rule, as it is instead the rule breaking that explains why the sport suffers.

This is not to say that enhancement drug use in sports does not constitute a harm, but only that policies governing sports are rarely fully clear or considered at a philosophical level, and frequently blur the line between (real) harm, including harm to others and harm to society, and (mere) offense. Unpacking these claims is crucial to understanding when claims of harm to society demand attention.

Consider the argument made in previous decades about the harm constituted by the use of hallucinogens, which pose little if any risk of harm to the user (aside from the few instances where a person believes they can fly after using LSD, for example). Hallucinogens were made illegal in large part because they were considered a threat to social cohesion. The idea was that society requires its members to share a fundamental perception of the world, and hallucinogens are precisely those pharmacologic agents that alter or distort perception—in other words, they disrupt our ordinarily shared worldview. Hallucinogens permit one to do just as Timothy Leary suggested: "Turn on, tune in, drop out." Many of those who experienced the alternative perception provided by the drugs decided not to retain their original position in society. In a sense, the individual might have been saying, "I may live here, but I am not like you, and I choose to no longer be part of your group."

This was viewed as harm to society because it threatened social cohesion. Some thought that government officials overreacted to the use of hallucinogens in the 1960s and 1970s, blaming Vietnam War protests and other social phenomena on the drugs, and arguing that psychoactive substances were one of the greatest threats to America. But were these officials right to be so concerned? In nearly every society, hallucinogens are used only in socially prescribed ways or not at all. Either it is a deep, often sacred, part of the social fabric, or it is abhorred and prohibited. Rarely is there a middle position concerning hallucinogens.

Interestingly, the sanction for using hallucinogens is not unique to humans. In dozens of studies on the effects of hallucinogens on social animals, the intoxicated animals became socially isolated and frequently caused substantial functional harm to the group. They are often attacked and killed by the herd. For example, cows will shun a fellow cow intoxicated by locoweed.[12] Rats will kill one of their own intoxicated on hallucinogens—but not, apparently, one intoxicated by alcohol or other toxicants.[13] Individuals dosed with LSD are notoriously disruptive to tight social communities such as wasps, bees, newts, and fish. For example, the neon tetra, a tropical fish in the Brazilian Amazon, swims in enormous schools so highly polarized that each individual is precisely one body-length distance from the others; this inter-fish distance is apparently necessary for the school to swim as a unit. Just five LSD-dosed fish are sufficient to destroy the decorum of the group. When the same study was done in a similar group— African cichlids—the school quickly disappeared as the weaker individuals were gobbled up by cannibalistic neighbors.[14]

While this seems to suggest that a separate category of harm to society makes sense, ultimately it is difficult to separate it from harm to others. After all, isn't society just made up of people, and aren't they the ones who ultimately are harmed by any "harm to society"? In the end, unless "harm to society" is determined in some objective way (would appeal to majority opinion be the right way to determine this?), it is difficult to see how the category of "harm to society" is really anything but shorthand for "morally wrong"—a criterion unlikely to provide guidance and easily collapsing into something like "offense." Where harm to society does not

12. Paul M. Gahlinger, "The Addiction of Cows," in *Cows: A Rumination,* ed. C. Hileman (Cincinnati: Emmis Books, 2004).

13. Ronald K. Siegel, *Intoxication: Life in Pursuit of Artificial Paradise* (New York: E. P. Dutton, 1989).

14. R. D. Chessick, Jean Kronholm, Mortimer Beck, George Maier, "Effect of Pretreatment with Tryptamine, Tryptophan and DOPA on LSD Reaction in Tropical Fish," *Psychopharmacology* 5 (5)(1964): 390–92.

appear to amount to a claim that something is morally wrong, it appears to be subsumed by harm to others. For instance, isn't the problem with a dip in economic productivity or a "tragedy of the commons" situation the likelihood that future humans will lack choices they otherwise would have had, and are thereby harmed? If so, then talking about a category of harm to society may simply cause more confusion, as it would be a metaphor for harm to others, which is already a concept riddled with complexity and confusion.

While there are interesting and important debates about how to identify morally relevant harms and whether and to what extent considerations of harm to society should drive drug policy, it is impossible to resolve them here. This admittedly confusing picture has been sketched only to expose the often-unexamined complexity underlying the claim that drug policy should be designed to prevent harm and facilitate benefits. Unsurprisingly, the different disciplines or silos navigate this complex picture differently, often leading to inconsistencies and incoherence in drug theory and policy.

Harm and Benefit within the Framework of Drug Policy

While people (often implicitly) disagree about the role different conceptions of harm should play in discussions of drug theory and policy, appeals to harm prevention remain central—if not indispensable—in evaluating drug policy in all areas. Such disagreements do not cripple discussions of drug policy as long as the contentious nature of claims about harm is kept in mind, so the assumptions made in the different silos can be identified and discussed. What, then, are the different conceptions and types of harm that underlie the vast array of drug policies, and are they consistent when viewed across the board?

These questions are central to understanding and evaluating drug policy because control over drug use is most often justified by appeal to the risk of harm. This is true in each sphere of drugs—prescription pharmaceuticals, OTC drugs, herbal remedies and dietary supplements, common-use drugs, religious-use drugs, sports-enhancement drugs, and illegal drugs. If drug use poses no risk of harm to the user, other individuals, or society, then controlling its use must be viewed as unjustified, whether by government or private parties. However, this limitation on intervention, while uncontroversial, is hardly ever relevant: *every* drug has the potential to do harm if used in excess, under certain circumstances, or in combination with certain other drugs. However, *every* drug—with a few exceptions, such as Sarin—may also be said to have the potential to produce benefits, if used properly. Of course, assessments of harms and benefits can change over time as new information is gathered and novel drug applications are considered. For example, *botulinum* toxin was originally thought to have no benefit, but now has become an important medication in treating certain muscular and pain disorders; it has also become a favored treatment of cosmetic medicine under the name Botox, injected to eliminate unwanted wrinkles from an aging populace as well as to solve other perceived aesthetic flaws. Yet for many drugs, disagreements rage about what counts as benefit and can be more volatile than disputes about what counts as harm.

Consider the range of agreement and disagreement about the effects of the use of drugs. Improved health in the form of better physical functioning of the body is usually counted as a benefit. Improved psychological function in the form of lessened psychosis, depression, agitation, and other mental illness is also usually counted as a benefit. Enhanced pleasure or experience is often but not always counted as a benefit, and altered mental states, pharmacologically induced "insight," and hallucinatory states are only sometimes counted as a benefit—by hippies and advocates of religious drugs, it is said, but no one else. Instead, altered mental states are much more often counted in public policy as a harm. The question here is what interests of a person are legitimately protected—certainly physical health and probably the capacity for normal psychological functioning, but what about pleasure, fantasy, and experiences described as involving visions or insight? Should these count negatively, positively, or not count at all?

Because nearly every drug has the potential to harm or benefit depending on its use, it might seem straightforward to conclude that drug policy should be designed to reduce the risk of harm while facilitating benefits—assuming the disagreements among various silos or professional disciplines about what constitutes a benefit or harm could be resolved, and there were some way to determine the relative weight that should be ascribed to each. All parties, at least in theory, should be able to agree that harms should be avoided and benefits facilitated. And in theory, control over drug use is designed to do just this. Yet in practice the picture is quite different, and accounts for some of the greatest conceptual confusion about drugs.

Harm and Abuse: The Federal Framework of Drug Control

The policy structure that comes closest to this model of weighing harms and benefits of drug use is that of the federal system (outlined in chapter 3), which involves several classificatory schemas. The system may not be fully coherent in organization, and while its underlying intention is to mitigate harm, there is a great deal of both legal and popular confusion. Perhaps the simplest way to approach the issue is to differentiate between two distinctive risks of drug use: biological toxicity and deleterious behavior. Both of these are harmful, but in very different ways.

The first—harm resulting from the toxicity of a drug—is perhaps the most straightforward. The FDA may prohibit a drug if it is deemed to be excessively toxic. More likely, toxicity is mitigated by restricting drug administration to licensed professionals. With the tremendous increase in drug development in the 1950s, it became clear that nonprofessionals could not be expected to have sufficient knowledge about many of the new medications. For example, inappropriate use of antibiotics could lead to direct illness, indirect illness (by increasing risk of other infections), and population drug resistance. All these continue to be seen in countries in which antibiotics are not restricted, with consumers using them in a cavalier fashion, which, in turn, has led to many drug-resistant infectious organisms. For example, syphilis is one of the historically most devastating sexually transmitted diseases. The invention of penicillin brought hopes that this disease would be vanquished. However, penicillin was so overused (and incorrectly used) that strains of penicillin-resistant syphilis arose, and the disease is now not only a continuing problem, but also much more difficult to treat. The same has been true of numerous other infectious diseases.

The 1951 Durham-Humphrey Amendment created a category of drugs that carry the following prescription legend: "Caution: Federal law prohibits dispensing without prescription" because drugs in that category normally cannot be used safely by laypersons without the supervision of an appropriately trained health professional. This effectively restricted a large proportion of drugs to administration only by an appropriately licensed professional, namely, a medical doctor for prescribing and administering (or ordering the administration) and a pharmacist for dispensing and managing therapy.

If the risk of harm is low enough, in contrast, the drug is not limited to prescription by a trained health professional. Dosing recommendations and other advice is given in the package insert, often also on the outside of the package, and even in advertisements.

Common-use drugs, such as alcohol, tobacco, and caffeine, are also available without consultation with a trained health professional, but here the risk of harm is addressed in a different way. Warnings are printed on the package or bottle, and purchase is restricted by age, but in general, the adult user is assumed to be competent to use these products responsibly. Although not identified as such, the federal framework implicitly considers the risk of harm from using herbal remedies and dietary supplements to be low enough that a prescription is unnecessary. This assumption stems from the apparent absence of any pharmacological value in the substance, with herbal remedies not held to prescription standards largely because they are not validated as medications. In other words, if the substance has no effect, it is unlikely to cause harm. Homeopathic remedies, for example, can hardly be considered toxic when they are composed of nothing but water or lactose—they are sometimes diluted so much that not even a single molecule of the supposedly healing substance is present. Therefore, it would be nonsensical to make homeopathic remedies a prescription drug.

Harm resulting from illegal drug use is often seen as an entirely different problem. Here, the concern is not so much toxicity, but rather the public health threats posed by drug-use behaviors. To clarify the distinction, it is necessary to examine the individual's motivation for using a drug. If someone needs a drug remedy for a health complaint (or preventative), this may be accomplished by consulting a physician or by self-medicating with an OTC drug. However, if the motivation is to use the drug for recreational use, sports-doping, or other prohibited or illegal purposes, this sort of drug-using behavior can result in physiological and social harms to the individual, other people, and society in general.

Harm and Abuse: Differing Conceptions

In different fields, abuse may be defined or understood in quite different ways. In some areas, as seen in the previous chapter, abuse of a drug can be defined as "use despite adverse consequences": in other words, if a person is using a drug with the knowledge of the risk of harm and that harm actually does result, this could be abuse. Using cough medicine (containing the OTC drug dextromethorphan) for a cough is not abuse. However, a competent person who takes large quantities of this cough medicine in order to become intoxicated is assumed to know the risks of harm—intoxication and its consequences—and is therefore "abusing" the cough medicine—even though doing so is not illegal. Another quite different stance is sometimes employed in the legal field: here, abuse is equated with illegal use. While using OTC cough medicine for intoxication is not illegal and therefore might not be understood as abuse, the use of prescription drugs without actually having a prescription is unlawful; it is often understood as abuse, independent of the reasons for which the drug is taken—whether to treat an illness or to get high.

In order to address the harm resulting from the abuse of drugs, an entirely different regulatory apparatus was developed. This approach looks at drugs not from the point of view of toxicity, but rather from an assessment of each drug's likelihood or severity of abuse. Addictive drugs, for example, may be relatively nontoxic, and yet they pose a tremendous personal and social threat by the behaviors of addicted individuals. Opiates such as codeine, hydrocodone, morphine, and heroin are all fairly benign drugs from a biological perspective. They produce drowsiness and can be fatal in overdose, but otherwise do not cause much injury in themselves. (Toxicity from adulterated substances, unclean needle injection, and so on are tangential issues not directly due to the drug.) However, easy availability of opiates was historically associated with social disorder, as described in chapter 2, because of widespread addiction.

The Controlled Substances Act, described in chapter 3, provides the basic regulatory schema to address drug abuse. Enacted in 1970, the Act has been modified many times and replicated in state and international laws. Both its prescription and controlled-substance regulations address harms posed by abusable drugs. However, these drugs also have benefits—otherwise, the need for regulation would be moot and complete prohibition would be in order. The challenge for any regulatory apparatus is to restrict drugs that pose harm while simultaneously allowing availability for those who have a legitimate need for the drugs' benefits.

This challenge is present in both prescription and controlled drug regulations, and there are special categories of drugs in both that escape the simple schema. With regard to prescription drugs, for example, there are cases in which a drug poses toxicity but remains over-the-counter for historical reasons. Under what might be considered a grandfathering clause, aspirin is available OTC although its potential toxicity might reasonably make it a prescription drug, as it was in India until 2006, when it was changed to OTC. The adverse outcomes from inappropriate aspirin use are significant—ranging from stomach bleeding in susceptible individuals to Reyes Syndrome, an often-fatal interaction between a viral illness like flu or chickenpox and aspirin use, especially dangerous in children. Clearly, aspirin should be used only with considerable care and awareness—precisely the reasons a drug would normally be restricted to a physician's prescription.

Conversely, there are drugs that are prescription but pose little evidence of harm. This most often occurs when the drug is new and there is insufficient information about possible toxicity. The FDA is highly restrictive in this regard and has been slow to approve OTC sales of prescription drugs. Other nations, especially in less-developed countries but also in Europe and Canada, allow many more drugs to be sold without prescription. Not surprisingly, there is considerable debate about the merits of the FDA's approach. Some argue that the cautiousness is less due to pharmacological concerns than to social, political, or economic concerns. For example, tryptophan is an amino acid that has long been sold OTC along with other amino acids (e.g., lysine and argenine). People buy them in the belief that they have medicinal benefits, but there is no scientific evidence to support these notions. In 1989, a contaminated batch of tryptophan caused a minor epidemic of eosinophia-myalgia syndrome, a disabling and sometimes deadly autoimmune disorder. A public panic ensued, and the government responded by prohibiting sales of tryptophan—with some restrictions continuing to this day without any significant pharmacological rationale. But is one necessary? In other words, is it enough to restrict the use of tryptophan that the drug has no known benefits and some risk of harm? If such a substance should be made available, it appears that only the value of respecting free choices, even unbeneficial ones, would weigh against the restrictions.

The Controlled Substances Act, with its lists of drugs classified into five Schedules of control, is also rife with inconsistencies and exceptions. One of the most prominent involves religious-use drugs. Peyote, as seen in chapter 3 and discussed again in chapter 6, is classified as Schedule I (the most highly restricted), but it is available to Native American individuals who are permitted to use it in their religious practices. Sports-enhancement drugs are another class of drugs permitted for use in some circumstances as OTC or prescription, but they are prohibited in the practice of competitive sports.

The limitation on steroids and other performance enhancement drugs in sports is not by government regulation (though in the case of baseball, this was threatened in the wake of a congressional inquiry in 2005) but instead a restriction put in place by private organizations like the various professional sport associations, the U.S. Anti-Doping Agency, and other national sport federations subsumed under the World Anti-Doping Agency (WADA). Nonetheless, the effect of private restrictions can be as thoroughgoing as if they were imposed by the state, with significant consequences for use in professional competitions. The principal differences are that sports-enhancement drugs are not criminalized or otherwise legally prohibited, and they remain available to athletes who leave the sport.

Is there a clear distinction between harm and abuse? It is often intimated that the distinction is largely circular. On the one hand, drug abuse is often viewed as the use of an illegal substance; this account makes no reference to the harm caused by the drug use other than the fact of violation of the law. Such an account of abuse would be circular if abuse consists only in violation of the law; such a view overlooks the rationale that specific drugs are prohibited or regulated because of their capacity to cause harm. Thus, as is to be considered shortly, the federal Schedule, which categorizes drugs according to their potential for abuse, might be said to be circular in concept under one of these understandings, if it regulates "abuse" but fails to recognize that the very possibility of abuse is a function of this classification itself. On the other hand, if abuse is defined in terms of actual harm rather than in terms of legal violation, this circularity in the Schedule does not arise, but the question of whether drugs of abuse actually do cause harm looms large. Thus, it is tempting to say that the Schedule is either circular and hence vacuous, or empirically not fully supported.

Part of the Problem: The (Mis)categorization of Drugs within the Regulatory Framework

It is one thing, however, to remark that drug policy conforms to the framework of prescription legend and controlled-substance Schedules in theory, and quite another to observe whether it does so in practice. Clearly, there are bizarre discrepancies between the theoretical framework and the way in which specific drugs are categorized. These discrepancies account for many of the inconsistencies in policy outlined in the earlier chapters of this book, and they are a major source of disagreement in public discussion in all areas across the board. Many of these questions have already been asked. Why, for instance, is heroin classed as Schedule I but morphine as Schedule II despite their functional equivalence? How can ephedra, when marketed as a dietary supplement, remain essentially unregulated, while its active ingredient, marketed as the medication ephedrine, is a fully regulated prescription pharmaceutical? And how can we reconcile the fact that in one case, that of the prescription drug, the sponsor must provide evidence of safety and efficacy to gain FDA approval for marketing while in the other case, that of the "herbal drug," the FDA must show evidence of "unreasonable risk of illness or injury" to take any regulatory action against the marketing of the same substance? Why is ibogaine Schedule I, when it has anti-addictive properties? Why is peyote in the Schedule at all, given its low potential for abuse? In contrast, why is aspirin unscheduled, when it poses reasonably substantial risks of harm to users? Aspirin is extremely widely used—it can be found in practically any medicine cabinet—but there is general agreement among experts that aspirin would be prescription-only if it had been introduced in the twenty-first century rather than in 1899. Why is marijuana, to which no fatalities have been directly attributed, a Schedule I drug, while tobacco and alcohol are not scheduled at all, though they are estimated to account for approximately 400,000 and 75,000 deaths a year, respectively, and both tobacco and alcohol are more addictive? There may be reasons for some of these seemingly inconsistent placements. For example, because heroin has two extra acetyl groups attached to the morphine molecule, it is more addictive—though it is identical to morphine once *inside* the brain, as the two acetyl groups are shed when they cross the blood-brain barrier. Yet such differences may not always explain placement in the Schedule adequately. In general, does the placement of different drugs in the different categories of the federal framework and the specific levels of the federal Schedule make sense when viewed from across the board? For many, perhaps most, drugs, the answer may be yes, but for others the answer is clearly no—and these are often the flashpoints in public controversy.

In chapter 2, we also explored the historical reasons for such miscategorizations. Some stem from political pressures at the time specific legislation or other control was enacted, often infected with racism and xenophobia. The criminalization of cocaine was due in part to public fears over drug-induced impulses of black males in the South. Likewise, the connection between Chinese railroad workers and opium provided an impetus for the drug's prohibition. And the association of Mexican immigrants and marijuana helped inspire a criminal ban on pot. Other miscategorizations of drugs were based on simple misunderstanding. While L-tryptophan was restricted because of harm from a single bad batch made with a toxic vehicle, for example, ibogaine was made illegal because of legislative misinformation. Ibogaine, derived from a plant in Africa and thought to control craving, has never been a problem of abuse in the United States. Yet it is listed in the Controlled Substances Act under Schedule I, the highest level of restriction, apparently because legislators mistakenly considered ibogaine a variant of LSD. Similarly, bufotenine is illegal, even though it has no psychoactive effect and can scarcely be imagined as an abused substance, given the disagreeable effects from its ingestion. It appears that bufotenine became illegal because lawmakers took seriously a humorous newspaper article in Australia with a fictitious report of people licking toads to get high.

What was at work in these erratic acts of drug prohibition can be described as a mistaken harm-benefit analysis. Harms and potential harms were hugely exaggerated and routinely conflated with abuse, and whatever benefits existed (especially those evident primarily to users rather than to onlookers) were virtually completely overlooked.

It would be tempting to say that these misclassifications are at the root of any conceptual and practical trouble over drugs. Indeed, these misclassifications do play a major role, and they are the focal point for much of the contemporary critique of drug policy. Recognizing these misclassifications, based on inappropriate and inadequate rationales for the categorization of specific drugs, presents a major opportunity for reclassification and thus the development of more consistent, coherent, comprehensive drug theory and policy.

To be sure, drugs sometimes are reclassified. Consider the example of GHB (gamma-hydroxy butyrate), the so-called date rape drug. It is a very simple substance common in industrial solvents. Due to its structural similarity to the inhibitory neurotransmitter, gamma-amino butyrate, it is a rapid-acting depressant drug. GHB was very popular in the 1980s and was legally sold as a nutritional supplement typically used by body builders to increase body mass. When the risk of abuse and harm—including addiction and overdose—became apparent, however, restrictions were put on its sale. But users were either unaware of this risk or in denial of it, and GHB became a favorite of the club drug scene. As use proliferated, there was a corresponding increase in the number of emergency admissions, date rapes, and deaths. In 2000, the drug was rescheduled under Schedule I, putting it in the company of heroin and LSD at the highest level of restriction. In 2002, however, new research showed that this drug did have a valuable medical use in treating narcolepsy. It was once again allowed, in another formulation known as sodium oxybate, under Schedule III (with additional restrictions). In this example, the shifting risk/benefit calculation has determined the type of restriction and the way in which the drug is classified and reclassified within the federal framework and scheduling system. Another example that may arise soon is Ecstasy, a compound currently under investigation as a possible therapy for post-traumatic stress syndrome.

As mentioned before, all drugs risk harms and almost all promise benefits. Thus more sensitive, appropriate reclassification could become a central element of comprehensive drug reform. For example, aspirin—a compound trusted by millions over the years—might be reclassified as a prescription drug in light of the newly understood risks it presents. Marijuana might be demoted from Schedule I to a level more consonant with its comparatively nonharmful pharmacological properties, though of course some regulation (e.g., age restrictions on purchase, or prohibitions of use in specific situations like driving an automobile) could still be appropriate. All herbal remedies and dietary supplements would need to be scientifically assessed; some would be prescription-only, others would become OTC, and still others might be prohibited altogether.

Some of the overall reclassifications in such a thoroughgoing reassessment would seem startling, in contrast to our current policies. Tobacco, for instance, might find itself in Schedule II—in keeping with the evidence that it is America's most dangerous drug at least in terms of mortality—or perhaps even Schedule I. Alcohol might find itself subject to prescription control, so that its health benefits would not be outweighed by its harmful effects. The typical prescription may allow a glass or two of red wine per day, but not much more. To be sure, the social consequences of such drastic changes in classification might need to be taken into account—as was not effectively done in Prohibition—but the rationale for reclassification would remain intact.

Yet even if radical recategorization of drugs were possible and could be effectively done within the rationale of the Schedule, it does not reach fully to the bottom of what accounts for the current distressful situation. Drug theory and policy appears inconsistent, indeed incoherent, when viewed across the board; and while the miscategorization of drugs based on a chaotic political history is surely part, it is not the whole problem.

The Root of the Problem? Inconsistent Foregrounding and Sidelining

Return for a moment to the full spectrum of drugs across the board: prescription pharmaceuticals, OTC medications, herbal medicines and dietary supplements, common-use drugs like alcohol, tobacco, and caffeine, religious-use drugs, sports-enhancement drugs, and illegal drugs. Under the account of weighing harms and benefits explored just now—which is assumed to be central, at least in theory, to the federal framework and scheduling system for management of drugs—a practical reform would involve confirming or reassessing the harms, risks of abuse, and benefits posed by each drug, followed by reclassification on this basis.

But there is a deeper incongruity at work as well. This involves not only disagreements about what kinds of harms and benefits count—the disciplinary silos talk past each other on these accounts, too—but whether harm itself is foregrounded or sidelined in relation to benefits. All drugs pose harms if misused; most familiar drugs also offer benefits, even if the benefits are merely perceived and lack objective verification. But the degree to which the harms or the benefits are "foregrounded" or "sidelined"—made central or left out of any risk/benefit calculation—varies dramatically from one area of professional concern to another. This is one of the deepest difficulties in the conceptual underpinnings of drug theory and policy with respect to harm, related to the fissure in the conceptual underpinnings of the notion of addiction. It is here that real trouble is born.

Appeals to harms and benefits typically fall into rough categories: physical harms and benefits, psychological harms and benefits, societal harms and benefits, and economic harms and benefits. These categories are imprecise and often overlapping, but nonetheless important. What is central to the troubled discourse about drugs is that harms and benefits in each of these rough categories are disparately weighted in different areas of drug theory, policy, and practice. As will be seen, the physiological benefits of drug use play a larger role in the harm-prevention policies that govern prescription drugs; benefits of this sort but also benefits in ease of access play a larger role in considerations about OTC status; and benefits of access but not physiological benefits play the largest role in policies governing herbal drugs and dietary supplements, where concern about harms plays little role. Benefits associated with common-use drugs—especially alcohol—are very heavily advertised and, except for routine label warnings and some public service campaigns, harms are often sidelined in the public consciousness. With religious-use drugs, harms are assumed to be at stake but a competing benefit, religious freedom, is sometimes (but not always) foregrounded. In sports-enhancement drugs, by contrast, freedom of choice is completely sidelined, while two sorts of harm are foregrounded: physical risk to the athlete and, more prominently, harm to the sport itself. With illegal drugs, only harms—physical harms, psychological harms, and social harms—are foregrounded, while benefits are completely sidelined; no harm versus benefit weighing is tolerated in the case of public policy concerning illegal drugs at all.

To reiterate, all drugs risk harms, especially if overused, and virtually all also offer benefits. What characterizes the differences between the multiple silos of theory and policy about drugs most prominently, though, is the way in which considerations of harms and benefits are assessed and emphasized. Let's explore for a moment in somewhat greater detail how this foregrounding and sidelining works.

Prescription Drugs: Foregrounding of Physical and Psychological Benefits: Alertness to Physical and Psychological Harms

Concern about physical or psychological harms and benefits to the user play the primary role in prescription-drug regulations. As all pharmacy and medical students are taught in their introduction to the therapeutic use of drugs, every decision should be based upon the ratio of the potential benefit to the potential risk associated with the use of the particular drug, for the particular patient and indication for which the drug is intended, and at that particular time. Students are taught to prescribe a drug if: (1) the drug is appropriate for the use; (2) no factors indicate that use by the particular patient would be inappropriate (e.g., impaired kidney or liver function that could adversely effect the metabolism of the drug in the patient's body); (3) the drug would be effective for the intended use, as indicated by scientific (not merely anecdotal) evidence; and (4) the drug is appropriate at this particular time in the course of the disease or disorder. In some cases, the authority to make this decision about weighing harms and benefits is given to the patient. In a process known as "informed consent," the patient is given a summary of the information and allowed to make the choice. In practice, however, the patient is usually swayed by the evident preference of the medical professional and by the way the information is provided. Since the patient and medical professional are in any case (ideally) both participants in a therapeutic alliance, the patient is likely to follow the advice. Whether the decision is made by the medical professional or the patient, the primary focus is on what benefit the use of the drug is likely to provide an individual patient in treating his or her condition or disease, tempered by how the toxicity (expected inherent adverse effects) and side effects (adverse effects that occur for some users) of the drug may affect the health of that patient.

With some drugs, the concern is not limited to individual patients. Regimens for antibiotic drug use reveal direct societal concerns. For example, if the drugs are not taken as prescribed, then their use will only increase the resilience of viruses, contributing to large-scale problems of antibiotic resistance. Mandatory immunization also provides as much a benefit for society as it does to those immunized, contributing to herd immunity that protects all.

Furthermore, policy concerning whether to categorize a particular drug as a prescription medicine does not always focus exclusively on the health effects for individual patients or health benefits to society more generally. Often decisions about categorization within the scheduling system—for example, whether drugs are to be prescription-only, limited prescription-only, OTC, or something else—provide incentives for manufacturers to produce the next generation of drugs. As long as a drug is classified as prescription-only, then most health insurance plans will pay for its use, and thus, the price of the drug can be kept relatively high because the market choices of individuals do not work to force the cost down. Along with patent protection, this encourages drug manufacturers to expend resources to create the next "miracle drug" based on their own financial self-interest. The downside is, of course, the increased costs of health insurance to cover the added expense of the prescription drug. The decision of whether a drug is classified as a prescription drug, or remains so, is often made in light of these economic concerns. Yet the background consideration here is how to foster the continuing development of new drugs that will benefit individual patients in the future. So while it is financial benefit to the pharmaceutical firm that appears to be central, the underlying rationale for considering economic incentive structure is ultimately the physical and psychological benefit of future patients.

Over-the-Counter Drugs: Foregrounding of Benefits of Access and Choice: Some Alertness to Harms

These same economic concerns also influence which drugs become available over the counter. Yet economic benefit is not the only concern in this area. If the drug can be used safely by the average person, then consultation with a health professional seems unnecessary, and attention to drug labeling becomes crucial. The FDA determines whether the patient or consumer can safely use the drug without monitoring by a professional, and in such cases it requires that sufficient information for safe use by the average person is included on package labeling. Conversely, if the responsible government agency determines that monitoring by a health professional is required for safe use of the medication, the labeling is written for trained health professionals (i.e., not on the level that the average lay person would be able to comprehend), and the drug is placed on the prescription legend.

OTC status does not assume that a drug cannot be harmful. Even though the risks of harm from the use of OTC drugs are reduced, they are still considerable. For example, overuse of Tylenol (acetaminophen, or as it is called in the U.K., paracetamol) may cause liver damage, and overuse of ibuprofen can lead to ulcers or depression. In fact, most OTC drugs, if taken in sufficiently large amounts, can carry with them all of the risks associated with prescription counterparts—in effect, overuse is tantamount to using the drugs at prescription strength. Two 200 mg Advil, for example, is the recommended adult dosage for this over-the-counter version of ibuprofen; but four Advil is equivalent to one 800 mg. Motrin, a prescription drug, restricted to prescription use because of the substantial risk of harm its use can involve. Thus it is not only the significance of the potential harm to the user that explains why some drugs are classified as OTC, but also the likelihood that the average user will be able to use the drug appropriately.

What is foregrounded in the case of OTC drugs, however, is a benefit: the user having easy access to drugs that treat common, comparatively minor conditions. If people had to see a medical professional to relieve a headache, increase alertness, or treat a bee sting, then they likely would never bother, or perhaps practitioners would be swamped. The problem the drug is designed to solve may no longer be present by the time the drug could be purchased. And if prescriptions were granted in anticipation of such circumstances, then the prescription would seem superfluous: the medical professional would likely just inform the patient of what is already printed on the label.

Common-Use Drugs: The Advertising of Benefits, Sidelining of Harms

What about common-use drugs? Even though they are largely unregulated like OTC drugs, the harms and benefits associated with common-use drugs such as alcohol and tobacco are much more complicated and controversial. Alcohol and tobacco are some of society's most deadly drugs in use. They can kill the consumer—either rapidly, as in alcohol overdose, or slowly, as in smokers' diseases. And even when they do not kill, they can cause significant liver or lung damage, or lead to depression. Tobacco use alone has been linked to over 150 diseases. And even something as benign as caffeine can cause sleep problems, anxiety, stroke, or a nonfatal heart attack, and can lead to significant withdrawal symptoms when it becomes unavailable.

Furthermore, common-use drugs do not just pose risks to the user. Alcohol use is estimated to lead to 50 percent of the deaths on American highways every year. It poses significant risks to fetal development, and, when associated with alcoholism, can lead to poor parenting skills, high conflict in the home, and ultimately a cycle of abuse perpetuated by the formerly abused child. Tobacco use, it is now believed, also poses significant health risks to others in the form of second-hand smoke. And it is said to pose substantial risks in pregnancy: according to a 1995 study, there are "an estimated 19,000 to 141,000 tobacco-induced abortions, 32,000 to 61,000 infants born with low birthweight, and 14,000 to 26,000 infants who require admission to neonatal intensive care units. Tobacco use is also annually responsible for an estimated 1900 to 4800 infant deaths resulting from perinatal disorders, and 1200 to 2200 deaths from sudden infant death syndrome."[15]

In addition, some of the most significant harms associated with common-use drugs are societal. The health care expenses linked with common-use drugs is staggering. Tobacco use alone accounts for an estimated 7 percent of all health care costs in the United States. The societal damage caused by the effect of alcoholism on families, while difficult to estimate, can also be substantial.

15. J. R. DiFranza and R. A. Lew, "Effects of Maternal Cigarette Smoking on Pregnancy Complications and Sudden Infant Death Syndrome," *Journal of Family Practice* 40)4)(Apr 1995): 385–94.

Even something as seemingly trivial as worker "smoke breaks" collectively imposes some economic costs on society through lost productivity.

With all these harms, why aren't common-use drugs simply prohibited, or at least classified as prescription drugs? The advice medical professionals would provide is no secret: tobacco should be avoided altogether, and alcohol and caffeine should be used only in moderation. But if the dangers are already well known and yet the harms persist, then why aren't these drugs made illegal? This would certainly be the case if the consideration of harms were foregrounded and that of benefits sidelined, as occurs in other areas of drugs. The reason comes in part from the history of Prohibition, as discussed in chapter 2: the harms caused by the effort at complete suppression would significantly outweigh even these considerable harms. While society does regulate the age at which these drugs can be used, restricting them altogether would only lead to a black market, the loss of the ability to ensure quality, and uncontrolled (and hence untaxable) distribution.

There is, of course, another reason. Despite the significant harms caused by the use of these drugs, the alleged benefits of common-use drugs have greatly impacted public perception. Prior to the recent tobacco settlements, advertisements for tobacco products—cigarettes, cigars, and chewing tobacco—associated them with pleasure, prestige and power, virility and sex. Alcohol ads continue to do the same: drinking is fun, sociable, sophisticated, and makes you feel good. Although the advertising of these products has been curtailed in specific venues in recent years[16]—for instance, bans on tobacco or alcohol billboards near schools—public perception still views these drugs as bringing pleasure, a substantial and immediately obtainable benefit. The same is true for caffeine products: coffee is "rich" and "satisfying," cola drinks are "refreshing," and high-caffeine drinks mean "power" and "energy."

Common-use drugs, thus, like virtually all other drugs, involve both harms and benefits. Alcohol in excess brings devastating physical, psychological, and social harms; but there are significant benefits to the use of alcohol in moderation. The risk of heart disease is reduced by a glass of red wine every evening, and the easing of anxiety makes alcohol in moderation

---

16. This trend, however, is reversing as so-called commercial speech is gaining more protection under the First Amendment. Troy L. Booher, "Scrutinizing Commercial Speech," *George Mason University Civil Rights Law Journal* 15(1)(2004): 74–79.

beneficial as a "social lubricant." Nicotine and other substances in smoking products may be devastating to the respiratory tract when consumed in quantity or over an extended period of time (as the habitual smoker does), but nicotine is also a powerful and effective cognitive stimulant. Similarly, as discussed above, there is some evidence that caffeine, while constituting a risk for some susceptible users with preexisting cardiac conditions or specific genetic traits, also appears to provide health benefits, such as protection against diabetes.[17] Coffee may also protect against alcoholic cirrhosis.[18] In any case, the use of caffeine also clearly provides the benefits of sociability and custom, evident at the office coffee pot or with the afternoon tea.

For common-use drugs, public perceptions and the siloed assessment of drug abuse professionals may be to a considerable degree inconsistent: the public and those who advertise to them see common-use drugs in a way that foregrounds benefits, while in contrast, addictionologists and others who work with alcohol abuse and smoking cessation programs are likely to see harms as foregrounded and benefits as on the side, if relevant at all.

Herbal Remedies and Dietary Supplements: Sidelining of Harms; Foregrounding of Benefits and Choice

What about herbal remedies and dietary supplements? They add yet another layer of complexity. The public perception is that these drugs do not pose significant risks of harm because they are "natural." Indeed, they are widely perceived to promise health benefits—even if health claims are not permitted to be stated explicitly on the package. Yet use of these drugs may risk harms. Many of these drugs are chemically identical to their counterparts produced in the lab, which appear on the prescription schedule. Their herbal and dietary-supplement versions, however, may contain contaminants like lead and mercury that the pharmaceutical Good Manufacturing Practices code safeguards against. Harms of other sorts may also be a risk. For example, the perception of these drugs as an "alternative" to

17. Mark A. Pereira, Emily D. Parker, Aaron R. Fulsom, "Coffee Consumption and Risk of Type 2 Diabetes: An 11-year Prospective Study of 28,812 Postmenopausal Women," *Archives of Internal Medicine* 166 (2006): 1311–16.

18. Arthur L. Klatsky, Cynthia Morton, Natalia Udaltsova, and Gary D. Friedman, "Coffee, Cirrhosis, and Transaminase Enzymes," *Archives of Internal Medicine* 166(2006): 1190–95.

seeking the advice of a medical professional—a physician or pharmacist—often results in people failing to obtain the drugs (or advice) they really need. Consider flu sufferers who refuse to see a doctor because they believe they will be cured by echinacea, something now known to have no benefits for those with influenza.

It is true, of course, that some herbal medicines and dietary supplements do provide significant benefits. For instance, Vitamin C (ascorbic acid), a drug necessary for the growth and repair of human tissues, generally boosts one's immune system when taken in moderate amounts. But if used to excess, it can shift the acid/base balance in the body, and if taken in very large doses, it can cause diarrhea, kidney stones, and serious drug interactions.

One of the most prominent "benefits" of herbal remedies and dietary supplements has little to do with physiological effect on the user: it is the (psychological) benefit of personal choice. This perceived benefit has played a major political role in the enactment of DSHEA, perhaps coupled with the assumption that individuals should be encouraged to take responsibility for their own health. With increased access to Internet data, it is assumed that information about these drugs will benefit people by allowing them to care for themselves. The problem with this view is not only that it typically takes specialized training to evaluate drug-related data, but also that information available on the Internet or on the labels of many herbal medicines and dietary supplements can be misleading. The complementary and alternative medicines can yield both benefits and harms, but in public perception they promise almost all benefit.

Religious-Use Drugs: Concern about Harms; the Benefit of Religious Freedom

The benefits and harms associated with the religious-use of drugs complicate the picture even more. As seen in chapter 3, the sacramental use of the Schedule I drug peyote was federally exempted for one group, Native Americans, and for one religious organization, the Native American Church, pursuant to special statutory and regulatory recognition. In the church, peyote is believed to be not a drug at all but a manifestation of Jesus Christ. Such reasoning allows Native Americans in the military to consume peyote, for instance, and at the same time deny using a psychoactive drug when questioned. Until recently, however, federal courts have been very reluctant to extend this exemption to other races or religions claiming sacramental use of otherwise prohibited drugs (with the exception of the Supreme Court's 2006 ayahuasca decision), particularly against a background concern that any further exceptions would undercut the Schedule's treatment of illegal psychoactive drugs. One rationale for exempting peyote (and possibly ayahuasca), for example, is the claim that its use in religious ceremonies is unlikely to spread to secular contexts, and therefore the harms that justify restrictions are unlikely to occur. In contrast, it is believed that allowing use of marijuana by Rastafarians, for instance, would spread to secular contexts. Such concerns are not necessarily unfounded. Although the wine used in Catholic Church ceremonies during Prohibition came in such small quantities that the harms associated with alcohol use were thought to be effectively mitigated, orders for wine by the Church during this period increased dramatically.

The benefits of religious drug use are assumed to be obvious. It is not just that religion is valued in society, that facilitating its practice is desirable, or even that religious practices foster group cohesion, respect for codes of ethical conduct, and so on; it is that religious freedom itself is a basic value to be preserved. In this sense, allowing exceptions for religious-use drugs is seen as largely a benefit, despite the risk of harm that is predicted if the practice were to escape its bounds.

Sports-Enhancement Drugs: Foregrounding of Harms to Athlete and to the Sport Itself; Complete Sidelining of Benefits

What about sports drugs? Excellence in athletics has been promoted in almost all societies. The underlying purpose of sports, it is often assumed, is to raise the overall fitness and public health of the population, to give reign to competitive spirit, to encourage group involvement, to provide models for youth, and to entertain. If sports champions were able to achieve their superiority by using drugs, it is often argued, it would undermine this social goal; therefore, drug use cannot be tolerated in sports that are exemplars of fitness and fair competition. Some "sports" that do not serve these ideals may use drugs, it is assumed, like professional wrestling; the fact that most of these "athletes" may achieve their physique by use of anabolic steroids seems irrelevant to all involved. However, if the same body-building drugs were used by, say, high school football players or Olympic athletes, it is argued, a considerable harm would occur not only to the players, who may feel compelled to use drugs to compete, but to the sport as a whole. If drug use were rampant in high school football or professional basketball, for example, these sports would be tarnished. They would no longer be exemplars of fitness and fair competition; they would no longer serve to encourage public health; and they would become physical grotesqueries, dangerous models for growing children and indeed for society as a whole. Football, baseball, and basketball are as central to society as any other major cultural institution, so it is argued, and thus allowing drugs at all would bring substantial social harm.

To be sure, sports drugs, like other drugs, also offer benefits. Steroids, for example, offer increased strength, stamina, and capacities for tissue repair. They enhance alertness, overcome injuries, and make possible more sustained and vigorous play. But these benefits are not the focus of scrutiny—all attention is focused on harms. The weighing of harms and benefits is simply not part of amateur or professional athletic policy for most prominent sports. Harms—both to the players and to the sport—are foregrounded, and benefits are completely sidelined.

Illegal Drugs: Foregrounding of Harms, Complete Sidelining of Benefits

Illegal drugs are perhaps the most controversial category of drugs. Because their classification is often the result of idiosyncratic political pressures, it may be unsurprising that this category also exhibits the most inconsistency. The rationale for classifying a drug as illegal might appeal to the risk of physical or psychological harm to the user (something true of all drugs, at least if overused), but it may be preceded or followed by other claims involving harms. Politically motivated restrictions have often involved explicit or implicit arguments that a drug poses harms—indeed, that the drug is particularly dangerous—when used by specific racial, ethnic, or socioeconomic groups. Claims about harms may also involve assertions that the drug is a gateway to more dangerous drugs, that drug use will harm the "social fabric," that it will undercut economic productivity or stifle other valuable social enterprises, or that it will damage the public health and drive up the cost of health care. So even if its use is not directly harmful, it is claimed, the drug will lead to harm in some extended chain of causation.

It is true that there are well-known and significant health risks associated with the use of certain illegal drugs, even irrespective of their illegality. If overused, some recreational drugs can have serious pathological effects. For example, cocaine can cause significant and often irreversible cardiovascular toxicity. Methamphetamine users may suffer from the ravages of severe hypertension, stroke, or myocardial infarction. And it has been widely asserted (though these claims may be exaggerated) that babies born to cocaine, heroin, or methamphetamine-using mothers are often born addicted to these drugs and sometimes suffer brain damage unless the condition is recognized and treated in the early days after delivery.

There are also psychological harms associated with the use of many illegal drugs—agitation, depression, hallucinations, paranoia, and so on—although it is difficult to separate the effects from the drugs and the effects due to their illegality. In addition, there are the risks of harm to others posed by intoxication. A marijuana-using air traffic controller may not cause direct harm to himself, but he may imperil the lives of hundreds of others by his diminished competence. A cocaine-using boat captain may crash the vessel and similarly imperil the passengers. It is for this reason that the federal government initiated a broad drug-testing program in the 1980s. Under the provisions of this law, not only federal employees but also many employees in private companies with federal contracts must be regularly tested for five common drugs—opiates, marijuana, amphetamines, cocaine, and PCP—based on the assumption that companies with drug-using workers will expose others to harm, including other workers, passengers, and consumers. The harms of drug use are also said to cause higher operating costs due to increased absenteeism, decreased performance, higher incidence of illness, and so on.

It is entirely true to say that many of the drugs that are currently illegal can cause severe harms to users, third parties, or society in general. High levels of harm are often associated with high levels of use—high-dosage use, chronic use, addictive use, use in inappropriate circumstances—although there are also cases of first-time, "moderate" use of drugs like Ecstasy or cocaine that prove fatal. Some drugs (e.g., heroin) work by mimicking neurotransmitter activity; others (e.g., Ecstasy) can work by destroying neurotransmitters altogether. The public perception is that the greatest harm occurs with fatal overdose, though the public rarely recognizes that most fatal overdoses do not involve street addicts, but instead a person who overdoses on correctly prescribed prescription drugs—a function, of course, of the much greater numbers of people using prescription drugs than street drugs. Indeed, according to the Centers for Disease Control and Prevention, poisoning from prescription drugs has become the second largest cause of unintentional death in the United States.[19]

Yet some illegal drugs present little risk of harm to the user or to others, but are nonetheless listed in the Controlled Substances Act. Many, if not most, of these drugs are hallucinogens. LSD, peyote, DMT, psilocybin, mescaline, and marijuana do not present major biological risks of harm to the user, are not physically addictive, and present no evident harm to others when taken in an appropriate setting (though they might, for example, if taken while driving a car or flying an aircraft).

There is another kind of harm in the picture: many illegal drugs appear to be associated with criminal behavior. What is to be made of this? The drug-criminal behavior link is the basis of a distinct argument about harm, in addition to claims already considered about physical, psychological, and social harm caused by use of these drugs. Criminal behavior associated with the obtaining of drugs, its environments, and its penalties, both on the street and in the courts, can also bring with it physical, psychological, and social harms. Many sorts of claims about the harms of criminality are made in discussions about drugs,—for instance, that street gangs survive primarily on the revenue from dealing in illegal drugs, that people are afraid to go outside in their own neighborhoods due to the violent nature of those dealing in the black market of illegal drugs, and that trade in illegal drugs funds terrorists. Teasing apart claims about harms due to

19. According to the Centers for Disease Control and Prevention 2007 report on deaths 1999-2004, this trend can be attributed primarily to increasing numbers of deaths associated with prescription opioid analgesics (like OxyContin) and secondarily to cocaine and prescription psychotherapeutic drugs (e.g., sedatives) overdoses, and cannot be attributed to heroin, methamphetamines, or other illegal drugs. *Morbidity and Mortality Weekly Report, online at* http://www.cdc.gov/mmwr/preview/mmwrhtml/mm5605a1.htm.

the physical effects of the drug itself, claims about harms due to the effort to obtain the drugs, and claims about harms due to consequences of having used the drugs, is of course central to a clear account of harms caused by illegal drugs. But such analysis is rarely provided. For instance, are infections from intravenous drug use due to the dangerous nature of the drugs or the fact that the quality of materials goes unregulated? At the center of controversy is the allegation that the most significant harm caused by illegal drugs results from their classification as illegal, not from the pharmacological nature of the drugs themselves.

Public dispute often flares when the foregrounding/sidelining in the Schedule's classifications are challenged. For example, current disputes over the medical use of marijuana involve the assertion that benefits have been overlooked while harms have been exaggerated. Cocaine also has legitimate medical uses, though this discussion is even more constrained. Discussions of perceived benefits of various illicit drugs like increased artistic creativity, enhanced self-awareness, and enhanced sexual performance are almost never publicly discussed—except, of course, by users themselves.

Conceptual Fissures: Addiction and Harm

Return for a moment to the central fissure discovered in chapter 4 when examining the two principal accounts of addiction, the 2001 AAPM/APS/ASAM consensus definition favored in clinical medicine and pain management circles, and the DSM diagnostic criteria typically used in psychological and drug-abuse settings. For one of these accounts, addiction is defined as "continued use despite harm"; for the other, it is not. But what is clearly relevant here is whether the substance in question is in a group—a siloed area—in which harms are foregrounded, and what sorts of harms or benefits are under consideration.

That is why is seems strange, for example, that Harry, the weekend cocaine user of chapter 4, failed to meet the criteria for addiction under one of these definitions: the drug he was using is associated almost entirely with harm in public perception. For cocaine and the illegal-drug category in which cocaine falls, harms are foregrounded and benefits completely sidelined. It also seems strange that under one of these definitions, Carl the coffee drinker did count as an addict, even though the drug he was using, caffeine, is one for which public perception works just the other way around: benefits for this "social beverage" are foregrounded and harms almost completely sidelined. This is despite the fact that, though in differing probabilities, both cocaine and caffeine can give pleasure, both invite continuing use, and both can be unhealthy or even fatal. The examples of Harry and Carl seem strange, almost completely counterintuitive, because society's conceptual assumptions are already shaped by the foregrounding/sidelining patterns characteristic of all areas of drug talk, not by any clear look at Harry's or Carl's drugs or drug use.

Thus chapters 4 and 5 have uncovered two of the deepest conceptual confusions about drugs: confusion about addiction, and confusion about harm, including what counts as harm and the degree to which harm is foregrounded or sidelined. This pair of confusions is, at the root of the overall confusion about drugs. They compound each other. Differing postures vis-à-vis each of these confusions are adopted within each of the silos—some using one rather than the other definition of addiction, and some using one foregrounding of harms rather than others. The result is that these differing silos—however well-meaning and cooperative, and however dedicated to the public welfare they may be—cannot really talk with each other in any deeply meaningful way about drugs—not in theory, not in the construction of policy, and not in clinical, consumer-oriented, or law-enforcement practice concerning drugs.

6

DILEMMAS OF DRUG MANAGEMENT AND CONTROL: CASE PUZZLES AND STUDIES IN CONFLICT

Case Studies: Dilemmas of Drug Management and Control

Policies governing the regulation of drugs and drug use both in the United States and elsewhere often seem neither consistent nor coherent when viewed in a comprehensive way. But what practical difference does this make? This chapter looks at a variety of dilemmas in drug management and control, offering case studies to illustrate these problems. Some are real, some are fictional, but none come with easy answers. In fact, solutions to such dilemmas are difficult in part because they rest on inconsistent foundations, the sorts of conceptual fissures and gaps between various silos of drug-related concerns that have been explored. The structure and some of the relevant background for these cases is sketched here, but they are primarily intended for further discussion.

Case #1: Opioid Drugs for Pain—Is the Solution Worse Than the Problem?

Mrs. Jones is an eighty-four-year-old nursing home patient with metastatic breast cancer complicated by osteoporosis that has resulted in several vertebral compression fractures. During the times she is lucid, Mrs. Jones says she suffers from severe pain. The pain service recommends changing her medications from ibuprofen alone to ibuprofen plus morphine, an opioid typically used in such a setting.

Mrs. Jones's daughter has legal power of attorney to make healthcare decisions for her mother. "Don't give Mom morphine," she insists. "It might kill her, it'll make her out of it, and in any case, it'll make her addicted."

Should Mrs. Jones's daughter be overruled?

Case 1: Concerns about using opioids in clinical medicine are shared by patients, family members, and physicians. Family members sometimes refuse these medications out of ignorance, perhaps like Mrs. Jones's daughter. Yet many physicians and other clinicians are also subject to misinformation and, especially, confusion about the nature of addiction and whether it would be wrong in a case like this to let addiction develop.

Poor pain management by clinicians often results from inconsistent laws, definitions, and regulations pertaining to medication control. To be sure, effective pain management frequently requires a multimodal and interdisciplinary approach. However, medications remain the cornerstone of care for the majority of patients, whether in the form of over-the-counter drugs like NSAIDS or prescription drugs like opioids, with the latter continuing to be the most effective analgesics for most moderate to severe pain. But because opioids are associated with potential toxicities and concerns about abuse and addiction, a maze of real and perceived laws, regulations, and precautions pertaining to their use has evolved, and many clinicians hesitate to use opioids consistently, even when they are medically indicated. Indeed, many doctors are reluctant to use opioid drugs at all—even when the patient would clearly benefit.

Concerns about opioid use in cases like that of Mrs. Jones could potentially occur hundreds of thousands of times a year in the United States alone. Many patients have significant pain at the end of life, and although physicians may attempt to relieve pain, the Drug Enforcement Administration focuses on abuse of the opioids often utilized in end-of-life pain and seeks to limit their use. Of course, the DEA is joined by concerned family members, patients, and clinicians who are apprehensive about the risks of addiction.

Inconsistent use and under-use of opioids in clinical medicine has been well documented.[1] The suboptimal patient care that results has precipitated numerous professional education efforts from organizations such as the American Medical Association (AMA), the Joint Commission on Accreditation of Health Care Organizations (JCAHO, the accrediting body for most American hospitals), and even the DEA, the federal government's vanguard of drug warfare. The AMA published a four-part series of monographs on pain management for primary care physicians that encourages the use of opioids at appropriate doses when clinically indicated, typically at the apex of an ascending ladder that begins with NSAIDS.[2] The JCAHO implemented standards in 2001 that require accredited health care organizations to increase their focus on effective pain management plans.[3]

1. http://www.medsch.wisc.edu/painpolicy/.

2. American Medical Association, *Pain Management* series, Chicago: American Medical Association, 2003, online at http://www.ama-cmeonline.com/.

3. Online at http://www.jointcommission.org/.

And the DEA, in collaboration with the Last Acts Partnership and Pain and Policy Studies Group at the University of Wisconsin Medical School, published an important document entitled "Prescription Pain Medications: Frequently Asked Questions and Answers for Health Care Professionals and Law Enforcement Personnel" (FAQ document) in 2004.[4] This document received broad praise for clarifying important issues about the risks of addiction in using opioids for pain, and was lauded as an important step toward balance.[5]

But allegedly because the DEA feared that a physician facing discipline would be able to appeal to the FAQ document as a defense to inappropriate use of opioids in treating pain patients, it removed the FAQ document from its website and requested that the two other sponsoring agencies do the same with their internet postings. The FAQ document was published in 2005 in a peer-reviewed journal, however, and therefore is still available.[6] Nonetheless, the DEA action had a chilling effect on clinicians treating patients for pain, increasing their concerns about prescribing opioids in the face of seemingly excessive regulatory oversight of their otherwise medically indicated actions.

Essential to sorting out this dilemma is clarity about what is meant by *addiction*. Pain-management clinicians have been loathe to acknowledge that their medication practices might result in addiction, but whether these practices actually do so is a function of which definition or diagnostic criteria are applied. To be sure, Mrs. Jones would become physically dependent upon morphine, although not addicted according to the 2001 AAPM/APS/ASAM consensus definition presented in chapter 4. Conversely, she might meet the *DSM* criteria for "substance dependence" (the condition more serious than "substance abuse"), since she would exhibit at least the minimal three out of seven criteria for that condition: tolerance, withdrawal,

4. David E. Joranson, Russell K.Portenoy, "Pain Medicine and Drug Law Enforcement: An Important Step Toward Balance," *Journal of Pain & Palliative Care Pharmacotherapy* 19(1)(2005): 3–5.

5. Arthur G. Lipman, "Does the DEA Truly Seek Balance in Pain Medicine? A Chronology of Confusion That Impedes Good Patient Care," *Journal of Pain & Palliative Care Pharmacotherapy* 19(1)(2005): 7–9.

6. Drug Enforcement Administration, "Prescription Pain Medications: Frequently Asked Questions and Answers for Health Care Professionals and Law Enforcement Personnel," *Journal of Pain & Palliative Care Pharmacotherapy,* 19(1)(2005): 71–104.

and the termination of important social, occupational, or recreational activities. Furthermore, the probability of pseudoaddiction or iatrogenic addiction to opioids in patients with pain is also a function of which definition of addiction is used. While the incidence of iatrogenic addiction is said to be low, it may be lower under one definition than another. Mrs. Jones will be "using" morphine for the remainder of her foreseeable life. Whether she technically is considered an "addict" is largely a function of conceptual categories.

The traditional, somewhat cavalier answer has been to say that Mrs. Jones is an old lady in a nursing home, and it does not really make any difference whether she is addicted to morphine or not—at least, not the kind of difference it makes when a high school adolescent, a middle-aged businessman, or a street junkie is addicted to an opioid. After all, she would not have to mug someone on the street or rob a store to get it. Another, more evidence-based answer is to observe that iatrogenic addiction is uncommon except in patients with a history of substance abuse, personality disorder, or severe affective disorder.[7] Still another response would be to question the label of addiction or dependence in this case. Imagine, for instance, that after a "miracle cure" has become available and used to treat Mrs. Jones, her cancer totally disappears, and with it, all her pain. At this point, would she have difficulty in being weaned from her opioids, which would be necessary due to the potential discomfort of withdrawal? If the answer is "no," she was no more "addicted" to the drug than is a diabetic to insulin. As considered by many workers in the area, addiction/dependence is always to be considered in relation to the behavior. It depends on inappropriate use of the substance (which, admittedly, is at times subject to debate). Consider that Mrs. Jones has not given up "important social, occupational, or recreational activities" to use drugs; it is her underlying cancer that is responsible for this phenomenon. Indeed, the cancer and not the opioid is the direct cause of the "positive" *DSM* criteria.

<hr />

7. Arthur G. Lipman, editorial, "Does Opiophobia Exist Among Pain Specialists?" *Journal of Pain & Palliative Care Pharmacotherapy* 18(2))(2004):1: citing Porter and Perry; J. Porter, H. Jick, "Addiction Rare in Patients Treated with Narcotics"; S. Perry, G. Heidrich, "Management of Pain during Debridement: A Survey of U.S. Pain Units"; J. L. Medina, S. Diamond, "Drug Dependency in Patients with Chronic Headache."

But even if all agree that Mrs. Jones will become addicted, what exactly would be wrong with addiction in her specific situation? Among those considered in chapter 5, one answer is that much of the harm of addiction results from the antisocial and criminal behavior that addicts engage in to secure their drugs. Clearly, this would not apply in the case of Mrs. Jones: her medications would be prescribed by her physician and paid for by Medicare or her supplemental insurance benefit until she dies. But if criminal behavior in drug seeking is not a problem, then why should it make a difference if Mrs. Jones is an addict? And if criminal behavior is not a problem in others—recall Harry, the weekend cocaine user from chapter 4, who although he broke the law in using cocaine did not commit crimes like theft to support his habit—why exactly should it matter if they, too are addicts? Is addiction a social risk, a moral failing, or something else?

Then, too, it is important to explore the DEA's rationale for suppressing the FAQ document that provided information to prescribers and law enforcement personnel about the use of opioids for pain. A variety of different rationales can be imagined, including:

1. Removing protection from opioid-prescribing physicians who may be prescribing to addicts.
2. Decreasing the possibility of opioid diversion from clinical supplies to the street.
3. Protecting nursing homes residents from the overuse of opioids.
4. Reducing the frequency of narcotic addiction in the United States.
5. Setting a model for younger people.

Some of these are suggestive of "primitive thinking"—for example, the notion that morphine is inherently "evil" and must be banned in all circumstances. Others involve consequentialist views about what would be best for society as a whole, even if Mrs. Jones herself is left to suffer. Yet others may involve distributive views about payment of costs, allocation of physician time, or any number of other factors. In the end, it might be difficult, if not impossible, to discern the actual rationale for the DEA action, which may not even be derived from the underlying justification for the agency's very existence. But that does not mean it cannot be asked whether plausible rationales on the part of the various parties in Mrs. Jones's case form a coherent picture—certainly not that all parties must be acting under the same actual motivation or to pursue the same immediate goals, but that the overarching theory and policy about drugs "hangs together" in an intelligible way.

So how does one go about resolving this one of the many dilemmas to be considered? First, look past the apparent defensiveness of pain-management clinicians in insisting that they do not cause addiction, as well as the seeming cowardice of physicians who fail to treat patients in pain adequately to avoid addiction at all costs. Also disregard the apparent disingenuousness of the DEA in the attempted suppression of the FAQ document. What plausible rationale remains for understanding or revising these actions? Of the multiple possible rationales for drug policy considered here (especially in chapter 3), which one seems to fit best all aspects of Mrs. Jones's case? Would an autonomy-based practice be the best policy here, or one that takes as its central rationale a paternalist protection of vulnerable parties? At the level of individual decision making, there are clear answers to the case of Mrs. Jones: if she is lucid and competent, her wishes to be out of pain should prevail, and thus, presumably, she should receive the ibuprofen plus morphine that pain service recommends. If, on the other hand, she is not competent, the decisions of her legally appointed surrogate, her daughter, should rule.

But this is just to answer the question at the level of individual decision making. It is not possible to answer the more general questions of policy concerning the use of opioids in pain management in an easy way. Should policy be constructed so that it favors an autonomist approach—what the patient wants, the patient gets—or should it be constructed to protect not only patients but also the rest of society from the potential abuse of a sometimes dangerous drug? What is important here is to observe whether the answers to similar questions in other cases in this chapter appeal to the same sorts of principles. If they do, that would suggest that they occur within a coherent, comprehensive system of theory and policy about drugs—or whether one sort of principle is used on this occasion, but on the next a different principle is employed, without any *reasoned* basis for the difference. That is what lies at the basis of the issue of drugs and justice.

Case 2: The answers to these questions seem to depend on whether sport-doping policy is consistent in prohibiting the use of exogenous agents on the grounds that they interfere with the fairness of competition, while prohibiting

Case #2: A 30-Kilometer Cross-Country Ski Race: What Counts as Doping?

Mary is a cross-country skier who is just about to compete in an Olympic trial race for a 30-km event. She has been using erythropoietin (EPO) on a daily basis for the week leading up to the event. Prior to the race, Mary undergoes a blood test that reveals her hematocrit to be 49 percent. She is relieved, recognizing that if her hematocrit were to reach 50 percent or greater, it would be counted as unsafe during an endurance race, and she would be disqualified from the event. Mary comes in second during the trial race, but she is randomly selected for testing after the event as well. The blood and urine specimens are sent to the laboratory for analysis.

Sarah is a cross-country skier participating in the same event. For the week leading up to the event Sarah has been sleeping in a nitrogen tent to boost her red blood cell count. Her pre-race hematocrit is also 49 percent. Sarah wins the 30-km event. Because she won the event samples are also collected for doping control and sent to the lab for testing.

In the laboratory, the elevated hematocrit in Mary's blood sample is confirmed and it is found that her hemoglobin and reticulocyte counts are also elevated. The EPO in Mary's urine is determined to be exogenous and she is suspended from skiing competition for two years. Further testing of Sarah's blood reveals her hemoglobin and reticulocyte counts to be the same as Mary's. EPO use is suspected, warranting further tests on Sarah's urine. No exogenous EPO is detected in Sarah's urine and her finish in the 30-km event stands.

Both Mary and Sarah worked to enhance their performance in ski racing and both managed to increase their hematocrits to 49 percent, just below the level considered a risk to safety, yet Mary was disqualified from skiing for two years while Sarah's victory was upheld and her future career unimpeded. Is this a fair policy? Is a nitrogen tent more acceptable than EPO to elevate hematocrit as a means to improve performance?

the use of environmental situations used to boost performance. As a matter of background, there are two stages of disqualification under Olympic policy. First, disqualification can be based on safety, for instance, if the hematocrit is 50 percent or greater during an endurance race. Second, disqualification can be based on the origin of performance-enhancing agent—in this example, one is an exogenous drug and the other is an environmental condition that stimulates the endogenous secretion of the same substance. The first stage allowed both Mary and Sarah to compete, their hematocrit being below 50 percent. But the second stage differentiated between these two athletes, penalizing Mary but not Sarah.

EPO is a hormone excreted by the kidney under conditions of low oxygenation that exerts an effect on the bone marrow to produce red blood cells. These red blood cells act to increase the capacity of the blood to carry oxygen to tissues such as muscles. EPO can also be administered by injection to have the same effect. Alternatively, a nitrogen tent can be used to decrease the atmospheric oxygen that an athlete breathes, frequently while sleeping; the body senses the decreased oxygen and secretes EPO to increase the red blood cells and thus increase oxygen to tissues. The physiological effect of the use of endogenous EPO, injected EPO, and nitrogen tents is the same—all produce a rise in the red blood cells and thus the hematocrit—but only the use of injected EPO counts as a doping violation. The nitrogen tent stimulates the body's normal EPO and is not detected as a doping violation.

While the World Anti-Doping Agency (WADA) does not condone the use of nitrogen tents (and is moving to prohibit their use), there is at the present time no way to distinguish the rise in EPO produced by a nitrogen tent (or high altitude for that matter) and normal endogenous excretion of EPO. The injection of EPO to boost performance is banned in sport because it is deemed an exogenous substance that mimics an endogenous process, much as testosterone is used to increase muscle strength.

Is a policy that bans exogenous EPO appropriate when EPO secretion can be stimulated by other means? If nitrogen tents are also banned, as may become the case, will athletes who live at high altitudes have an unfair advantage over athletes who live at sea level? Should training at altitude (even without nitrogen tents) be banned if not all athletes have the opportunity to stimulate their own secretion of EPO?

> ### Case #3: Prescription vs. Over-the-Counter Drugs—Is the Difference Due to Safety or to Profit?
>
> In 2003, the pharmaceutical manufacturer AstraZeneca requested and obtained approval from the FDA to change its prescription heartburn medication, Prilosec, to over-the-counter status. This change was requested at the time the patent for Prilosec was about to expire. Simultaneously, AstraZeneca introduced a new prescription drug, Nexium, which is therapeutically comparable to Prilosec, although with a slightly different dosing format.
>
> Is this a legitimate medical distinction between a prescription drug and a nonprescription drug?

Case 3: Over-the-counter (OTC) drugs are deemed acceptable for medical use without the necessity of monitoring by a health professional. OTC drugs must contain labeling that is appropriate for use by non-clinicians (so-called "lay persons") and include adequate instructions for use, including dosing and precautions. Some medications are available in lower strengths as OTC medications, such as ibuprofen 200 mg tablets (e.g., Advil) and in higher strengths as prescription medications, such as ibuprofen 400, 600, and 800 mg tablets (e.g., Motrin). Obviously, patients can take multiple 200 mg OTC tablets that are available without prescription to get the same effect as taking prescription-strength tablets. However, the labeling for the OTC tablets cautions against exceeding the recommended OTC dosing unless instructed to do so by a physician.

Beginning in 1972, the FDA has reviewed drugs for conversion from prescription to OTC status. It has approved conversion of more than forty primary medications based on extensive clinical experience that indicates these previously prescription drugs are safe for OTC use. Until recently, all petitions to consider such switches have been from the pharmaceutical industry. Such actions appear most commonly when the manufacturer is about to introduce a new prescription alternative for the same indication, such as the case of AstraZeneca's application to move Prilosec to OTC status and replace it with the new prescription drug Nexium. This allows the manufacturer to focus on OTC public marketing of the branded product Prilosec and at the same time promote the new prescription drug Nexium to health professionals. Thus, the company has a greater financial benefit than if it had just a single drug: patients either pay directly for the OTC medication or pay for the more expensive prescription medication (usually by their medical insurance, which normally does not cover OTC medications). In this way, the company is able to market to various types of consumers, both insured and uninsured. Yet except for its slightly different dosing format, Nexium has neither general clinical advantages nor greater risks than the older product Prilosec. For some drugs, like Motrin, the risks associated with higher dosage may be said to justify restriction to prescription availability, but for others there may be little additional risk or benefit.

More recently, health maintenance organizations (HMOs) that pay for their beneficiaries' prescription medications but not for OTC medications have initiated such petitions to move drugs from prescription to OTC status, motivated by the prospect of substantial savings if the drug is OTC and thus not covered by their health plans. Insurance companies commonly have similar policies. The conversion of medications—for example, the antihistamine Claritin—has resulted in many patients having to pay for expensive drugs themselves when their insurance previously had covered the costs.

These scenarios raise concerns about distributive justice. Ought public policy, such as that promulgated by the FDA in its review of drugs for prescription or OTC status, serve first to protect the health of the individual consumer, to protect the interests of the manufacturer, or to shield health insurers from certain drug costs? The apparent inconsistencies in drug theory and policy in such cases are not solely issues of conflicting financial interests among manufacturers, insurers, and patients. This is hardly news in a for-profit health care economy. Instead, the problem is how a policy ostensibly intended to protect patients—who are assumed to be incapable of correctly judging their own interests in the matter of drugs—is utilized to serve other interests.

The inconsistency stems from pharmacologically identical drugs, neither one with clinical advantages over the over, occupying both prescription and nonprescription status. If the drug is dangerous when misused, or for other reasons requires monitoring by a health professional for safe use, then it would seem that *both* versions belong under prescription status. Indeed, only 40 percent of physicians responding to a 1995 survey (a time when the movement for reclassification was gaining traction) approved of reclassification of drugs from prescription to OTC status,[8] although it was not clear that safety was their primary concern. Today, however, there is little objection from physicians to reclassification.

Conversely, if the drug is safe for the consumer to use with adequate package information but without professional monitoring, then there is little justification—other than commercial advantage to the manufacturer—for assigning it prescription status as well. What cannot be maintained, however, without apparent violation of the basic principle of justice, *"treat like cases alike,"* is the dual-status assignment of identical drugs. Or is there something wrong with the way the distinction is drawn between prescription and OTC drugs?

Case 4: Caffeine is by far the most commonly consumed drug in the world and is socially accepted almost everywhere. In the United States, it is usually ingested in the form of coffee, tea, and carbonated drinks like Coca-Cola and Mountain Dew. Many other caffeinated drinks (maté, "smart" water, and high-energy drinks like as Jolt) and caffeine preparations (e.g., "stay-awake" tablets such as NoDoz and headache remedies such as Midrin) are also available without restriction. A molecular scientist who also owns a café in Durham, North Carolina, has developed a way to add caffeine to baked goods—"Buzz Donuts" and "Buzzed Bagels," he calls them.[9] Inventors have developed a soap, "Shower Shock," said to provide transdermal absorption of caffeine equivalent to two cups of coffee within five minutes, claimed to be faster than the oral administration route of coffee,[10] although it is not clear that the caffeine molecule is actually absorbable in this way. AdvoCare International of Texas makes a caffeinated "sports drink"

8. Lori R. Jacobs, "Prescription to Over-the-Counter Drug Reclassification," *American Family Physician* 57(9) (May 9, 1998): 2209–14.

9. Associated Press, "US Scientist Brings Caffeine Buzz to Baked Goods," *International Herald Tribune Americas,* January 29, 2007.

10. Reuters, MSNBC, "Caffeinated Soap Perks Up Your Shower," April 20, 2007, online at www.msnbc.msn.com/id/18230175/.

powder that is marketed to children in two strengths: KickStart Spark for children 4-11 years old, which contains 60 milligrams of caffeine (equivalent to about a cup and a half of coffee) and other stimulants, and AdvoCare Spark, for children 12 and up, with 120 milligrams of caffeine (about as much caffeine as three cups of coffee or three 12-ounce colas).[11]

As in the example of Carl in chapter 4, compulsive coffee consumption might be considered an addiction according to at least one widely accepted

---

Case #4: Caffeine Consumption: The Marketing of Addiction?

Tony is six years old. He walks into Starbucks one summer day, orders a venti latte, sits down, and drinks it. The next day, Tony returns and has another latte. In fact, he continues to return day after day. Is there any problem in serving Tony lattes on a regular basis?

Susie is also six years old. With her allowance, she goes to the corner market and buys a bottle of Jolt Cola, a highly caffeinated soda that appeared in her favorite movie, Jurassic Park. She buys another bottle of Jolt the next day and the next. Is there any problem in selling caffeine drinks to Susie?

Many workplaces maintain coffee pots or allow coffee-vending machines. Is this a problem? What about truck drivers who use caffeine tablets to stay awake on the road, or students who use caffeine and other cognitive enhancers to study for exams? What about caffeinated baked goods that circumvent coffee's bitter taste, or shower soap that dispenses caffeine for dermal absorption—allegedly stronger and quicker than coffee? If Starbucks opens a coffee stand in the lobby of the local hospital, is this a problem?

---

11. Duff Wilson, "A Sports Drink for Children is Jangling Some Nerves," *New York Times,* September 25, 2005.

set of criteria. Other definitions of addiction require harm to the user, yet caffeine habituation does not appear to be harmful for most people. The preponderance of clinical evidence indicates that consumption of as many as five cups of coffee daily is not associated with adverse physiological, social, or psychological effects for most persons, although high consumption often does cause insomnia and jitteriness. But as mentioned in chapter 4, caffeine consumption may contribute to increased risk of stroke or nonlethal heart attack in some predisposed individuals or people who have specific genetic variants. Most commonly, however, the only adverse effect is withdrawal headaches among chronic users. Indeed, coffee has been claimed to have health benefits ranging from protecting against liver disease to preventing diabetes, and its psychoactive properties in promoting increased alertness and cognitive acuity are well known.

Caffeine in OTC drugs such as NoDoz and Anacin is regulated as a drug by both the Food and Drug Administration and the Federal Trade Commission. Caffeine in carbonated beverages and other drinks is regulated by the FDA as a food rather than a drug. Foods that have natural forms of caffeine, such as coffee, tea, and maté, are essentially unregulated. Under DSHEA, the Dietary Supplement Health and Education Act, caffeine in dietary supplements is subject to minimal, if any, regulation, even though the amount and potency may far exceed that of other preparations. Yet the physiological effect of caffeine from all these sources is the same.

Caffeine is freely available to almost anyone, without restrictions by age or limits on quantity. Indeed, it is available even in jails and prisons, where the use of any other psychoactive substance is highly restricted. Given the arguably addictive nature of this drug, not to mention its evident psychoactive properties and its infrequent but potentially serious adverse effects for some people, it is remarkable that it should be so free of restrictions.

What if caffeine had not previously existed and was now introduced as a new drug? If the risk of addiction were considered central and it were considered a threat to society, it could be classed as a controlled substance, due to its arguably addictive properties. In comparison to other controlled substances (marijuana and peyote, for example, both of which are Schedule I), caffeine might be considered more dangerous, with more adverse effects (headache, jitteriness, arrhythmias, possible stroke) and far greater likelihood of overdose. In 2006, the American College of Emergency Physicians, reviewing records over a three-year period at the Illinois Poison Control Center in Chicago, reported 256 cases of medical complications from ingesting caffeine supplements, largely by young people (average age, 21) either to stay awake or for a feeling of euphoria. Twelve percent of these overdose cases required hospitalization, including treatment in intensive-care units.[12] In a consistent regulatory system, caffeine presumably would be restricted at the same level as equally dangerous drugs. In the real world, then, the disparate classifications—marijuana and peyote as Schedule I, for instance, but caffeine as OTC, a food, or altogether unregulated—appear to reveal a major inconsistency in current classificatory systems. In fact, caffeine is actively marketed even to children (in colas) and hospital patients (in coffee); and neither Tony nor Susie, both six years old, had any difficulty obtaining it.

Does this make sense? Should drug regulation be based entirely on cultural precedent while disregarding pharmacologic and addictive properties? Does consistency speak for greater restrictions on caffeine, or for reduced restriction of other habit-forming or addictive drugs that are psychoactive and potentially dangerous to some people?

Case 5: Opioid concerns have been exacerbated in recent years by the abuse of the long-acting opioid analgesic OxyContin. This powerful and effective pain medicine, now available in high-dose controlled-release tablets, offers the advantage of delivering an effective dose of the opioid oxycodone (similar in potency to morphine) in a single tablet. The dosage form is designed to release the medication over twelve hours, thus removing the necessity for patients having to take lower dose oxycodone tablets every four hours.

However, many drug abusers know that the controlled release characteristic of OxyContin tablets can be overcome by crushing or chewing them. Doing so is dangerous and even lethal, particularly when taken together with other drugs.[13] As of 2006, the DEA has verified 146 deaths in which

---

12. "Young Americans Abusing Caffeine," NewsMax.com Wires, Tuesday October 17, 2006, reporting on the presentation of Danielle McCarthy at the 2006 meetings of the American College of Emergency Physicians.

13. Arthur G. Lipman, Editorial, "What Have We Learned from OxyContin?" *Journal of Pain & Palliative Care Pharmacotherapy* 17(1)(2003): 1–4.

Case #5: Is a Drug Manufacturer Responsible for Abuse?
The OxyContin Controversy

Should Purdue Pharma continue to manufacture and distribute OxyContin, given its high potential for abuse? In recent years, the preparation of oxycodone marketed under the brand name Oxy-Contin has become a favorite of opioid abusers, replacing heroin in many states. Along with the increase in abuse, there have been many overdose fatalities. Some commentators have argued that OxyContin is a more insidious drug than heroin because it is obtained more easily from diverted prescriptions and does not have the risks of adulteration that are characteristic of heroin. Others point out that precisely because it is manufactured under strict controls, it is to be preferred to street heroin.

The diversion and recreational use of pain-management pharmaceuticals is one of the fastest-growing areas of drug abuse. Is Purdue Pharma responsible for the harm stemming from abuse of OxyContin? Indeed, should pharmaceutical companies that manufacture pain medications or other abusable drugs be responsible for abuse of their products, or responsible for abuse if they manufacture drugs in a dosage form that can be abused?

OxyContin was the direct cause or a contributing factor; an additional 318 deaths lacking acetaminophen or salicylates in the toxicology findings most likely involved OxyContin as well.[14] Both health professionals and law enforcement officials recognize the growing problem of prescription-controlled substance abuse, which may soon exceed illicit drug abuse.[15] The U.N.-affiliated International Narcotics Control Board annual report

---

14. www.deadiversion.usdoj.gov/drugs_concern/oxycodone/oxycontin7.htm.
15. "Increase in Poisoning Deaths Caused by Non-Illicit Drugs," *Morbidity and Mortality Weekly Report,* 54(02)(Jan 2, 2005): 33–36.

for 2006 found that in parts of Europe, Africa, and South Asia prescription drug abuse has already outstripped many illegal drugs, including heroin, cocaine, and Ecstasy.[16] Still others suggest that OxyContin has become a "gateway" drug—both a drug of abuse in itself and a lead-in to other drugs from illicit sources.

Defenders of OxyContin claim that the media and some politicians have exploited this *cause célèbre* to attack the pharmaceutical industry, suggesting that the facts about OxyContin are distorted and the criticisms failed to note that the drug was being taken illegally with intent to induce effects that the users knew could be dangerous.[17] Moreover, the notoriety associated with this legitimate, clinically useful medication has led to extensive litigation and increased fear among clinicians in utilizing this and other important opioid medications. The result has been needless patient suffering.

What tensions between the domains of prescription pharmaceuticals and illegal recreational drugs does the case of OxyContin reveal? Should Purdue Pharma continue to produce OxyContin in its current form, or only in forms that cannot be so easily abused? It has invested significant resources in an attempt to develop a tamper-resistant tablet by incorporating a naloxone additive, but has not so far been successful. Which consideration should take priority: convenience of administration for pain patients, or the risks of diversion into recreational use? Which professional group should decide this issue: clinicians involved in pain management or criminal justice and substance abuse authorities?

OxyContin appears to present a classic conflict in drug regulation—the calculus of harm versus benefit, and correspondingly, the conflict between medicine and criminal justice, between free trade and social responsibility, and ultimately between individual autonomy and governmental paternalism. Consider, for instance, recent legal decisions that have held tobacco companies liable for the harm resulting from the use of their products, even when the consumers were aware of the risks. Indeed, the trend to

16. International Narcotics Control Board, Annual Report, "Abuse of Prescription Drugs to Surpass Illicit Drug Abuse, Says INCB," press release No. 4, March 1, 2006, online at http://www.incb.org/pdf/e/press/2007/annual-report-press-kit-2006-en-4.pdf

17. Lipman, "What Have We Learned from OxyContin?"

pursue actions against firms perceived to be distributing dangerous products has moved as far as lawsuits against firearm manufacturers, automobile
manufacturers for unsafe design, and fast-food chains for their contribution to obesity, though most have failed. Should Purdue Pharma, despite
its attempts to develop a naloxone additive, be similarly implicated for the
harm from OxyContin abuse?

Case #6: Religious Drugs: Peyote and Beyond

Red Eagle, a Native American, and John, of European ancestry,
are members of the Native American Church and the Peyote Way
Church of God, respectively, and both use peyote as a religious
practice. Diego is from Brazil; he is a member of the União do
Vegetal Church, and uses ayahuasca as a religious practice. Isaac
is a recent immigrant to the United States from West Africa; he
is a follower of the Bwiti religion, which uses iboga root as a
sacrament. Mustafa is an immigrant from the opposite coast of
Africa, Somalia, and he chews khat while reciting Islamic prayers
and reading sacred texts; although khat-chewing enhances his
religious practice, he says, it is not part of his religion in itself.
Maurice considers himself a Rastafarian and smokes marijuana
as a religious rite, while his roommate, Thomas, rejects organized
religion but uses marijuana as a way to connect with his "inner
spirituality."

Case 6: Two of these individuals are acting within current U.S. law;
the other five are not. At issue for these five individuals is the possibility of criminal prosecution under federal law for their drug consumption,
but the outcome in each case might well turn on distinctions that may
be unsustainable upon further investigation. As discussed in chapter 2,
Native Americans who are members of the Native American Church, like
Red Eagle, are exempted regulation from the Controlled Substances Act
in their "nondrug use of peyote in bona fide religious ceremonies," which
was further extended to any Native American who practices "a traditional

Indian religion."[18] As held by the U.S. Supreme Court in 2006, the Religious Freedom Restoration Act (RFRA) prevents federal—but not state—officials from placing a substantial burden on the religious use of drugs without a compelling justification. This ruling protects the sacramental use of the hallucinogenic tea ayahuasca by members of the União do Vegetal church, which would include Diego. However, none of the practices in the other examples cited in this case are permitted under federal law: John's use of peyote in the Peyote Way Church of God, Isaac's use of iboga root as a Bwiti sacrament, Mustafa's chewing khat while reciting his prayers, Maurice's use of marijuana in Rastafarian religious practices, or Thomas's personal use of marijuana for spiritual enlightenment.[19] It might be asked, then, which of these practices should be free from interference by law enforcement and whether the resulting pattern has any semblance of consistency and coherence.

Consider the express exemption of peyote use by Native Americans under federal law. Although the essential aspect of this political policy would appear to be the "nondrug" use of an otherwise banned substance "for bona fide traditional ceremonial purposes," the exemption has not been explicitly extended to the sacramental use of drugs by members of other groups or religions. After the Supreme Court's 2006 ruling in favor of members of the União do Vegetal Church—and, in particular, the Court's rejection of Native Americans having a "unique relationship" with the federal government as a justification for disparate treatment—the sacramental use of otherwise banned drugs by non-exempted groups and churches would seem to be eligible for legal protection. If members of federally recognized Indian tribes and congregants of the União do Vegetal Church can ingest peyote and ayahuasca, respectively, why should members of other races or churches (e.g., the Church of the Toad of Light) be precluded from consuming peyote or the hallucinogenic excretions of the Colorado River toad *(Bufo alvarius)* as part of their religious ceremonies? Indeed, could any drug use be defended

18. 21 Code of Federal Regulations 1307.31 (citing as authority 21 U.S.C. §§ 821, 822(d), 871(b)); 42 U.S.C. § 1996a (extending exemption to members of Indian tribes).

19. It might be noted that John could be protected from a *state* prosecution. See, e.g., *State v. Mooney*, 98 P.3d 420 (Utah 2004) (concluding that exemption applies to Native American Church members who do not belong to a federally recognized tribe).

by the user claiming that such use is part of a religious practice, protected by the First Amendment or, more likely today, RFRA?

The government might argue that the different treatment of these religious groups could be based on the history and tradition of sacramental drug use. As mentioned in chapter 2, for instance, peyote has been used in religious contexts for thousands of years. This may seem to suggest that the historically established ingestion of a drug is bona fide religious use but that more recent practices are less verifiable as such. Perhaps other religions that are already established with a history of drug sacraments should fare better in obtaining exemptions.

But consider the Bwiti religion of West Africa that uses the iboga root as a sacrament in its religious ceremonies. Iboga root contains ibogaine, a Schedule I substance that has some chemical similarities to LSD. Bwiti has not yet appeared in the United States and thus has not made a request for a religious exemption for its consumption of iboga. Clearly, Bwiti would satisfy criteria for a bona fide religion in the context of drug use (or "nondrug" use). It could not be claimed that the church existed solely for the sake of protecting a drug use practice, which might explain why some other religions have been denied the exemption—a rationale that, ironically, would cut against the exemption provided for the Native American Church, which was established explicitly to protect peyote consumption. Moreover, there would be no legal distinction between the classification of exempted substances and the drug used by Bwiti. Like peyote and ayahuasca, ibogaine is listed as a Schedule I substance, and it has been classified as a dangerous substance by WHO's World Health Assembly since 1967—despite the fact that it has no addiction potential and indeed has been tested and marketed, under the trade name Endabuse, as an anti-addiction medication.[20] Moreover, the case of Bwiti seems remarkably similar to the situation of the Native American Church and União do Vegetal—traditional indigenous religious practices under "Western" scrutiny—so it seems natural to ask whether the courts should treat them similarly.

If peyote and ayahuasca are exempted, shouldn't ibogaine (or, for that matter, marijuana and any other religious-use drug) be exempted as well? What about culturally used drugs that may be associated with religious

20. Gahlinger, *Illegal Drugs,* 299–306.

practice in some regions, but are not actually part of religious rites per se, like khat? Is there any plausible limit to recognizing drugs used in traditional religious practices around the globe? There are numerous drugs that have historically been used in a religious context. These include the mushroom *Amanita muscaria*, Broom (*Cytisus scoparius*), Calamus (*Alcorus calamus*), Coleus (many species), Datura (many species), Doña Ana (*Coryphantha macromeris*), Hawaiian Baby Wood Rose (*Argyreia nervosa*), Henbane (*Hyoscyamus niger*), Kava (*Piper methysticum*), and Morning Glory (*Rivea corymbosa*), to name just a few. Should all these drugs be prohibited, peyote included, even though they have very little abuse? On what viable basis could the cases of peyote, ayahuasca, ibogaine, khat, marijuana, and the many others be deemed "unlike" and their religious adherents undeserving of equal treatment under the basic principle of justice? Indeed, it can be argued that all historically used psychoactive substances have had at least some religious use. Certainly, all have been used in ceremonial contexts, and religion itself is difficult to define. Most pre-industrial societies did not separate religious from nonreligious activities in daily life—in a sense, it could be said, everything was sacred.

Beyond the specific challenge posed by the case of the Bwiti, there are deeper theoretical issues to be considered. Presumably, a long-standing church whose sacramental drug use is already well established is best positioned to gain an exemption similar to the one made for the Native American Church. But this may be only a pragmatic consideration. So far, the courts have used the language of a "bona fide" religion, but have been understandably reluctant to give criteria to define this concept precisely.[21] To say that a group does not qualify for the exemption is not, by itself, to say that the group is not a bona fide religion, because government may have a compelling interest in not extending the exemption even to an admittedly "bona fide" religion. But the appearance of inconsistency is strong in allowing exemptions for some members of some groups but not for other members or for other groups, all of whom seek to use these substances in religious ceremonies. It may thus seem entirely inconsistent that the Native American Church and União do Vegetal have been able to secure protection for their religious practices while

21. Troy L. Booher, "Finding Religion for the First Amendment," *John Marshall Law Review* 38 (2004): 469.

the Peyote Way Church of God and the Church of the Toad of Light have not. Moreover, is it a belief in a deity or membership in an organized church that makes some belief system a "bona fide" religion? What makes one belief system as opposed to another a "bona fide" religion? Is the real problem whether something is a bona fide religion, or, rather, whether it is possible to know whether something is a bona fide religion? In other words, is it the sincerity or the possibility of faked sincerity that is most important?

The hypothetical cases of the seven individuals using drugs in connection with religion—two in compliance with federal law, five violating it—suggest the following question: What if a dissident from an organized religion uses marijuana as a means to reach a higher level of consciousness, commune with nature and fellow believers, or obtain some other spiritual goal? Why aren't his actions a "religious" practice? At times the U.S. Supreme Court has suggested that such practices would qualify as "religious." The most notable example is the Court's willingness to extend a federal statute that exempted religious conscientious objectors from the draft to include those with "deeply held moral, ethical, or religious beliefs" against war, even though the Court recognized the objector was only "religious in the ethical sense of the word," whatever that means.[22] One could even imagine a religion that required khat chewing or marijuana smoking at regular intervals. Should the government be required to demonstrate a compelling interest in refusing to extend the exemption to that group?

If only some religions are to be included in this exemption, criteria for legitimacy of religions would have to be established. And even assuming a religion is "bona fide," how is membership to be determined? For instance, if members are allowed to use peyote or ayahuasca in their religious ceremonies, by what test are we going to evaluate whether an individual is a member of the church? What if it does not define membership? Like some contemporary religions, imagine that people are simply invited or come by themselves, attending once a week or once in a lifetime. They might present themselves with their birth name, their spiritual name, or some other given or self-selected name. There may be no documentation of their presence at a ceremony or other participation in the church. What does membership mean in this context?

22. *Welsh v. United States*, 398 U.S. 333, 341, 343–44 (1970).

Federal law has been interpreted to mean that only Native Americans can participate in the religious use of peyote, but the definition of "Native American" may depend on an arbitrary quantum of aboriginal ancestry. The federal statutory exemption defines the term "Indian" as "a member of an Indian tribe," meaning "any tribe, band, nation, pueblo, or other organized group or community of Indians ... which is recognized as eligible for the special programs and services provided by the United States to Indians because of their status as Indians."[23] Although many tribes (and many states such as Texas) use a standard of one-quarter Native American ancestry, the Ute Indian Tribe of the Uintah and Ouray Reservation requires 5/8 "blood quantum," for instance, while the Eastern Band of Cherokee Indians of North Carolina only demand 1/16 Cherokee ancestry. Not only do the criteria have a seeming arbitrariness about them, but a separate constitutional infringement could arise should the federal government seek to prevent, for instance, a non-Native American congregant from sacramental use of peyote— namely, a violation of that member's right to "equal protection of the laws" without regard to race. The União do Vegetal does have membership criteria; however, many ayahuasca-using groups do not have organized membership. (Indeed, it can be supposed that the reason the União do Vegetal is the one involved in the legal case is *because* they are the most organized.)

In the past, law enforcement has argued that expanding the exemption for the religious use of drugs will likely lead to an increase in the nonreligious use of those drugs, which has been deemed sufficient to deny exemptions to otherwise bona fide religious groups and sincere religious users. After the Supreme Court's most recent ruling, however, this type of generalized argument is unlikely to be considered a compelling government interest to preclude sacramental drug ingestion, at least without some supporting empirical evidence. Does this permit one who merely claims a religious use to become a "law unto himself," as the Supreme Court suggested in 1990?[24]

There is a further problem in the law's treatment of this issue. This discussion has focused primarily on policies of the federal government, but the states need not recognize any federal exemption under their laws

---

23. 42 U.S.C. § 1996a(c) (extending exemption to members of Indian tribes).
24. *Employment Division v Smith*, 494 U.S. 872, 879 (1990).

(although the federal exemption would still apply to federal laws). Conversely, the states can exempt whatever religious drug use they wish regardless of federal prohibition. So under current jurisprudence, the federal government may be required to allow members of the União do Vegetal to use ayahuasca, for instance, but the states could criminalize this practice consistent with the "free exercise" provision of the U.S. Constitution. Yet surely the extent to which federal and state law can differ on an issue of such profound importance as the restriction of religious practice demands further reflection.

Whether there could ever be a compelling government interest—federal or state—in criminalizing *religious* drug use requires a closer examination of the underlying rationale for the regulatory structures in the first place. Is the rationale a paternalist one, to protect users of these substances from the harm it might cause? Most religious drug use involves hallucinogens, intended to provide a visionary spiritual experience. The various hallucinogens used in religious ceremonies are, in general, not dangerous to the user, particularly when ingested in protected circumstances like religious ceremonies. If paternalism were the rationale for regulation, virtually all such practices should be allowed, as long as the paternalistic rationale is applied on a case-by-case basis. Or if the rationale for prohibiting some use were a moralist one, a general disapproval of such practices or at least drug use in such practices, it would seem to call for prohibition of all religious drug use that falls within its moral reach, including those currently exempted. Is the concern fear of addiction? As it turns out, none of the substances in question are addictive in any of the common senses, unless the "regular use" involved in recurring religious practice is itself taken as evidence of addiction.

What about the apparent basis for the political branches' refusal to grant further exemptions, that the government is only preventing the spread of drug use and thus limiting exemptions to cases where use is not likely to spread? On this argument, it might seem sensible to permit peyote use for some Native Americans but not for non-Native Americans; to allow ayahuasca use if the drug is not generally sought; but to prohibit marijuana use for all Rastafarians on the grounds that use would inevitably spread. After all, peyote and ayahuasca are difficult to take (they are nauseating and induce vomiting) and therefore are not favored for

Case #7: Drug Interactions between Prescription and Alternative Medications

Mary Jo is a thirty-six-year-old white female who received a kidney transplant in April 2005. She was prescribed the usual array of medications to keep her body from rejecting the transplanted organ, including Cyclosporin A, and was considered stable for a period of several months. Indeed, Mary Jo was doing extremely well and was regarded as a model patient for diligence in cooperating with the anti-rejection regimen. In November 2005, however, her blood level of Cyclosporin A dropped precipitously, well below that needed to maintain the transplant effectively. She was admitted to the hospital for a variety of lab tests and a kidney biopsy.

After several days of inconclusive results, Mary Jo revealed to her physicians that she had been feeling a bit "down" due to all her medical problems. She had read about St. John's wort and its use to treat mild to moderate depression in a magazine. Intrigued, she had explored the findings by accessing several web sites and discovered that St. John's wort contains constituents that inhibit the reuptake of important neurotransmitters that regulate mood, similar to certain prescription antidepressants. She certainly did not want to take any more drugs, so she had thoughtfully investigated manufacturers, purchased a product standardized to contain 0.3 percent hypericin (the purported active ingredient), and carefully followed the dosing instructions on the label.

Mary Jo required a second kidney transplant in December 2005. Unknown to Mary Jo, St. John's wort interferes with cyclosporine, and by undercutting her anti-rejection drug regimen, she probably caused the need for another transplant. Who or what was at fault for this unfortunate turn of events?

recreational purposes, while drugs like marijuana are more pleasant to use in both religious and nonreligious contexts. But if an exemption is allowed only for Native Americans who use peyote, is it because non-Native Americans are more likely to use peyote in "drug" rather than "nondrug" ways? If the risk of spread in "drug" use rather than "nondrug" use is the underlying rationale for these seemingly inconsistent and thus potentially unjust decisions, then this rationale itself deserves closer scrutiny.

Furthermore, the tension between criminalization and protecting religious practices from government interference should be squared with society's considered opinions elsewhere. If all dangerous drugs in religious contexts were to be restricted or criminalized, shouldn't all dangerous religious practices be restricted as well? That might mean confiscating rattlesnakes from serpent handlers in Appalachia, forcing Jehovah's Witnesses to undergo blood transfusions, and requiring Christian Scientists to accept medical treatment. Likewise, societal opinions about prohibiting drugs used in religious contexts also would need to be squared with opinions about how to regulate substances that are legal but otherwise restricted in differing contexts of age, athletic condition, and health status. Nonetheless, it seems that a more compelling defense is needed to sustain a drug law exemption made available to Red Eagle and Diego but not Maurice or Isaac, at least if like cases are to be treated alike.

Case 7: St. John's wort has shown efficacy against mild to moderate depression in some but not all clinical trials. The hypothesized mechanism of action overlaps with that of prescription medicine, calling into question the classification of St. John's wort as a dietary supplement and not a drug. This plant is also known to stimulate enzymes in the body that normally metabolize both Cyclosporin A and many other important medications, including warfarin, digoxin, irinotecan, indinavir, carbamazepine, fluoxetine, simvastatin, and oral contraceptives. When metabolism is stimulated, these drugs are cleared more rapidly, producing a drop in blood levels—a so-called "drug interaction." No such information or warning is provided on the St. John's wort label, as would be required for prescription or OTC preparations. Even though Mary Jo carefully researched the clinical evidence and the products and followed the instructions, a drastic and very expensive medical procedure was required to save her life; indeed, the cost of kidney transplant surgery can cost as much as $150,000.[25]

Drug interactions can occur with prescription pharmaceuticals, "natural" herbal remedies, sports-enhancement drugs, and even common-use drugs, especially alcohol, all of which can potentiate the effects of other drugs. In Mary Jo's case, not only did the container of St. John's wort provide no information about possible drug interactions with Cyclosporin A, but it also failed to mention that the substance could, for instance, interfere with or neutralize the effect of birth control pills. Indeed, only later did Mary Jo learn that this phenomenon was so common that obstetricians sometimes refer to "St. John's wort babies," and that medical groups in Sweden and the United Kingdom have issued warnings about this interaction. Pressing for specific information about the nature of this herb-drug interaction, she found that a recent study estimated that St. John's wort reduced the effective dose of oral contraceptives by 13 to 15 percent.[26] Given her already existing difficulties with kidney function, Mary Jo was tremendously relieved not to have her medical outlook complicated by an unintended pregnancy.

Who or what is at fault for Mary Jo's need for a second transplant, when she had been such a model patient? Should any party be blamed, or was it just an "accident"? Who should pay for the second transplant? Should Mary Jo be held financially responsible, since it was needed because of her use of St. John's wort? Should her physician have been responsible in some way, if he failed to warn her of drug interactions between her Cyclosporin and any herbal remedies or dietary supplements she might also take? Should the manufacturer of Cyclosporin have placed warnings about drug interactions on its package inserts? Should the manufacturer of St. John's wort have placed a warning on the label of the bottle? Should the government, perhaps the FDA in particular, be blamed for failing to regulate St. John's wort in some way? Or should there be some other mechanism for warning

25. See http://www.emoryhealthcare.org/departments/transplant_kidney/patient_info.faqs.html, accessed June 8, 2006.

26. Patricia A. Murphy, Steven E. Kern, Frank Z. Stanczyk, Carolyn L. Westhoff, "Interaction of St. John's Wort with Oral Contraceptives: Effects on the Pharmacokinetics of Norethindrone and Ethinyl Estradiol, Ovarian Activity and Breakthrough Bleeding," *Contraception* 71 (2005):402–8.

patients like Mary Jo, who certainly did not wish to interfere with her first transplant or make her own health situation worse, about the risk of pharmaceutical and herbal drug interactions?

Case #8: What Do the Brain Scans Show? Should Parkinson's Disease, Obesity, and Methamphetamine Use Be Considered Alike?

Andrew has Parkinson's Disease, Bob is obese, and Charlie uses methamphetamines. Neuroimaging studies of all three show changes in brain morphology that substantially influence their behavior. Yet the three are regarded differently: Andrew as the victim of a disease, Bob as irresponsible for failing to exercise and control his diet, and Charlie as an addict. As far as current neuroscience can tell, changes in brain biology largely account for their patterns of behavior.

Does modern neuroscience's new ability to identify changes in the brain make it difficult to maintain traditional moral distinctions about responsibility for behavior? If Andrew's, Bob's, and Charlie's brains are affected in even somewhat similar ways, should their behavior be assessed in similar ways—for example, that Bob's girth and Charlie's cravings are not so different from Andrew's tremor?

Case 8: New research in neurotoxicity suggests that methamphetamine damages the same brain systems as those associated with Parkinson's Disease, the neurodegenerative disease with symptoms such as flat affect and, in later stages, a distinctive tremor and cognitive loss. Parkinson's selectively compromises a specific neurochemical transmitter system, the nigrostriatal dopamine pathway, and methamphetamine use can also damage this pathway. Although more controversial, it is also believed that the damage in Parkinson's Disease, like that done by methamphetamine, may be caused by exposure to an external toxin, possibly environmental poisons such as the pesticide Paraquat and heavy metals like manganese.

Both methamphetamine users and Parkinson's patients lose cognitive skills and can become very impulsive. In turn, obesity often involves deficiencies of dopamine transmitter pathways, probably in the nucleus accumbens. Likewise, methamphetamine can also affect the nucleus accumbens and cause deficiencies in the same dopamine receptors. While the dopamine systems in the human brain are numerous and extraordinarily complex, all three people suffer from damage to such systems.

Thus, the responses to Andrew, Bob, and Charlie may seem to be starkly inconsistent. In Andrew's case, his behavior is accepted and care is provided due to societal compassion about Parkinson's Disease. Cases such as Bob's are often met with social rejection—fat phobia, it is sometimes called—though when an obese person like Bob actually does develop diabetes, cancer, or cardiovascular disease, more compassion and care tend to be provided. But in the methamphetamine case, society may incarcerate a meth user like Charlie, even though the type of brain changes are similar to that suffered by the Parkinson's patient and the obese person. Except in prison settings and some urban clinics, there is little or no health care for the methamphetamine user, with the focus placed on the social destructiveness of the drug's use.

Is this inconsistent? Is it reasonable to be sympathetic with the clinical expressions in one case because society appreciates that the underlying cause is neurobiological, while with the other clinical problems it ignores the biology and public interventions lack compassion because the clinical presentation is deemed socially unacceptable? Society recognizes that Parkinson's Disease and illnesses associated with obesity can disrupt families, but public perceptions never equate these effects in any way with the social pathology linked with methamphetamine use. Is this inconsistent? Should behaviors resulting from similar brain changes be regarded as equally culpable (or nonculpable), even if the underlying causes are different? Or does it in fact matter how the brain changes came about, rather than what those changes mean now? (This case is thanks to Elen R. Hanson.)

Case 9: Depression is a human condition suffered on an immense scale. In the United States, an estimated 20 percent of women, and only a slightly smaller percentage of men, have depression. The disease ranges from a minor inconvenience for some to a crushing, catastrophically disabling illness for others. Indeed, depression can be fatal due to the increased risk of suicide. The social costs of this ailment are enormous, as are the human costs.

Case #9: Self-Medication for Depression? Antidepressants: Legal and Illegal

Janice and Karen are both in their early thirties. Both suffer from chronic depression. Janice is employed but Karen is not.

Janice has had years of psychotherapy as well as medical treatment. She has been prescribed lithium, Valium, Elavil, Prozac, Wellbutrin, and now Cymbalta. She says that with this new drug she has finally got it right, more or less, and that her depression is relatively under control for the first time in her life.

Karen, on the other hand, is not insured and has access only to emergency health care, which is not well equipped to treat chronic depression. Like Jane, Karen has tried to control her depression for years, although variously using alcohol, marijuana, amphetamines, cocaine, and, now buprenorphine, or "bupe," as it is known on the street. Karen too says that she now has got it "about right," but that her principal problem is frequent brushes with the law, when she is jailed or required to undergo drug treatment therapy, which cuts off her supply of antidepressant drugs.

What, exactly, is the relevant difference in these two cases? Both Janice and Karen have struggled with depression for many years; both have managed to continue their lives; and each has finally found a drug that controls the depression. Is there something unjust if Karen's drug of success is prohibited to her while Janice's is provided for her by prescription?

Depression stems either from an endogenous imbalance in a person's brain chemistry or an imbalance precipitated by the negative impact of some external event. Thus, drugs that alter brain chemistry can play a major role in depression. Some drugs cause or intensify depression, such as those that work by inhibiting various parts of the central nervous system. These include many pharmaceutical drugs used for treatment of medical conditions, and they can variously exacerbate preexisting depression, unmask latent depression, or cause depression in themselves. The drugs raise clinical dilemmas in medical practice about whether to add an antidepressant to a patient's treatment or instead to back off on the original therapeutic regimen. Interferon used to treat hepatitis C is associated with depression, for example, and drugs that intensify or cause depression can be found in other areas as well. Alcohol also inhibits the central nervous system and can complicate depression; so can common OTC drugs such as antihistamines. Some religious-use drugs, such as the hallucinogens, are psychoactive and can exacerbate preexisting psychiatric disease, including depression. Steroids used in sports enhancement, including androgenic steroids like nandrolone, can cause severe depressive reactions. Barbiturates and benzodiazepines—such as Phenobarbital and Valium, known on the street as "downers"—are also highly associated with depression.

On the other hand, there are drugs, especially central nervous system stimulants, that relieve some of the symptoms of depression. These include common-use drugs like caffeine, found in coffee, tea, colas, energy drinks, and various "stay-awake" nonprescription OTC medications like NoDoz (see case #4). The dietary supplement St. John's wort is a mild antidepressant, although it can cause clinically important drug interactions (see case #7), and other dietary supplement stimulants, such as ephedra, can provide transient relief of mild depression. Many sports-enhancement drugs are central nervous system stimulants, such as amphetamines. So is the common-use drug nicotine. Such stimulants also include prescription drugs like methylphenidate (Ritalin), which is indicated for a variety of disorders and lessens depressive symptoms. Methamphetamines are widely regarded on the street as "uppers," substances that relieve depression and brighten mood. For this reason, illegal Ritalin has a growing street market as well.

Several classes of prescription drugs are specific antidepressants. Prozac is best known, though there are several classes of antidepressants that are equally effective but that have very different side-effect profiles. These include the monoamine oxidase inhibitors (MAOIs) and the tricyclic antidepressants (TCAs) like amitriptyline (Elavil), both of which were introduced in the 1950s and have significant side effects. More recently, the selective serotinin reuptake inhibitors (SSRIs), the first of which was Prozac, are far better tolerated and can be taken by many more patients than the earlier classes. The newest therapeutic alternatives for the medical treatment of depression are serotinin-norepinephrine reuptake inhibitors (SNRIs) like duloxetine (Cymbalta), the drug Janice is taking.

About 70 to 80 percent of patients with severe depressive disorder (endogenous depression) respond to antidepressant pharmacotherapy, and a somewhat lower proportion respond to counseling or psychotherapy. Maximal response is achieved by using both, as Janice has done in this case. Ironically, however, some drugs both relieve depression and cause it. Opioid analgesics are central nervous system depressants that provide initial relief but make depression worse when taken chronically—which, in turn, can lead patients to increase their opioid intake in an attempt to lessen depression when, in fact, they are making it worse. Depression is common among opioid-dependent patients and has been associated with worse prognoses.[27]

Alcohol is a central nervous system disinhibitor that seems initially to relieve depression, but after ingestion in high amounts it rapidly induces depression. Stimulants may temporarily relieve depression, although they frequently cause wide mood swings and contribute to a rollercoaster, up-and-down pattern. For instance, cocaine can provide an initial, depression-relieving high, but this is followed by a depressive low. Methamphetamine also can be effective in the initial relief, but this spike is typically followed by a crash of intensified depression, reinforcing continued use of the substance to try to alleviate the condition. As such, these seeming "uppers" often cause a severe rebound depression, though they are not typically recognized by users in this way.

The environment of use can also make a difference in drug effect. For example, Ritalin and methamphetamine, both sympathomimetic stimulants, can be used in moderate amounts to control depression, but the environment in which meth and street Ritalin are used often contributes to overuse, thus producing the paradoxic rebound of depression. Other drug combinations can exacerbate depression, for instance, alcohol coupled with other depression-exacerbating drugs. And some drugs do not themselves affect depression, but can lead to a period of intense depression during withdrawal.

27. Edward V. Nunes, Maria A. Sullivan, Frances R. Levin, "Treatment of Depression in Patients with Opiate Dependence," *Biological Psychiatry* 56 (10)(2004):793–802.

Karen has tried all these things in her search for relief, often making her condition worse. However, Karen's new drug, buprenorphine—her "bupe"—is useful in the management of depression associated with opioid dependence because it helps reduce the craving for opioids. Several other more traditional prescription antidepressants are likewise effective, but she has no access to them. Illegal drugs, including many of those used recreationally, can also have profound effects on the user's level of depression, as Karen well knows. Indeed, many street users like Karen are also managing their depression with drugs, much as Janice manages hers, though without professional expertise and often with unintended toxicities and side effects. Karen has tried many street drugs in her largely trial-and-error search for an effective antidepressant, but she has found that bupe works for her.

Therein lies an irony. A clinical trial conducted at Harvard Medical School in 1995 demonstrated that a majority of treatment-refractory, unipolar, nonpsychotic, major depression patients could be successfully treated with buprenorphine, even after several other (non-opioid) traditional antidepressant medications failed to provide these patients with any measure of relief.[28] Buprenorphine is also indicated for the treatment of opioid dependence; the prescription form is combined with naloxone (Suboxone), an opioid antagonist, which is added to prevent the abuse of buprenorphine. But while the primary use of buprenorphine is for opioid addiction as well as for treatment of moderate to severe pain and perioperative analgesia, the FDA does not recognize buprenorphine as an antidepressant in the United States. This is largely because the manufacturer of buprenorphine has not conducted extensive clinical trials and has not petitioned the FDA to include depression as an indication. By trial and error, Karen has found a drug that might well be approved for her condition if an application were pursued by its manufacturer, but she can only get it on the street and at the risk of landing in the criminal justice system.

Given this broad picture of antidepressant and depressant drugs, consider the questions raised by the cases of Janice and Karen. Their drug use in seeking relief from depression may seem to be similar, even though one uses a

28. J. Alexander Bodkin, Gwen L. Zornberg, Scott E. Lukas, Jonathan O. Cole, "Buprenorphine Treatment of Refractory Depression," *Journal of Clinical Psychopharmacology* 15(1)(Feb. 1995):49–57.

prescription drug and the other uses an illegal one. Indeed, a drug court judge observes that as much as half of the illegal drug use that he sees is self-medication, much of it for depression. For some, meth is the cheapest antidepressant available, and other street drugs, like bupe, might be a close second.

Is it inconsistent to support a market in prescription antidepressants that costs billions of dollars a year, while measures intended to control illegal drugs effectively suppress a possibly cheaper, more available route of self-medication for depression? Do the dangers of illegal drugs—whether from the drug itself, its adulteration, or the externalities of black market distribution—outweigh the advantages (if there are any) of individual control of medication for depression? How should access to antidepressants be managed, across the board? Given the self-regarding character of drugs that affect one's own mood but do not typically have direct effects for other people, should "uppers" and "downers" that relieve depression or restrain mania be clinically managed by health professionals in treatment settings, self-managed by users on the open market, or approached with some other methodology? What about herbal antidepressants like St. John's wort and those in other categories? What about sports-enhancement uppers, widely used by amateur athletes who are not attempting to compete in venues like the Olympics where these substances are prohibited? Do the risks of depression-treating drugs require close monitoring, or does the importance of personal control in mood regulation speak for an open market in antidepressants and other mood-affecting drugs? Why should Karen be denied the relief that Janice has obtained?

Case 10: Although this vignette is played out countless times each day in the United States, the practice of punishing drug addicts for behaviors related to their addiction is legally problematic. To appreciate the jurisprudential dilemma, it is necessary to provide a sketch of two seminal U.S. Supreme Court decisions.[29] In the 1962 case of *Robinson v. California*, the Supreme Court considered a California statute that made it a crime for a person to "be addicted to the use of narcotics," punishable by up to a year in jail.[30]

---

29. For detailed analysis, see Erik Luna, "*The Story of* Robinson v. California, in *Criminal Law Stories: A New History of Ten Leading Criminal Law Cases,*" ed. Robert Weisberg (New York: Foundation Press, forthcoming).

30. Cal. Health & Safety Code § 11721, quoted in *Robinson v. California*, 370 U.S. 661 (1962).

Case #10: Drug Crime: Can the Government Punish Addiction?

Alan is addicted to heroin. During a recent encounter with law enforcement, a small bag of heroin and a syringe were discovered in Alan's coat pocket. Alan was arrested and charged with possession of heroin and drug paraphernalia, which could lead to his imprisonment for several months.

Alan protested that he is addicted to heroin and hence cannot help using it. He knows that it is illegal, but that doesn't make any difference to his physical cravings: Alan simply cannot control his needs, any more than he could control his symptoms if he had insulin-dependent diabetes.

The defendant, Larry Robinson, had been convicted under this statute based on testimony that he had needle track marks, discoloration, and scar tissue on his arms, coupled with the defendant's own admission of using narcotics in the past. The Court's opinion began by noting that government clearly had the power to regulate drug traffic within its borders, including imposing criminal sanctions for the manufacture, sale, or possession of drugs. But in this case, California was prosecuting Robinson for the "status" of narcotic addiction, which it described as an illness or disease. The Supreme Court opined, "It is unlikely that any State at this moment would attempt to make it a criminal offense for a person to be mentally ill, or a leper, or to be afflicted with a venereal disease."[31] With addiction thus characterized an illness, the Court struck down the California law as violating the constitutional limits on criminal penalties, famously noting that "even one day in prison would be a cruel and unusual punishment for the 'crime' of having a common cold."[32]

The immediate consequence of *Robinson* was to preclude the government from punishing an individual for drug addiction or, by obvious extension, alcoholism—but it also brought into doubt drug and alcohol-related

31. *Robinson*, 370 U.S. at 666.
32. Id. at 667.

crimes. Relying upon *Robinson*, for instance, a pair of federal appellate court cases decided in 1966 held that a chronic alcoholic cannot be punished for the crime of public drunkenness.[33] One of these cases reduced the winning argument to syllogistic form: "[Defendant's] chronic alcoholism is a disease which has destroyed the power of his will to resist the constant, excessive consumption of alcohol; his appearance in public in that condition is not his volition, but a compulsion symptomatic of the disease; and to stigmatize him as a criminal for this act is cruel and unusual punishment."[34] Similar arguments were made with regard to drug-related offenses, and the resulting confusion in the courts virtually guaranteed that the Supreme Court would have to address the issue of addiction and criminal justice once again.

In the 1968 case *Powell v. Texas*, the justices considered the constitutionality of punishing a chronic alcoholic for the crime of public intoxication. Defendant Leroy Powell had been convicted of this crime even though a psychiatrist testified that the defendant was compelled to drink due to the "disease" of chronic alcoholism. In a four-person plurality opinion, the Supreme Court distinguished *Robinson* from *Powell* by concluding that Powell was not being punished for his status but instead for "public behavior which may create substantial health and safety hazards, both for [himself] and for members of the general public, and which offends the moral and esthetic sensibilities of a large segment of the community."[35] Justice Byron White concurred in the result, providing the key fifth vote to uphold the conviction, although he wrote that punishment for public intoxication might be impermissible for an individual who could not avoid public places, such as a homeless alcoholic. In the drug context, the Constitution would thus bar a conviction "where the drug is addictive" and "for acts which are a necessary part of that addiction, such as simple use."[36] But in the present case, there was no evidence that Leroy Powell was unavoidably in a public place due to poverty or his state of extreme inebriation.

Because Justice White's vote was decisive in *Powell*, his concurring opinion would typically be viewed as controlling in subsequent cases—most

33. See *Easter v. District of Columbia*, 361 F.2d 50 (D.C. Cir. 1966); *Driver v. Hinnant*, 356 F.2d 761 (4th Cir. 1966).

34. *Driver*, 356 F.2d at 763.

35. Id. at 526.

36. Id. at 552 n.4.

important, that the Constitution bans punishment not only for being an addict but also for conduct that was compelled by and symptomatic of an addiction. This is not the current state of the law, however. Except for a few outlying cases, American courts have uniformly held that a defendant's addiction offers no defense to a prosecution for the purchase, possession, or use of illegal drugs. The *Robinson-Powell* doctrine has been interpreted as only precluding criminal sanctions for the "status" of addiction but otherwise permitting punishment for all other drug-related crimes. As a result, few if any barriers to punishment exist for drug crimes, even where the defendant is an addict and the relevant conduct is the product of his addiction—a seemingly erroneous interpretation that the Supreme Court has nonetheless failed or refused to correct.

Much of the reasoning seems to evince not just a silo mentality but, at times, a rejection of any interdisciplinary analysis of drug issues altogether. As Justice Hugo Black wrote in his concurrence in *Powell*, "medical decisions concerning the use of a term such as 'disease' or 'volition,' based as they are on the clinical problems of diagnosis and treatment, bear no necessary correspondence to the legal decision whether the overall objectives of the criminal law can be furthered by imposing punishment."[37] Subsequent lower court decisions have largely ignored the opinions of medical professionals and thus adopted an insular approach to problems of crime, drugs, and addiction. Some legal opinions have glibly claimed, for instance, that addicts always have a choice when they acquire and consume drugs, like participating in a rehabilitation program instead of giving in to their addictions.[38] However, such arguments appear to rely upon abstract notions of free will rather than the practical reality of human decision making and the consequences of addiction. Moreover, this approach is inconsistent with the modern legal movement to incorporate (or at least consider) science and the opinion of medical professionals in inherently empirical questions of causation and, perhaps to a lesser extent, culpability, such as those arising from mental illness.

Medical professionals must also share part of the responsibility for the law's discomfort with addiction-related claims in drug prosecutions. As discussed in chapter 4, the various clinical and scientific communities have

---

37. *Powell*, 392 U.S. at 541 (Black, J., concurring).

38. See, e.g., *United States v. Lyons*, 731 F.2d 243, 246 (5th Cir. 1984); *Moore*, 486 F.2d at 1183.

failed to provide a mutually understandable and usable definition of "addiction," and the *DSM* (a resource widely accepted by the courts for issues related to insanity) does not even recognize the term "addiction," instead offering definitions for "substance abuse" and "substance dependence," though the latter is tantamount to addiction. It is unclear precisely what a court would do with these terms, given that the *Robinson-Powell* doctrine uses and relies upon the concept of "addiction" in delineating between valid criminal sanctions and unconstitutional punishment. Without some agreement on terms and definitions, the medical profession is not well positioned to affect the jurisprudence of crime, punishment, and addiction.

Then again, one might ask whether the problem is not the failure of law versus that of medicine, but instead the incompatibility of these two disciplines, based on two different worldviews—one that largely assumes free will while the other takes a mostly deterministic perspective. Each profession is called upon to render judgments about inherently unique and often less-than-clear cases that cannot be so neatly categorized. Consider, for instance, an exchange in *Powell* between the prosecutor and defendant after the latter admits to having one drink on the morning of his trial but then stops drinking:

> Q. And you knew that if you drank it, you could keep on drinking and get drunk?
>
> A. Well, I was supposed to be here on trial, and I didn't take but that one drink....
>
> Q. So you exercised your will power and kept from drinking anything today except that one drink?
>
> A. Yes, sir, that's right.
>
> Q. Because you knew what you would do if you kept drinking, that you would finally pass out or be picked up?
>
> A. Yes, sir.

On redirect examination, however, defendant Leroy Powell was questioned by his attorney as follows:

> Q. Leroy, isn't the real reason why you just had one drink today because you just had enough money to buy one drink?
>
> A. Well, that was just give[n] to me.

Q. In other words, you didn't have any money with which you could buy any drinks yourself?

A. No, sir, that was give[n] to me.

Q. And that's really what controlled the amount you drank this morning, isn't it?

A. Yes, sir.

Q. Leroy, when you start drinking, do you have any control over how many drinks you can take?

A. No, sir.

In light of this testimony, how are we supposed to apply terms like "compulsion" and "volition"? Is it even possible to make an "either/or" assessment of whether Leroy Powell should be held responsible for public drunkenness?

One additional issue deserves mention. Even under the current conception of the *Robinson-Powell* doctrine and the disparate definitions of addiction in the medical communities, an entire class of drug prosecutions might be constitutionally dubious. To reiterate, current jurisprudence deems it impermissible to punish an individual for his addiction but acceptable to use the criminal sanction for his drug-related conduct, premised on the idea that the status of addiction can be neatly separated from the conduct of the addict. But what if addiction cannot be separated from and, in fact, may be defined by conduct? As will be recalled, the 2001 consensus definition claimed that addiction was "characterized by *behaviors*," including "impaired control over drug use," "compulsive use," and "continued used despite harm." Likewise, the DSM diagnostic criteria define its analog to addiction, "substance dependence," as including *behaviors* such as obtaining and using the drug. So if addiction is delineated by, among other things, acquiring and consuming drugs, it would appear that punishing an addict for purchasing, possessing, and using drugs would be tantamount to punishing his or her addiction in violation of the Eighth Amendment. Conversely, one could ask whether addiction is really a "status" in the sense supposed by the U.S. Supreme Court.

The question for all disciplines—law, medicine, psychiatry, philosophy, and so on—are the consequences of this potential reinterpretation of American jurisprudence. If the addict cannot be punished for his possession or purchase of drugs, can he nonetheless be held liable for drug trafficking or dealing?

Would this issue turn on whether his involvement in illegal drug transactions was in order to secure drugs for his own (addiction-driven) use, to take a portion of the drugs as his share of the profit, or to obtain money in order to pay for the drugs that his addiction drives him to use? And if the notion of addiction were extended this far, could an addict also avoid prosecution for theft, burglary, robbery, or prostitution if these crimes were undertaken to purchase drugs? Such queries would seem to demand serious interdisciplinary discussion of addiction and its appropriate treatment in the law.

Case #11: Is Ignorance a Defense? The Case of the Olympic Swimmer—and the Rower, the Thief, and the Cyclist

Consider the case of Brian, a junior elite swimmer who hopes to one day compete in the Olympics. His coach recommended the use of a dietary supplement because it was advertised to enhance the loss of body fat and facilitate the development of lean muscle, thinking that it would help Brian's swimming form. The coach was not worried that it would contain banned anabolic steroids, since they had recently become controlled by the 2004 Amendment to the Controlled Substance Act and presumably had been taken out of all dietary supplements. However, while participating in a swim meet, Brian tested positive for dehydroepiandrosterone (DHEA), a substance on the World Anti-Doping Agency list of banned anabolic steroids.

Incredulous, Brian insisted that he had taken nothing but a dietary supplement, which he had purchased at General Nutrition Center at his coach's recommendation. Brian's defense was unsuccessful, and he received a two-year doping ban from competitive swimming. What went wrong, causing Brian's athletic disgrace and in all probability ending his swimming career?

Case 11: As a substance that occurs naturally in the human body, DHEA is an endogenous steroid that is penultimate in the formation of testosterone and pivotal in the creation of estrogen. It is the most abundant of the steroids circulating throughout the body in humans between the ages of fifteen and forty-five. The exogenous DHEA that Brian consumed, however, is typically manufactured in China from the roots of yams. It is widely promoted to prevent or slow the loss of muscle, memory, and libido associated with aging, although studies in elderly men and women have generally failed to show benefits in mood, well being, activities of daily living, or cognition.[39] One study has shown that DHEA improved erections and libido compared to placebo.[40] The physiological replacement dose of DHEA is about 50 mg/day, although doses of 100 to 450 mg/day are often recommended by proponents of dietary supplements. As with many other dietary supplements, the quality control of DHEA is often poor, and, as seen in chapter 3, what is promised on the label does not always correspond to what is in the bottle.

Although the FDA banned OTC sales of DHEA in 1985, before the passage of DSHEA in 1994, many steroid precursors—including DHEA—were initially classed as dietary supplements, rather than as foods (e.g., caffeine-containing beverages) or drugs (e.g., NoDoz). As dietary supplements, these steroid precursors did not require FDA approval or regulation. However, the 2004 Anabolic Steroid Amendment to the Controlled Substance Act added more than fifty steroid precursors to the list of controlled anabolic steroids. This was in response to the claim that such precursors were being sold as components of dietary supplements, and their consumption could result in the type of athletic performance enhancement provided by anabolic steroids themselves (e.g., testosterone). Furthermore, athletes complained that the ingestion of supplements containing unregulated precursors could lead unknowingly to a positive doping test. As a result, most potential precursors are now controlled as Schedule III anabolic steroids and cannot be sold as components of nutritional supplements. Such substances include androstenedione ("andro"), the controversial substance taken by former St. Louis

---

39. Dennis T. Villareal, John O. Holloszy, Wendy M. Kohrt, "Effects of DHEA replacement on bone mineral density and body composition in elderly women and men," *Clinical Endocrinology* 53 (2000): 561.

40. Werner J. Reiter, Armin Pycha, Georg Schatzl, A. Pokorny, D. Gruber, J. Huber, Michael Marberger, "Dehydroepiandrosterone in the treatment of erectile dysfunction: a prospective, double-blind, randomized, placebo-controlled study," *Urology* 53(3) (1999): 590.

Cardinals baseball player Mark McGwire at the time he broke the single-season home run record in 1998.

However, DHEA was not included on the list as an anabolic steroid in the 2004 amendment to the Controlled Substances Act. The exclusion was intentional rather than an oversight, with the amendment beginning with the following definition: "The term 'anabolic steroid' means any drug or hormonal substance, chemically and pharmacologically related to testosterone (other than estrogens, progestins, corticosteroids, and *dehydroepiandrosterone (DHEA)*" (emphasis added). In combination, DSHEA and the 2004 Anabolic Steroid Amendment allow DHEA to remain unregulated as a dietary supplement and exempted as an anabolic steroid. Thus, DHEA is available to this day as an ingredient in dietary supplements without prior tests of safety or efficacy. And it is advertised as enhancing athletic performance despite being banned by the International Olympic Committee, the World Anti-Doping Agency, the National Collegiate Athletic Association, the National Football League, the National Basketball Association, and Major League Baseball.[41]

So why is DHEA exempted? On April 17, 2005, the *New York Times* quoted Representative Henry Waxman, Democrat of California, as saying that DHEA was protected "because of the economic pressures from the dietary supplement people that stand to make a lot more money by selling it." As of this writing, DHEA is still available and promoted as a "legal" testosterone precursor, causing confusion among purchasers and occasionally resulting in positive doping tests. As in the case of Brian, an unsuspecting athlete who assumes that the Anabolic Control Act actually controls *all* anabolic steroids and makes them illegal in OTC dietary supplements may ingest such a supplement and have to live with the unintended consequences.

---

41. Of all these sports organizations, Major League Baseball was the only one at the time not to ban steroids. Baseball officials had complained to lawmakers that the lawmakers' failure to write in zero-tolerance toward steroids into the federal law made it difficult for them to ban DHEA in their own drug policy. The executive vice president for labor relations at Major League Baseball was quoted as saying, "It is difficult, from a collective bargaining perspective, to explain to people why they should ban a substance that the federal government says you can buy at a nutrition center." Ann Kornblut, Duff Wilson, "How One Pill Escaped Place on Steroid List," *New York Times* April 17, 2005. Since then, however, Major League Baseball has also banned steroids and now tests for them.

Some claim that the current policy of excepting DHEA has benefits for the public by making available a substance that promotes good health and well-being and may stave off the scourges of old age. This line of argument can be countered not only with concerns about harm from adverse effects—such as acne, excess hair growth, liver dysfunction, hypertension, acute manic episodes, and harmful interactions with other prescription drugs—but also with charges that the entire policy of regulating anabolic steroids remains inconsistent and incoherent.

Most athletic organizations, including most professional sports, have a sort of strict-liability policy for prohibited drugs—that is, an athlete is "strictly liable" for what is found within his or her body regardless of the reason or intent of ingestion. This makes the claims of ignorance untenable. A professional athlete can appeal their positive doping test to their sport governing body for confirmation of accuracy of the test, and an Olympic athlete can appeal to the Court of Arbitration for Sport. In a very few cases, the reason or intention for the ingestion may be considered justified, for example, when an athlete had been taking a drug openly and continuously for medical reasons since before it was banned, like skeleton racer Zach Lund's use of finasteride, Propecia. But despite a small degree of discretion in the reviewing authority, in general an athlete's claim of ignorance will be no defense.

Should this be the case? Is the mere presence of prohibited drugs in a person's body a sufficient basis for the penalties imposed on him or her? Or does it make a difference how the drugs got there, and what the motivations of other involved parties were? Numerous reports show that dietary supplements on the market in the U.S. often fail to contain the substances indicated on the label and may contain other substances and contaminants.[42] To press this issue further, consider other cases in which ignorance might be claimed: Jeff the rower, Joe who becomes a thief, and Jacques the cyclist:

Is a strict liability-style policy too strong? What if one athlete purchases peaches at his local grocery, cleverly inoculated with nandrolone by another shopper who is rooting for another athlete? Is a policy of similar strictness appropriate elsewhere as well—schools, air traffic controllers, government

---

42. Gilroy et al, "Echinacea and Truth in Labeling"; J. Manning and J. C. Roberts, "Analysis of Catechin Content of Commercially-Available Green Tea Products," *Journal of Herbal Pharmacotherapy* 3(2003): 19–32. See also http://nccam.hi.gov/health/supplement-safety/ and http://msnbc.msn.com/id/188027830/.

employees—or are these situations different? Is it too extreme to reject categorically claims of ignorance? What about team sports, as in the case of Jeff, where one individual's ingestion of a banned substance—whether done intentionally or inadvertently—can disqualify all his teammates? Is this fair? Does it matter what professional area is at stake, for instance, athletics, public education, medicine, or transportation? If it were an airline pilot, the prospect of serious harm is clearly identified when performance-affecting drugs have been introduced into the pilot's body, even without his knowledge; the

---

Case #11 continued

Jeff is an elite Olympic athlete in the team sport of rowing. He trains regularly with his teammates and individually under the direction of the team trainer. Six months before the Summer Olympics his trainer recommends the use of a dietary supplement that promises a 50 percent boost in blood testosterone, resulting in increased muscle mass and strength. The trainer insists that the supplement contains only natural ingredients. After his boat wins an Olympic qualifying event, Jeff is chosen at random to have a doping test, which comes back positive for the drug nandrolone, an anabolic steroid. As a result, his team is disqualified from the event and thus prevented from participating in the upcoming Olympic games, while Jeff is suspended for two years. Both Jeff and the trainer claim that they did not know the supplement contained nandrolone, pointing out that neither the supplement's label nor any product advertisement mentioned the drug—yet lab analysis of the supplement reveals large amounts of nandrolone. The supplement manufacturer claims that the label was appropriate, and that if there were nandrolone in the product, it must have become accidentally contaminated.

Jacques, a top-seeded cyclist, is competing in the Tour de France. A spectator holds out a bottle of water at the roadside. While most professional cyclists pour such water over their heads rather than drinking it, Jacques is particularly thirsty at this moment, having already exhausted his own water supply, and drinks what is offered him. The spectator, rooting for another cyclist, had put nandrolone in the water. After he won the race, Jacques tested positive for nandrolone and was disqualified from winning. He was suspended from cycling for two years.

Joe is appearing in drug court, which he chose as an alternative to prison time after being convicted of theft to support his methamphetamine habit. The drug court requires that in order to remain out of prison, a person must submit to unannounced urine testing and must be clean. Joe fails his test this week, claiming that he doesn't know how meth got into his system. Joe's friends gave him some "vitamin" pills last week but didn't tell him they contained meth. In turn, his friends claim they didn't know.

same might be said about a neurosurgeon or crane operator. But is there the same prospect of serious harm if an athlete has performance-affecting drugs introduced into her body even without her knowledge, and if so, why does that push one way or the other for strict liability? And how much should administrative convenience play in such determinations? Resources will be expended and possible violators emboldened if a reviewing body moves from a no-excuses approach, to one of limited defenses, to full-fledged trials with the presentation of evidence and the allotment of burdens of production, proof, and persuasion on one party or the other.

In this context, ponder the consequences for a drug court (or any drug testing with legal, especially criminal, consequences). The public expense might be substantial if Joe, and all other defendants who test positive for methamphetamine, were allowed to claim ignorance of how the drug got into their bodies and demand some form of legal process. But the seriousness of the consequences for Joe—incarceration—may seem to require that an individual be allowed to defend himself from unjust charges. After all, it is not implausible that a person may unknowingly ingest drugs. Thus the question is which contexts, if any, justify a strict liability policy for drugs found within one's body: in drug court, in sports contexts, in employment situations, or whenever?

Case #12. Drug Court and the Unrepentant Heroin User

Hal is a long-time heroin user who leads an otherwise functional life. After being arrested for drug possession, he was given a choice. Hal could proceed through the traditional criminal justice system, and because he was only charged with possession and has no prior record, he could expect to receive a short sentence or possibly just probation, and then continue his life as before—although now with a criminal record. Alternatively, Hal could enter a plea in abeyance,[43] participate in a drug court program, and if he successfully "graduates," have the charges against him dismissed. But the program will last at least a year, and should he test positive at any time during that period, he could be put in jail.

Indeed, Hal might end up spending more time in jail than under the traditional system, which might involve probation alone or a short term of incarceration. Moreover, Hal is not sure he is interested in drug treatment, doubts that he can go an extended period of time without using heroin, and, quite frankly, doesn't understand what harm he has caused to anyone else. Yet if Hal is convicted through the standard process, he will face a variety of negative repercussions, including losing his job. What should Hal do? Is it right to put him to this choice?

Case 12: In 1989, the first drug court was established in Miami, Florida, as an alternative to the traditional approach to drug crime. As of spring 2006, there were more than 1,500 drug courts operating in the United States and another 400 in the planning stages—and as a result, every state and the District of Columbia, as well as territories like Guam and Puerto Rico and the

43. Typically, a "plea in abeyance" involves a guilty plea (or plea of no contest) by a defendant. Pursuant to a judicially approved agreement between the prosecution and defense, a judgment of conviction and resulting sentence are not entered at that time on the condition that the defendant comply with conditions stated in the plea agreement. In the present context, the condition is the successful completion of a drug court program.

reservations of numerous Native American tribes, have drug courts in operation or on the drawing board.[44] The impetus for developing drug courts included the perceived ineffectiveness of the traditional criminal justice model at reducing drug-related crime and rehabilitating offenders, as well as the enormous costs associated with processing and incarcerating drug criminals. As for the former, one study found that a population of fewer than 600 drug abusers was responsible for nearly 75,000 crimes over a twelve-month period.[45] Although not establishing that these crimes were committed *as a result of* the drugs their perpetrators used, the study did demonstrate that drug abuse and crime are often intertwined. In turn, it can cost more than $20,000 per year to house an incarcerated drug offender and thousands of dollars more in court costs to put him or her behind bars in the first place.

According to practitioners and proponents, the drug court model contains a number of key components, including early identification of suitable participants; non-adversarial, informal, and relatively frequent court proceedings; intensive drug treatment programs, heavy monitoring of participants through, among other things, recurrent drug tests; and immediate consequences for failure to meet program requirements. Drug court programs are (usually) restricted to nonviolent offenders who agree to plea in abeyance and enter the program instead of serving a jail or prison sentence. Although varying by jurisdiction, a program is typically twelve to eighteen months in length, with an average time to "graduation"—release from the court's strict monitoring—of twenty-two months. During the program, the participant will be required to undergo a drug treatment regimen backed by frequent drug tests and interactions with the drug court judge. For instance, they may have to submit to several random drug tests (typically urine analyses) per week and face a drug court judge in the company of a prosecuting attorney and his or her defense attorney and therapist every couple of weeks.

---

44. See Office of National Drug Control Policy, "Drug Courts," at http://www. whitehousedrugpolicy.gov/enforce/drugcourt.html.

45. Peter Finn and Andrea K. Newlyn, "Miami's 'Drug Court': A Different Approach," Program Focus. U.S. Department of Justice, National Institute of Justice, 1993, 13; specifically, the study found that a single set of 573 substance abusers in Miami were collectively responsible for 900 auto thefts, 6,000 robberies and assaults, 25,000 acts of shoplifting, and 46,000 larcenies and acts of fraud. See also Hon. Peggy Fulton Hora, Hon. William G. Schma, and John T. A. Rosenthal, "Therapeutic Jurisprudence and the Drug Treatment Court Movement: Revolutionizing the Criminal Justice System's Response to Drug Abuse and Crime in America," *Notre Dame Law Review* 74 (1999): 439–537.

If the drug tests are positive *for any reason*, the court is then allowed to issue sanctions ranging from a fine to mandatory community service to a jail sentence. It is also able to order an increased treatment regimen or any other therapeutic option. The particular sanction given is usually one suggested by the participant's therapist and agreed to by the judge, defense attorney, and prosecutor. Most important, a participant cannot "graduate" from a program until he or she is entirely "clean," meaning no positive drug tests for some extended period of time, such as six months. Although a participant agrees to a minimum of twelve to eighteen months of drug court treatment, they cannot leave the program once in it, and are often in the treatment program for a much greater period of time—on average, almost two years.

Drug court advocates point to substantial reductions in both recidivism rates and costs associated with drug offenders. Though studies of drug court performance have been plagued by inadequate research design, selection and reporting bias, and insufficient follow-up analysis, at least a few randomized studies have demonstrated statistically significant reductions in recidivism rates for drug court participants versus those dealt with through the traditional process.[46] Much of this comes from the melding of the criminal justice and medical models. The standard approach views drug crime as antisocial behavior that must be met with punishment, most notably, incarceration, and usually assumes that the defendant (and others) will be deterred from such behavior by the unpleasant consequence of imprisonment. Although the criminal justice model is effective by definition in its short-term coercion—sentences are *imposed* on the defendant, not freely *chosen* by him or her—they are notoriously ineffective at preventing future crime by drug users. In contrast, the medical model can be effective in treating many drug addicts in dealing with their behavior through a number of protocols. But drug treatment under the medical model is invariably premised on voluntary participation of the addict, and the drop-out rate of clients ranges from 80 to 90 percent.

Drug court, however, combines the coercion of the criminal justice system with the treatment of the medical model. Once in a drug court program, treatment is not optional, but mandatory. A participant might

46. See, e.g., Douglas B. Marlowe, David S. DeMatteo, David S. Festinger, "A Sober Assessment of Drug Courts," 16(2) *Fed. Sentencing Rptr.* 153 (2003).

minimize his time spent in drug court by refraining from drug use, but this will still entail at least a year in the program. Because a participant cannot opt out at any time and must obey the treatment recommendation or face incarceration, drug courts can actually force someone to undergo therapy even when the participant is unwilling or the regimen is difficult. Every two weeks, treatment recommendations can be suggested, altered, and enforced relative to what is considered to be the most therapeutically effective and appropriate in light of the given participant's situation.

Under the traditional approach, a drug conviction and subsequent prison sentence might occur many months or even more than a year after the time at which the offender actually used any drugs, producing a disconnect between the user's behavior and its legal consequences. By comparison, drug court participants frequently face a collection of attorneys, judges, and therapists, with the sanctions for violations swiftly imposed. Given that a sanction for drug use will come no later than two weeks after the offense, it will be vivid and relevant to the offense in the participant's mind, connecting the drug use and its punishment in an obvious and viscerally understandable way. Even this relatively short time span can be altered in appropriate circumstances, and the participant's therapy and drug court proceedings can be increased to occur as frequently as deemed necessary. Drug courts even have the capability of giving participants drug tests while they appear in court and sanction accordingly.

The high levels of contact between offenders and criminal justice actors and the temporal connection between violations and sanctions can have a powerful impact on a drug user, but there should be little doubt that the sheer length of time that a participant must undergo treatment gives the drug court much of its edge. In this respect, drug court contrasts with both voluntary treatment programs—these can end at any time on the participant's whim—and also with intensive detoxification programs, which typically last for no more than twenty-eight days in most cases. Drug court is guaranteed to last for twelve to eighteen months at least, and will not end until the participant has spent a full six months drug-free. This model might be described as a "twelve-step program with teeth"—no opting out and criminal punishment for those who fail. So in sum, drug courts are both quick in response to violations and lengthy in period of treatment, producing a regimen that Hal, our hypothetical unrepentant drug user, will surely find arduous, unpleasant, but in the end, may be effective at coercing him to give up his drug use.

The questions remain, however, as to which path he should take and whether it is appropriate to put him to this choice. From an autonomy-respecting perspective, there seems to be no justification for government to put Hal to the choice of (1) little or no punishment but a criminal record and its collateral consequences (i.e., loss of employment), or (2) coerced abstinence but no conviction and attached repercussions. But, of course, this viewpoint rejects the criminalization of drugs in the first place or, at least, would limit government interference to those situations where an individual lacked the capacity meaningfully to choose to use drugs or where drug use harms others. Conversely, a paternalistic approach might well find the coercion of drug courts perfectly acceptable; under a vision of the "good life" that rejected the use of all or certain intoxicating, addictive substances, drug paternalism might assume that the sober Hal of the future will be content with his transformation and the state justified in forcing the heroin-using Hal of today to forgo drug use.

The drug court model, as an appendage to the traditional criminal justice system, is not fully paternalistic and seems to take a somewhat curious middle course. If, in fact, paternalism justifies the drug court regimen, then why does a drug user have a choice about whether to participate in it? In other words, if we presume that drug courts are effective and lead to a better life for the user and society in general, why should an offender be allowed to opt out of the program up front rather than simply imposing it on him (and all other drug offenders)? Moreover, why have most drug courts been limited to low-level drug offenders—first-time drug offenders, for example, but not dealers? Shouldn't all drug offenders—and, for that matter, all offenders for any crimes who also use drugs—be required to participate in drug court? Part of the answer may lie in the insufficient funding for drug court programs, but some of it surely has to do with an assessment as to the disparate sympathy society holds toward different types of drug users.

Consider also the very notion of a "drug" court in the absence of other tribunals geared toward specific types of crime. For instance, why aren't there alcohol courts? Although there is a legalistic answer—namely, alcohol is legal but marijuana, cocaine, and heroin are not—shouldn't offenders who drink to excess (or drink at all) be put through the same institutional procedures as, say, marijuana smokers?[47] How about a kleptomaniac court—if there were some device that could detect when a habitual thief had stolen property once again, a type of urinanalysis for thieves, shouldn't that be implemented as well?

More generally, one might ask precisely whether it is appropriate to combine the therapeutic goals of medicine with the intentional infliction of painful consequences that is characteristic of the criminal justice system. To put it another way, is it right to try to cure addiction through the threat or imposition of punishment? Drawing upon case study #10, there may even be a valid constitutional objection to the drug court's use of criminal sanctions against a drug addict. If a drug court sends an addict to jail because of a positive drug test, isn't he being punished for his addiction? Under one (admittedly rejected) interpretation of the Supreme Court's decisions in *Robinson* and *Powell*, it would be cruel and unusual punishment to incarcerate an addict for his drug use. In a lower court case decided in the period between *Robinson* and *Powell*, a federal appellate court ruled that it was unconstitutional for an alcoholic to be required to abstain from alcohol as a condition of his probation.[48] It seems hard to differentiate that case from a situation where a drug court participant is required to forego drug use.

*   *   *

As mentioned at the outset of this chapter, these case studies are intended to illustrate problems in drug theory, policy, and practice. Solutions to dilemmas such as these are made difficult by inconsistent foundations— conceptual fissures and gaps between various silos of drug-related concerns. They are intended for further discussion; they are all important in the construction of consistent, coherent, comprehensive policy, but it seems doubtful that the reader will find easy solutions for any of them.

47. It should be noted that some jurisdictions have adopted "DUI courts," based on the drug court model, that integrate alcohol treatment for drunk driving offenders. See, e.g., http://www.aca-usa.org/ACA_old_site/duicourtshome.htm; http://www.ndci.org/dwi_drug_court.htm.

48. *Sweeney v. United States*, 353 F.2d 10 (7th Cir. 1965).

7

TOWARD JUSTICE IN DRUG THEORY, POLICY, AND PRACTICE

At the end of this work, the Grateful Dead's most famous reprise seems particularly apropos: "What a long strange trip it's been." The journey began with a discomforting recognition that the various disciplines' approaches to drug theory, policy, and practice are each dominated by a type of silo thinking, a kind of compartmentalization that easily results in inconsistency and lack of coherence across the broad spectrum of drugs, the very root of current difficulties. Next came a brief review of the history of drug regulation; this too exhibited the sort of compartmentalized thinking that has been the product of differing political concerns and pressures. Likewise, an examination of the underlying rationales for drug policy recognized the siloed nature of regulatory structures and the very different theoretical underpinnings of their rationales. It became necessary to look more closely at the accounts of addiction, dependence, tolerance, pseudoaddiction and iatrogenic addiction that are employed in various fields. This was followed by analyses of harm and benefit, core concepts at the root of inconsistency and incoherence in drug theory, policy, and practice. A set of case puzzles on drug management and control served to explore the problems endemic in silo-thinking and the failure to speak clearly or even agree on key terms within a profession, let alone among disciplines. It was hoped that these studies would reveal many tensions for the reader to consider, and perhaps address.

The path has been far from straight. The road has been filled with bumps and potholes. The signs have created confusion and at times pointed in different directions. And now that the end has been reached, readers might throw up their hands and say: *Does it have to be this way? Can't there be a consistent, coherent, and comprehensive approach to drug theory, policy, and practice?* The answer may well be "yes," but a series of fundamental choices will have to be made, each of them carrying distinct advantages and disadvantages, and each subject to a basic issue of governance, namely, political viability. Toward that end, the following will briefly lay out two quite extreme alternatives—both theoretically possible but unworkable in the real world—and then three practical alternatives, each of which could be realized if there were the political will to do so. This is not to say that society should adopt any one of these alternatives; they are laid out to stimulate further discussion within and among the different disciplines and between the governed and their governments. This book is a beginning, not an end.

Absolutist Policy Alternatives: Drug Anarchism and Total Drug Prohibitionism

A good starting point in determining the possibility of consistency in drug policy is to ask whether to regulate drugs at all. This question may appear a bit silly, given the current status of the modern regulatory state and the vast web of statutes, administrative regulations, court rulings, and so on, emanating from two and sometimes three levels of government (federal, state, and local), all of them controlling the production, distribution, sale, and consumption of drugs in all spheres. But although it may seem inconceivable, there once was a world without (much) drug regulation. As discussed at length in chapter 2, there was a time in American history when the substances now denominated as "drugs" were completely free of legal constraints.

It is, in fact, more accurate to describe drug regulation as a relatively recent endeavor preceded by millennia of few official limitations. As societies developed new societal needs, whether real or imagined, over the course of human history, governments attempted to control traffic in various commodities, including drugs, for a variety of reasons—for example, to raise taxes for the government treasury, to regulate public morals, or to enhance the general welfare. But the vast body of drug regulation, administered by layers of bureaucracies and law enforcement agencies, is by and large a phenomenon of the twentieth century, continuing on into the twenty-first. Although there were a few sporadic state regulations and schemes of taxation at earlier dates, the first broad federal law governing drugs in the United States arrived with the Pure Food and Drug Act of 1906, followed by the Harrison Narcotics Act of 1914 and the Food, Drug, and Cosmetics Act of 1938. Thus the huge regulatory system that looks so familiar today in the United States is less than a hundred years old.

Drug Anarchism

One alternative would be a world without drug laws of any kind. In the United States this would mean no Food and Drug Administration, no Drug Enforcement Administration, no Bureau of Alcohol, Tobacco, Firearms, and Explosives as it now exists, no Alcohol and Tobacco Tax and Trade Bureau, and no White House Office of National Drug Control Policy, the five principal agencies considered in chapter 3. Imagine no offices at any level of government to control production, distribution, or use of drugs of any sort. Private actions involved in producing, distributing, and using drugs would be constrained only by the "laws" of supply and demand. Metaphorically, it would be a large-scale version of the neighborhood lemonade stand, dependent only on the ability of the seller to provide and the purchaser to buy lemonade—but in this case, the product could be antihistamines, alcohol, antibiotics, anabolic steroids, coffee, cocaine, opioids, tobacco, anti-anxiety drugs, ayahuasca, whatever.

This "drug anarchism" approach certainly would offer a consistent, coherent, and comprehensive policy—covering all drugs and treating them all the same—without confused categories or distinctions. There may even be some who would find this approach attractive. But in general, it can be assumed that this hypothetical would be deemed unacceptable to contemporary society. Among other things, there would be no testing of pharmaceutical drugs before they become available, no consumer protections against adulterated or misbranded drugs, and no warnings or instructions on usage, with people taking grave and potentially lethal risks when they ingested a substance. In the absence of medical advice and prescription, some could become inadvertently addicted or dependent on dangerous drugs. Others would be injured or killed by users of drugs if there were no constraints on age or restrictions on context, such as bans on driving while intoxicated. The potential drawbacks from a wholly unregulated approach would span the entire pharmacopoeia and the entirety of human life and social interaction.

Although this picture may seem extreme, things looked pretty much like this before the beginning of the twentieth century. Because fewer drugs were available in earlier centuries and potentially dangerous machines (e.g., the automobile) were yet to be invented, the impact of anarchic drug-control policies may have been less. There were still certain controls in place, with social constraints and peer pressure playing a greater role in drug control. Nonetheless, much of the past has been a time of comparative drug-regulation anarchism, while drug control by state authority is a phenomenon of the present. Of course, it is sometimes quipped that there are some more recent natural experiments in complete drug deregulation—the "Summer of Love" in San Francisco 1967, roving Phish concerts, the summer gatherings of the Rainbow People, and so on—but these are local phenomena not established by public policy on a broad scale. Although drug anarchism may be an unacceptable option, it is nonetheless instructive to consider why. Before doing so, however, let's turn to the opposite extreme position.

Total Drug Prohibitionism

Now imagine a diametrically opposed response to the preliminary issue of whether to restrict or allow drugs: a regime in which all such pharmacologically active substances are prohibited. Under this approach, no substance defined as a drug would be legally available. A prohibitory stance would not produce a drastic change in circumstances for many illegal drugs, at least those that have no *legally* recognized medical use: marijuana, cocaine, some opioids, and most hallucinogens. As is true now, these drugs would all be unavailable through any lawful channel and their production, distribution, and consumption would be prohibited. The few exceptions that currently exist would be eliminated, such as state laws permitting the medical use of marijuana or the prescription of opioids for pain patients. For that matter, all prescription pharmaceuticals, as well as over-the-counter medicines, dietary supplements, and sports-enhancement drugs would be forbidden, whether or not medical professionals wished to prescribe or otherwise recommend their consumption. Common-use drugs like alcohol, caffeine, and nicotine would be banned in any of their consumable forms, meaning the end of not only coffee, for instance, but all caffeinated beverages. Such a legal ban on alcohol might bring back images of Prohibition during which alcoholic beverages were largely forbidden in the United States from 1920 to 1933, but a total ban would be even more extreme. Sacramental wine was exempted during Prohibition, for example, while a flat ban on all drugs would encompass religious-use drugs without exception.

Beyond the current war on drugs and America's failed experiment with Prohibition, one can see glimmers of outright bans in other real-life contexts. Amateur and professional athletic organizations can be quite strict on the use of drugs considered performance-enhancing, and there are faith groups that disavow some or all drugs. But in general, an absolute prohibition on all drugs of any kind has never occurred in human history, and with good reason. For most people, it would be unfathomable for society to preclude doctors from prescribing and their patients from obtaining any of the countless drugs that cure or diminish physical and psychological ailments. Under such circumstances, medical professionals would be limited to diagnosis, nonpharmacologic therapies, and maybe some basic advice in the absence of drugs (e.g., exercise, rest, drink water). Among others, the field of pharmacy might cease to exist as a discipline and profession. Although of seemingly lesser importance, people would have to forgo their morning (or afternoon) cup (or pot) of coffee, and the notion of a smoke break would disappear except as a metaphor for nondrug related activities. There would be no pubs or local bars, and no mixers or other social events with alcohol, tobacco, or caffeinated drinks.

This picture too is extreme, even more extreme than the drug-anarchism scenario. It has certainly never been done on a societal level. Yet among religious groups there is one vivid current example: Christian Science, which prohibits or strongly discourages the use of virtually all drugs. To be sure, some other religious groups prohibit or discourage the use of alcohol and/ or tobacco—for example, Muslims, Methodists, Mormons, and Southern Baptists—as well as illegal drugs, and some religious groups prohibit the use of stimulants: Seventh-Day Adventists, for example, discourage the use of hot spices and pepper. But Christian Science is distinctive in rejecting the use of pharmaceutical drugs used in the treatment of physical illness as well as other drugs. For Christian Science, healing is a matter of prayer, not bodily medicine, and the use of pharmaceutical drugs only reinforces the erroneous notion that the human being is a material object. The practices of Christian Science suggest that total prohibitionism, the complete rejection of all drugs across the board, is actually possible—although there is little reason to think such a policy could become a widespread, state-imposed, publicly supported phenomenon.

Clearly, neither of these absolutist approaches—a completely anarchic, unrestricted open market without any restraints, or a complete prohibition on drugs of all sorts—would be seen as workable or desirable in contemporary society, yet it is important to consider these extremes as a way of focusing on the challenges presented by a demand for justice in drug policy: for a consistent, coherent, comprehensive approach that requires good reason for any differential treatment of drug issues that occurs. Some drugs have enormous benefits in treating illness, enhancing performance, relieving pain, or giving pleasure; thus, clearly, not all drugs should be prohibited. Other drugs pose huge dangers to the user's physical, psychological, or social well being, or they present harms to others affected by the user; thus, not all drugs should be available without any regulation at all. But most drugs can do both, and this is what makes drug policy complex. The problem is not only balancing the harms and benefits of various sorts of drugs—any meaningful analysis must also include the harms and benefits of diverse policies designed to regulate drug use. These overarching concerns can help in the assessment of more practicable alternatives.

Real-World Policy Alternatives

Both absolutist regimes—the anarchic and the total prohibitionist—are mere theoretical possibilities, since neither approach can appropriately account for the fact that drugs can produce enormous benefits and also immense harms. While still extreme in their own ways, three more practicable, real-world policy options will be considered in turn. It is not our aim here to promote any one of these approaches as the "right" or "best" way to deal with drugs, but to recognize that each is at least consistent and coherent on its face, though they are incompatible with one another.

As the previous chapters have shown, there are huge inconsistencies and incoherence in drug regulation in the United States—and, to be sure, in much of the rest of the world—often resulting from historical events and sometimes sheer happenstance, inadvertently encouraged by intra-disciplinary, compartmentalized silo-thinking and professional uncertainty about core concepts and terms. For these reasons, it is important to rethink regulatory schemes derived from history's twisting path or unfounded, prejudice-ridden judgments if a measure of justice is ever to be achieved. The goal is not only greater clarity in the central concepts and terms that directly affect decision making, such as "addiction" and "harm," but also an account of overall consistency and coherence in policy. This will provide a basis for an honest, intelligible, and informed discussion, with many voices from varying areas of expertise. That is the reason for outlining three quite different but yet practically possible policy alternatives.

Informed discussion of these alternatives might begin with a small set of basic questions, which have a vague resemblance to the stereotypical reporters' questions and which will help guide interlocutors toward a consistent, coherent, and comprehensive approach to drugs:

- *Why*: Why should we regulate drugs in general or a drug in particular?
- *What*: What drugs should be regulated?
- *When and Where*: When and where should drugs be regulated?
- *Who*: Who should design and administer drug regulation?
- *How*: How should drug regulation occur?

These questions cannot be answered on a silo-by-silo basis; that is what leads to compartmentalization and disciplinary hyperspecialization, the root of current difficulties. Rather, to consider how these questions (and more) might be answered across the board, and as a way of exploring the broad range of possibilities for the regulation of drugs and drug use, consider three alternative approaches that fit somewhere between the theoretically tidy but practically unworkable absolutist extremes. As is evident, neither drug anarchism nor total prohibitionism would be sustainable in the contemporary world. The three policy options considered here, although in a sense also extremes, are nonetheless workable, real-world candidate policies. What is of interest, for now, are the advantages and disadvantages they each have, and the types of questions they each raise.

An Autonomist Approach

Imagine first what might be called an autonomist, "consumer-sovereignty" approach that stresses the notion of individual autonomy (respecting the voluntary, fully informed choices of individuals) limited only by the harm principle. This is not just the unworkable allow-all-drugs-without-restriction anarchist view discussed earlier, but a considered public policy for drug management. Such a view assumes that each adult is capable of making an informed, voluntary decision concerning whether to produce, distribute, sell, purchase, and ingest whichever drugs he or she chooses so long as harm is not caused to others. It is a simple policy—at least on the surface—dedicated to maximizing individual freedom, subject only to plausible constraints about harming others, and seemingly realizable in a free market. It fully meets the conditions for maximizing the liberties of the buyer to make voluntary, fully informed choices in a way that is morally defensible, namely, subject to the harm principle restriction.

Such an approach would permit competent adults to use drugs as they wish with only a few constraints. It would permit age and competency limitations, under the assumption that minors and individuals of diminished mental faculties are incapable of making a fully informed and voluntary choice concerning drugs. It would also be compatible with—indeed, require—regulations regarding accurate labeling and informational disclosure (arguably subject to considerations regarding commercial speech), since individuals cannot make fully informed and thus voluntary decisions if they do not know the nature of the substances they are purchasing and consuming. Of the types of drug control now on the scene, it comes closest to the over-the-counter model: drugs must have adequate labeling and warnings for consumers, but are freely available for purchase. It differs, however, in that in the current United States (though not in some other countries) it is largely low-risk drugs that are marketed OTC, while under the autonomist model proposed for discussion here, virtually all drugs would be available that way.

Both conditions on this autonomist model impose substantial limitations, but ones that this view deems appropriate. The first would permit the development of laws prohibiting actions that harm others, not only assault or fraud but specific matters involving drugs, for example, poisoning from pediatric antibiotic syrups, failed cancer therapy due to counterfeit anti-cancer drugs, or irresponsible use of antibiotics that contributes to antibiotic resistance. Thus, competent adults would be free to use drugs as they wish provided their drug-caused actions do not harm others. The second condition would require access to full information about risk/benefit considerations of all drugs, including such considerations tailored as much as possible to an individual's own environment, physical constitution and health status, genetic susceptibilities, and so on.

In this autonomy-emphasizing, consumer-sovereignty scenario, a principal role of governmental bodies would be to ensure that manufacturers and suppliers of drugs—whether entrepreneurial pharmaceutical giants or home meth labs—provide comprehensive, accurate information about a drug's pharmacological action, including physical benefits and harms, psychoactive activity, effect on social interchange, long-term effects, and so forth. Misleading and slanted information would not be tolerated. The assumption here would be that entities that produce drugs for human consumption can be held responsible for providing full, accurate information to the prospective user about the pharmacological, toxicological, and beneficial effects as well as modes of use for any drugs it offers for sale. The central objective is to maximize the informed and voluntary character of a user's choice. Under the autonomist model, it is the consumer who decides whether to use drugs and which drugs to use; government or other regulation serves primarily to protect the voluntary, informed character of that choice, without dictating what it should be, as well as to prevent harm to others. The consumer is sovereign, as long as he or she does not harm others.

In this autonomist scenario, laws and policies may play a major role in prohibiting the manufacture, sale, or consumption of drugs that will cause the user to harm others, or will cause third-party harms in other ways. Drugs that uniformly produce behavior that harms others could be prohibited, but other restrictions would not be imposed. As seen in chapter 5, there clearly would be disagreement about what counts as harm, whether harms are outweighed by benefits, and how great the likelihood of harm-causing behavior would need to be to warrant prohibition—all questions that must be answered in practice. In principle, however, this view is consistent as only harm-causing drugs (whatever they are) would be illegal;

the use of all other drugs would be allowed. Note that this scenario underwrites the prohibition only of drugs that cause harm *to others*—informed and voluntary harm to self would not be a basis for making a drug illegal.

An autonomist model is compatible with various views about methods of drug control where restriction or prohibition is justified. For example, it is sometimes asserted that the only effective method of stopping drug abuse is social opprobrium. In earlier times, this may have pointed to a simple solution—stop drug abuse by making it unfashionable—and until Prohibition, this was a fairly effective deterrent to alcoholism. With Prohibition, however, nonlegal social deterrence was replaced by legal deterrence, which some have described as far less effective and may have resulted in even more alcohol abuse. More recently, social opprobrium has been credited for a 50 percent reduction in tobacco smoking, and while there are age restrictions on tobacco access, there are no legal penalties on "abuse" of tobacco by heavy users or chain smokers. The autonomist model is also compatible with substantial, legally enforceable restrictions or prohibitions on drug use that may constitute harm to others. The same chain smokers who are not prohibited from causing harm to themselves are now legally restricted in certain jurisdictions as to where they may smoke and thus harm others—for instance, not in restaurants, not in bars, not in public buildings, and not underneath the air intake vent outside a building.

While an autonomist model may seem to presuppose that drugs will be manufactured only by private entities, it need not make such an assumption. This model would be consistent with the possibility that some drugs might be government-manufactured—vaccines, for example, or orphan drugs for medical conditions that affect so few people that manufacturers see no financial gain in developing them, or perhaps even drugs for which purity and consistent strength has not in the past been assured, such as marijuana, echinacea, or Ecstasy. Drugs produced by the government still would be subject to requirements about accurate information and non-misleading advertising, as well as the prevention of harm to others. Again, what is central in this scenario is not so much the exact structure of any agencies and manufacturers involved, but the crucial expectation that it is primarily the user who decides whether or which drugs to use.

Under this autonomist scenario, the current categories of prescription and illegal drugs, indeed all drugs, would be treated in a way analogous to OTC drugs, stressing that accurate labeling regarding drug contents, indications, appropriate dosages, as well as warnings about side effects and drug interactions would be required. Doctors might make recommendations to patients but would not control their choices; doctors would be more like consultants than gatekeepers. At an abstract level, this approach is consistent, coherent, and comprehensive, leaving the choice to the competent individual whether to enter into voluntary exchanges for drugs and to consume the same. Here, the picture is one in which the prospective user is ensured access to reliable, full information about any drug he or she may consider using, for whatever reason, but leaving the ultimate decision to the consumer.

This would only begin to frame the discussion, however. As observed in chapter 3, the notion of autonomy raises intricate issues of free choice. How do we know when someone has adequate mental capacity to grasp and assimilate knowledge about drugs, and who is to make this gate-keeping judgment of the cognitive capabilities of the relevant decision maker? What type and amount of information is necessary for a fully knowledgeable decision-making process on whether to consume drugs? And what are the necessary conditions for adequate reflection and deliberation of this information by an otherwise competent individual? Then, too, there are issues of harm prediction and the assessment of the likelihood of specific harm to others. As discussed in chapter 5, the issue of harm can be incredibly tricky, freighted not only with normative considerations but also with the residue of historical bias.

There would be many problems. A drug policy based on this autonomist rationale would have to decide which types of harm or risk of harm are intolerable, like using vision- or judgment-impairing drugs while flying an airplane, or allowing the private use of highly lethal drugs (e.g., sarin) at all. It would need to determine just how much information, in what detail, would be required to ensure that individual choice would qualify as fully informed. It might need to decide what forms of penalty are appropriate for violations and who pays the bill for the care of those harmed, including both users and others harmed by drug use.

If more than one type of harm could justify regulation, it might be necessary to provide some methodology to order and compare the relative harms—for example, an approach to deciding whether physical harm to another is worse than psychological harm, or the other way around. Most important, there must be some agreed-upon process for assessing the weight of a given harm, the factors that lead to its occurrence, and level of severity that will then be utilized by an agreed-upon decision maker in establishing a drug regulation. But this raises further problems. Would the alleged harms to others caused by methamphetamine use, for example, be assessed by a pharmacologist, a toxicologist, an addictionologist, an economist, a pathologist, a sociologist, a medical practitioner, an applied ethicist, or a combination of these professionals? How would considerations of harm to others be kept distinct from concerns about harms to self? And would the selected harm assessors then decide an appropriate policy for methamphetamine consumption, or would they simply provide information to be utilized by a separate entity—an agency or political body, for instance?

There would be still further problems. Assuming some level of regulation were implemented in order to prevent harms to others—say, from methamphetamine consumption—how would that regulation be enforced? Should law enforcement seek a criminal prosecution? Instead, should the harmed individual bring a private tort action against the user of the drug? Might the government institute a civil suit on behalf of the aggrieved individuals or society at large? Could enforcement occur outside of court proceedings via private regulations or social norms, such as internal action by non-governmental organizations (e.g., the International Olympic Committee) or the scorn of private individuals, like family, friends, and neighbors? While the autonomist approach is attractive, many questions must be answered before it can take the shape of a viable alternative. One thing is important to understand, however: an autonomist model need not mean more drug use; it means, rather, more user choice in the use or nonuse of drugs.

A Medical-Model Approach: The "Drug Decision Specialist"

Another approach might be described as a medical model, premised on the primacy of the judgment of medical experts—in other words, one that begins with the notion that health care professionals, not politicians or bureaucrats or would-be users and consumers, should be central in determining whether an individual should have access to a given drug. This is in part paternalist, but it also is a model that incorporates notions of physician responsibility and the fiduciary obligation to patients that protects individuals from professional whim. While the prospect of paternalism is currently somewhat out of fashion in medical ethics, it resembles the medical model of several decades ago by assigning a major role to a physician-figure. It is not fully paternalist, however, in that it does not assign full control to this individual.

A version of this partly paternalist approach already dominates the landscape of prescription pharmacotherapy. By law, a patient must receive a prescription from a licensed prescriber in order to obtain certain drugs; this requirement is understood to be based on a medical assessment of the potential benefits and harms from consumption. The pharmacist is legally required to provide the user information about drug effects and interactions, and he or she also controls dispensing. Under the medical model that is relevant here, a treating clinician would diagnose an individual's condition and physical, psychological, and emotional needs. Taking into account a particular drug's risk of harm from side effects and toxicity, as well as the likelihood of addiction, dependence, overdose, and so on, the clinician would then decide whether to prescribe a particular drug for the patient's consumption, limited by restrictions on the number of doses dispensed at a time and the number of refills that may be obtained. This partly paternalist approach casts the medical professional as the protector of an individual's well-being, sometimes contrary to the prospective user's own autonomous choices, by virtue of the health professional's extensive knowledge and training in the subject matter at hand.

This scenario does to a great extent describe the world of prescription pharmaceuticals—but it is currently confined largely to the medical sphere. Thus, the second practicable alternative would expand this picture to cover not just the medical sphere, but all areas of drug use altogether. So, for example, a consistent, comprehensive policy governing drugs might warrant the development of analogous specialists, beyond physicians, whose role is to assist prospective users of all drugs in deciphering and understanding the often very complicated information available to them, and in prescribing those that are appropriate for a given person. It would be an entirely new approach in some areas of drug use, entirely familiar in others. For instance, one can envision quasi-medical "drug decision specialists" playing the same gatekeeper role for the use of herbal remedies—helping consumers interpret the huge and variable bodies of information that might be relevant in light of their health status, genetic patterns, or social situations.

It also seems possible to imagine specialists whose particular role is to help users of common drugs decide when, how much, and how to avoid too much—an "alcohol-coach," say, something like a personal trainer who assists individuals wishing to use alcohol in deciding how best to do so without damaging themselves or others. For an athlete, part of the role of the drug-decision trainer or coach would be to supply concrete, specific, accurate information about enhancement drugs, explaining the difficult tradeoffs between enhanced performance and long-term health risks. Such a counselor, equipped with genetic testing capability, might help the athlete to understand the dangers if he or she is considering using a particular drug—for instance, whether the individual is one of the 14 percent of the population for whom hyperthermic reactions to Ecstasy are likely, thus risking death, or instead has no such genetic disposition and can use the drug with relatively low risk. After all, in some athletes particular drugs may be fatal, though they would not be a risk for others. And, clearly, these "drug decision support specialists" would also be available to help someone decide whether or not to use cocaine, for example, or statins for lowering cholesterol, beta-blockers to reduce performance anxiety in giving a speech or playing the violin, or solvents to sniff for pleasure. Drug decision specialists might play an extremely important role in preventing overdose. They might stress to a client who had previously been using cocaine but had been clean for some time that renewed use of this drug must not start again at the same dosage level—the client's tolerance will have dropped while he was off the drug, and the same dose in his current state could be fatal.

Within the boundaries of legitimate health care, pharmacists are increasingly assuming such roles as medication monitors and advisers in collaboration with physicians and other clinicians. Drug decision specialists might function something like this, acting as repositories of information about drug use in all conditions, whether clinical, social, religious, competitive, or cosmetic. Among other things, drug decision specialists would need to consider the propriety of hard and fast rules, or rules of thumb, versus individual discretion with regard to prescribing for drug consumption. Some general regulations may be perfectly sensible, such as limitations on age. For instance, it would be unacceptable to most observers for a doctor or drug decision specialist to prescribe marijuana, cocaine, or heroin to a thirteen-year-old based on the assessment that the teenage patient is so precocious physically, psychologically, and emotionally as to justify having access to the drug. There may be, however, other drugs that are sometimes used clinically, sometimes recreationally, that would be appropriate for a particular child—say, Ritalin. Conversely, with the advent of new scientific techniques to detect unique risk factors associated with drug problems, it might be appropriate for a decision maker to deem certain otherwise competent adults ineligible to purchase alcohol, tobacco, cocaine, caffeine, and so on, based on their social, psychological, and genetic predispositions toward drug abuse, dependence, and addiction. It is well known that alcohol does not appear to harm some people even in moderate quantities but carries substantial risks of abuse and physical harm for others, and the same is true for various other drugs. There are obvious risks of social and racial stereotyping under this scenario, but the underlying point is that different individuals may respond differently to the same drug, and a patient-centered, client-oriented professional would be the best and most sensitive party to help individuals recognize this.

Supplying the prospective user with information about the benefits and harms of various kinds of drugs—whether for curing illness, enhancing performance, or pure pleasure—is not all the drug decision specialist would do (as that would already be possible under the autonomist model). He or she would also play a determinative role in controlling the use of drugs by writing, or refusing to write, prescriptions. In this model the drug decision specialist would provide prescriptions not only for medicines to treat illness but also for drugs to enhance function (like Prozac) or provide pleasure (like Viagra). She would also cover the entire range of drugs, including those consumed for religious purposes, sports enhancement, and social and common use, like alcohol, tobacco, and caffeine, as well as drugs currently classified as illegal. The specialist would be committed to minimizing harm to her client and to others affected, but would not be limited to the medical uses of drugs.

As with the autonomist approach, a range of questions would have to be addressed and assorted obstacles overcome under this medical model approach. Although it is often assumed that the highest ethical standards apply to physicians and other health professionals, cases abound of doctors inappropriately prescribing or denying drugs to patients, friends, family members, and even themselves. The issue is further complicated by the economic incentive structures that affect medicine no less than any other profession. As the *New York Times* editorialized in 2006, "New evidence keeps emerging that the medical profession has sold its soul in exchange for what can only be described as bribes from the manufacturers of drugs and medical devices…. It is long past time for leading medical institutions and professional societies to adopt stronger ground rules to control the noxious influence of industry money on what doctors prescribe for their patients."[1]

Other ethical questions might arise with regard to a health professional imposing his or her own personal moral stance, as has been seen in controversies surrounding the refusal of some pharmacists to fill prescriptions for birth control or the so-called morning after pill. Would it be all right for drug decision specialists to deny a patient access to marijuana, for instance, because of their revulsion to "pot heads"? Would it be permissible to force these specialists to do so against their moral beliefs? Moreover, would the medical model be practical for all drugs across the board—for example, would it be plausible public policy to require a drug decision specialist's prescription to purchase a six-pack of beer, a carton of cigarettes, or even a can of coffee? These possibilities may seem silly, and yet such a model could save the lives of those at risk for alcoholism, those who would become chain smokers, or those (admittedly few) at risk for tachycardia or stroke associated with high levels of caffeine, as well as those at risk of overdose with harder, more addictive drugs where tolerance may develop more readily. To be sure, this degree of paternalist surveillance is only possible when the professional in question has extensive knowledge of the user and can predict how he will react and act toward others under the influence of a particular drug.

Perhaps the most important aspect in which the drug decision specialist would play a role not now occupied by reliable professionals is that of the coach for pleasure and enhancement of physical or mental performance, as

---

1. Editorial, "Seducing the Medical Profession," *New York Times*, February 2, 2006, A24.

well as relief of symptoms and avoidance of pain. As shown in chapter 5, current theory, policy, and practice about drugs is often characterized by inconsistent foregrounding and backgrounding of harms and benefits. In some areas, like prescription drugs, herbal drugs, and common-use drugs, benefits tend to be foregrounded and harms minimized or not disclosed; in others, like sports enhancement drugs and illicit drugs, harms are emphasized to the virtually complete exclusion of attention to benefits. The drug decision specialist would regard all drugs, across the board, with equal attention to both harms and benefits, in an effort to help the client achieve the best balance between them, given the client's own individual physiology, genetics, interests, goals, and values. Thus pleasure-seeking might be coupled with health protection, not viewed as at odds, as is now often the case.

It might even be argued that a medical-model drug decision scenario could reduce the social disparities and health costs associated with drug use in different economic groups. Leaving aside the question of how it might be financed and what private or government health services or agencies would provide it, under the drug decision specialist scenario, street people would have access to the same counseling and prescription services as high-status executives. Both the street user and the patient in a pain medicine clinic would have the necessary information and clinical oversight in their use of narcotics, with the goal of improving the quality of life for the person involved and preventing harms that person might cause to others. The enforcement costs and social disparities associated with a vast underground market in some drugs would disappear, as would the health damage and health care costs produced by dangerous substances. Drug decision specialists would attempt to aid their clients by finding whatever drugs might be most suited and least damaging in responding to their pain levels, their health problems, their anxieties, their desire for altered states of awareness, or simply their desire for pleasure—that is, whatever motivates their interest in using drugs. However financed and whether such drug decision services are provided through the government or by other means, it could be far cheaper than the current arrangement.

Yet still there would be concerns. For example, if there were an entire profession dedicated to coaching and gatekeeping marijuana consumption or the use of diet drugs and sleeping medications, there may be reason to worry about the resulting incentives. Would such individuals have a personal interest in their clientele continuing to use drugs regardless of whether it is in the consumers' best interests? How could a reasonable level of professionalism be maintained, and what sorts of training and licensure would need to be instituted? Strong emphasis would have to be placed on notions of professional responsibility and the fiduciary obligation not to harm or take advantage of one's clients. Such inherent conflicts of interest already exist in scenarios in which licensed professionals profit from selling a product, such as optometrists testing patients' eyesight and prescribing corrective lenses when the optometrist owns the business that sells the eyeglasses.

To be sure, there may be limits to the level of paternalism that a society would accept. The notion of drug decision specialists beyond doctors, although intriguing, would raise concerns in addition to those about requisite education, licensing, or professional standards. To some extent, physicians and, increasingly, pharmacists already play this role with respect to prescription drugs, but the drug decision specialist in this thought-experiment would provide assistance and professional control in the use of drugs across the board, whether in medical, social, religious, sports, or recreational contexts.

A Centralized, Super-Regulatory Approach

A third approach to drug issues might involve reconfiguring our piece-meal regulatory entities into a centralized, nationwide agency governing all drugs, across the board. This approach could involve the creation of a single body tasked with evaluating and regulating the entire pharmacopoeia, legal and illegal, across the country, including the formation of policies that overcome the silo mentalities of the various areas of current drug regulation as well as the development of a consistent, coherent rationale for drug regulation across the board. For a start, it might begin by reclassifying drugs that seem wildly out of place in the current regulatory scheme. Given what is now known about their risks, aspirin might be moved to prescription legend, for example, and marijuana might be moved down from Schedule I ("high risk of harm or abuse with no known medical application") to a less restrictive or perhaps a nonrestricted status. Alcohol and nicotine would move onto the scheduled list by virtue of their potential for addiction. Coffee, colas, and "high-energy" high-caffeine drinks might be sold with warning labels, less blunt than those on cigarettes but none-theless important for those susceptible to certain conditions, and warning labels for caffeinated drinks marketed to children might be particularly important. After adequate testing for safety and efficacy, alternative medi-cines would assume appropriate places, some in the restricted schedules, some OTC, some unregulated altogether.

The overall task of this single body would be to develop a comprehen-sive policy for the regulation of all drugs on a logical, scientifically well-supported basis and with clear, unambiguous accounts of such notions as addiction and harm. Under a centralized super-regulatory approach, this single body would presumably be a governmental agency of some sort—perhaps, indeed, an intergovernmental, international agency coor-dinating drug policy throughout the world. Given the impact of drugs around the globe, this super-agency would presumably have the high-est status—a cabinet position within a government's executive branch or perhaps a key position at an international body like the World Health Organization within the United Nations, at least if there were an interna-tional health-related institution with regulatory power. In a U.S. version of a centralized, nationwide bureaucracy, all current federal agencies—the DEA, FDA, ONDCP, TTB, ATF, and many other acronym bureaucracies—and their analogues in the various states might be combined into a unitary organization charged with harmonizing, promulgating, and enforcing all drug laws.

Such a process would in some ways mirror the consolidation under the Department of Homeland Security of various existing agencies, from FEMA to the Coast Guard, all brought together in one centrally coordinated, over-arching agency. With a neutral name such as the Department of Drug Man-agement, this entity would oversee regulation in all areas, from prescription pharmaceuticals and herbal remedies to common-use, religious-use, sports-enhancement, and illegal drugs, regardless of whether they are used in hos-pitals, workplaces, churches, playing fields, or private homes. To accomplish its across-the-board goals, it would also have to include agencies not cur-rently part of the governmental regulatory structure, like the U.S. Anti-Doping Agency (which monitors and regulates performance enhancing drug use in some sports). It might also include officials from religious groups that use drugs, like the Native American Church or the União do Vegetal, and representatives of industries, schools, and workplaces that utilize or restrict drugs. The use of dextroamphetamine to increase alertness and reduce fatigue—whether by long-flight or sleep-deprived fighter pilots, astronauts, or long-haul truck drivers—would fall under a single regulatory roof.

Instead of creating yet another layer of bureaucracy, however, it is possible to imagine a fresh start, where the existing public and private agencies would be scrapped in favor of a new super-agency made from whole cloth. The exact responsibilities entrusted to such an agency would have to be determined, but it would undoubtedly be one of the largest entities in any government, one with enormous influence and power. Such an agency would not necessarily need to impose a uniform policy on drug use; rather, its purpose would be to ensure that any differences in drug regulations are supported by legitimate reasons—neither racist, ideologically skewed, or idiosyncratic rationales, nor reasonless moralizing, but good reasons supported by sound science and coherent social policy.

Such an agency would face substantial challenges. For example, the United States and many other countries are becoming increasingly multicultural. Immigrants and aboriginal peoples often retain aspects of their historical culture, including drug use. Any blanket drug prohibitions developed by a highly centralized super-agency might risk being discriminatory to some. Immigrants from West Africa who practice the Bwiti religion may make claims to be permitted the sacramental use of ibogaine, for example, just as Catholic or Jewish immigrants from Western nations might seek exemption for sacramental wine if they were to relocate in countries that ban alcohol. Ideally, a centralized regulatory schema would protect public health and safety while maximizing individual autonomy, freedom of religious practice, and the pursuit of happiness, even though the challenge of devising a regulatory system that is offensive to none and acceptable to all would be immense on a nationwide level, let alone on an international scale.

The inevitability of change provides an additional challenge for a centralized regulatory approach (though it would be a challenge for the other two models as well). Modern drug discovery, compounding, and synthesizing proceeds at an astonishing rate—witness not only the successes of the pharmaceutical industry but the resourcefulness of the sports-enhancement field in developing undetectable ways to improve performance without violating existing prohibitions. Redesign and marketing of common-use drugs changes the picture for consumers, as for instance in high-caffeine drinks targeted at athletes and children, or energy drinks that contain alcohol. At the blink of an eye, new drugs come into and out of fashion on the club scene. Rapid change in today's drug landscape is simply a function of modern technology that allows innovation to proceed at a much greater rate than ever before. It is likely that even an ideal regulatory apparatus would become inadequate and obsolete as entirely new categories of drugs appear, posing problems that are now scarcely imaginable. The result is a co-evolution of drug use and regulatory demands, with the risk that any large, centralized agency would always be running a good bit behind.

There would be other challenges and disadvantages to a highly centralized super-agency of this sort. These include the usual problems of bureaucracies: internal conflicts and inefficiencies, self-interest in bureaucratic perpetuation, the risk of political hijacking, insensitivity to local values and conditions, and the temptation to impose a uniform conception of the good on the populace. Maybe these drawbacks could be avoided, given that at least some bureaucracies are effective, enlightened, and sensitive contributors to public well-being. Nonetheless, a super-agency of this sort would wield extensive authority. The hope would be that this power would be wielded to promote a more consistent, coherent regulatory scheme for all drugs than currently exists under a welter of incompatible agencies, rather than just exacerbating the bureaucratic problems associated with myriad organizations.

These three approaches—autonomist, medical model, and centralized super-regulatory—are all real-world alternatives that could be adopted by society. To be sure, these three approaches are far from the only possibilities, and each admits of numerous variations. It is not yet possible to conclude that any one of them is the best or even an effective approach, as difficult questions remain for all models, as well as for the current status quo. Such scenarios are nonetheless informative in discovering what might be the losses as well as gains with greater consistency, coherence, and comprehensiveness in drug policy.

It is important to remember that legislation and regulation are not the only means of controlling behavior. Social norms of family, friends, colleagues, and communities, including social opprobrium, can also limit behavior and may well be superior to the sledgehammer response of criminal law enforcement. In fact, it is most likely that a more consistent, coherent, and comprehensive drug scheme will rely upon a host of control mechanisms, with differing levels of regulation for certain categories of drugs and possibly distinct entities making decisions over access, whether they are government agencies, professional societies, treating physicians, religious organizations, or the affected individuals themselves. This might involve an amalgam of the three models presented here—provided that the amalgam is constructed in a consistent, coherent way rather than pieced together from a happenstance background history.

A Plan for Better Drug Theory, Policy, and Practice?

Although we have made no attempt here to provide solutions to all the questions posed in this book, it does not mean that creating a more consistent, coherent, and comprehensive drug policy is simply too difficult, and therefore the best that can be done is tinkering at the edges and correcting only the most extreme inconsistencies. On the contrary, wholesale changes are possible, and indeed necessary for drug policies to become (more) just. This book has argued that a noncompartmentalized, interdisciplinary approach to addressing the inconsistencies in drug policies is essential in meeting this goal. A system riddled with inconsistencies and challenged by incoherence in many of its basic rationales and theoretical commitments is not just one of the "happy incidents of the federal system," in Justice Brandeis's words—that is, the beneficial result of a governmental system that allows individual states to make their own social-policy choices. Instead, it is a behemoth that rests on an insecure foundation, fractured along basic conceptual lines and without adequate justification for many of the apparent injustices it perpetuates.

The Effect of Siloed Hyperspecialization

Among the obstacles to the development of policy that is consistent, coherent, and comprehensive is the continuing trend toward specialization in academia, clinical practice, and research, which encourages academics and professionals to focus on narrow fields and create such complex scholarship that the views of outsiders are not taken seriously. To be sure, high levels of specialization have many advantages in encouraging rigor, careful focus, and high intensity and quality of research. But highly siloed hyperspecialization, born of compartmentalized institutional structures, has its disadvantages too. Many of these are particularly apparent in drug-related contexts.

If there is to be any real progress on issues involving drugs, it is crucial that the various professions and silos within the professions open up their conversations to include those from other fields in a truly interdisciplinary discussion. Each of the professions has something to say about each drug category, but they are often speaking only to themselves, within their own silo—doctors to doctors, lawyers to lawyers, philosophers to philosophers, and so on.

When attorneys and judges talk about the "war on drugs," for instance, one can predict the topics and interchange with some degree of certainty. There might be discussion about whether drug criminalization actually deters potential offenders or simply increases the price of drugs and potential profits in the black market. Maybe the exchange will focus on whether drug offenses harm communities through rampant, open-air drug dealing and gang activity, or whether instead it is the act of criminalizing drugs that indirectly destroys neighborhoods by imprisoning breadwinners and family members and taking away entire generations of young people. Or maybe the conversation will focus on whether drug war enforcement and mass incarceration is "winning" the war, and if not, whether some alternative like drug court might better serve the societal interests at stake. Rarely, however, will lawyer/lawyer or attorney/judge talk include an informed discussion about the meaning of addiction or philosophical reflection about the nature of harm. And when the discussion strays beyond recreational drugs into prescription pharmaceuticals, religious-use drugs, or sports-enhancement drugs, the form of argument simply repeats itself. Whether OxyContin, ayahuasca, or human growth hormone should be part of (or excluded from) the drug war is a question answered by legal responses: What does the federal law say and how should it be interpreted? Are there constitutional issues involved and what is the likely legal outcome? How will this affect law enforcement officials? By opening up the conversation to other professions, not only will the answers be different but—still more important—very different questions will be asked.

When doctors discuss these issues, in contrast, they are far more likely to talk about the pharmacological properties of drugs: what substances affect what bodily functions in what ways, what doses might affect different individuals in different ways, how grave the harms or substantial the benefits might be from one formulation of a drug or one delivery mechanism in contrast to another. Even within a silo or between closely related silos, professionals face gaps in understanding. Not infrequently, pain management professionals accuse chemical dependency practitioners of being unaware of pain management issues, and chemical dependency professionals often consider pain management practitioners naive about substance abuse. And these two disciplines are usually considered to be closely allied—they are both fields with extensive areas of clinical practice and with a commitment to preserving the health and well-being of their patients.

Siloed hyperspecialization within different areas of concern about drugs also cloaks differences of foregrounding and backgrounding between fields. Pain management professionals, for example, typically hold that public policy should serve to facilitate the control of pain in medical contexts like terminal cancer or whole-body pain, while addictionologists and chemical dependency specialists often take a more nihilistic approach to drugs: their primary worry is about the potential for abuse, not the potential for inadequately treated pain—even though it is often the same drugs they are discussing. One sees the benefits of these drugs in the foreground; the other sees the risks of harm. Then, too, clinicians from both camps fail to communicate effectively with investigators, and both commonly lack an appreciation of the perspectives and obligations of policymakers. Even the term "drug" may have different meanings to those in different areas. To lawyers and judges it may connote "illegal substance"; to doctors it typically means "curative agent." Most health professionals tend to interact and communicate primarily with other health professionals, especially those in the same or allied specialties, as do those in law, social sciences, and philosophy.

A further consequence of siloed hyperspecialization is that professionals in each silo are not getting input they need from other disciplines—doctors need help from lawyers, lawyers need help from doctors, and both need help from biomedical and social scientists, sports professionals, and religious practitioners, as well as from advocates, regulators, enforcers, activists, users of drugs of all sorts, and ordinary citizens. This is not to say that there is value merely in having numerous perspectives thrown together before policy decisions are made or that rigorous methodologies should be abandoned. Each discipline must retain its own methodologies when interacting with other disciplines, and perhaps even adopt rigorous methodologies of other disciplines when appropriate, much as political scientists have come to incorporate economic analysis. Communication is a prerequisite, not the cure. But currently there are few or no communication conduits from one sphere to another—somewhat like emergency civilian and military communication systems that differ from, and are incompatible with, each other; or local telephone systems and computer networks that either do not work together or interact only with complex translational systems that fail to convey much that is essential to understanding fully the world at hand.

That is what this project has hoped to do, to change the very way in which drugs and justice are discussed. By talking with other professions about the entire spectrum of drugs, a given discipline certainly will hear new answers to questions that it has pondered for years with the same set of responses, and in the process come to pose new questions that were never part of the stock discourse within their discipline. It is this enhanced, interdisciplinary dialectic that makes the goal of justice in drug law, policy, and practice a real possibility. In coming to appreciate the insights of those who work within other silos than our own, we have gained insights into our own disciplinary myopia and have been forced to recognize that many of the truths that we held are in fact not generalizable outside our own professional circles.

Evidence of Change

While the complexities of intra-silo specialization may make it difficult, if not impossible, for any one person to master every discipline, it remains possible for everyone to collaborate with people working within other disciplines. Indeed, greater inter-silo contact and collaboration may be beginning to happen, with some promising evidence of increased communication and interaction on drug issues. For example, a group called the International Association for Pain and Chemical Dependency has recently formed to further an effective dialogue among professionals over tensions between pain medicine and addictionology, and it is not coincidental that several of the principals in forming this new association are the same professionals from pain medicine and addiction medicine who jointly developed the AAPM/APS/ASAM consensus definition examined at length in chapter 4. The concerns of drug courts, as described in chapter 6, combine law, social work, psychology, and sociology under the tent of the criminal justice system. Some dietary supplement manufacturers are beginning to use pharmaceutical Good Manufacturing Practices to help demonstrate that they are making quality products, and a body of careful research is beginning to develop about some herbal substances, including glucosamine, chondroitin, gingko, and ginseng. The FDA has issued a new advisory concerning dietary supplements and many kinds of alternative medicine, including "energy medicine," "manipulative and body-based practices," and "mind-body medicine."[2] Americans are also beginning to look abroad for research on dietary supplements, especially to Germany.[3] After two decades of FDA experience in reclassifying prescription-legend drugs to over-the-counter availability,[4] there is greater contact between the pharmaceutical and OTC silos. The OTC drug phenylpropanolamine, an oral decongestant, was removed from the market because of toxicity when used incorrectly. Another example, from 2006, is found in the DEA's announcement of its intent to overturn its own two-year-old policy limiting prescribers' authority to write multiple prescriptions for controlled substances for consecutive time periods (this reversal resulted from interaction with the pain medicine community and pain patients).[5] Some federal judges are starting to use scientific criteria—specifically that of pharmacological similarity—to reevaluate the 100-to-1 crack-powder cocaine drug quantity

2. Online at http://www.fda.gov/cber/gdlns/altmed/htm.

3. See e.g. Mark Blumenthal, senior ed., *The Complete German Commission E Monographs: Therapeutic Guide to Herbal Medicines* (Tr., from the Bundesinstitut fur Arzneimittel und Medizinprodukte, Germany) (Austin, Tex., American Botanical Council, 1998). This system was developed by a German expert committee, the Commission E, established in 1978, to evaluate the safety and efficacy of herbal medicines.

4. Marian Segal, "Rx to OTC: The Switch is On," online at http://www.fda.gov/bbs/topics/CONSUMER/CN00012c.html.

5. Drug Enforcement Administration, Department of Justice, Notices, "Dispensing Controlled Substances for the Treatment of Pain," See Federal Register 71 (September 6, 2006): 52716–52723] From the Federal Register Online via GPO Access [wais.access.gpo.gov], [FR Doc E6–14517].

discrepancy in sentencing, and by 2007 Congress was considering several bills that would alter or equalize this ratio.[6] Caffeine may be viewed as an abusable drug, not merely a social beverage.[7] Harm reduction projects have expanded from alcohol to drug use, making a point of including not just professionals concerned with illegal drugs, but patient advocates, social activists, and users themselves. Attempts to develop evidence-based policy for illicit drugs have much in common with the assessment of pharmacologically active substances in other spheres, particularly prescription drugs. Particularly significant, a group of British researchers has developed a "rational scale" to assess the harm of drugs of potential misuse: heroin, cocaine, barbiturates, street methadone, alcohol, ketamine, benzodiazepines, amphetamine, tobacco, buprenorphine, cannabis, solvents, 4-MTA, LSD, methylphenidate, anabolic steroids, GHB, Ecstasy, alkyl nitrites, and khat.[8] Their method involved using a nine-category matrix of harm with an expert Delphic procedure, and while this is still subject to some of the silo effect—different experts in different areas—it nevertheless represents a substantial effort to employ uniform methods to scrutinize both legal and illegal drugs. These researchers found that their assessments of harm—the drugs above are listed in descending order of harmfulness as judged according to this matrix—differed considerably from those embodied in current regulatory systems in the U.K. and elsewhere. While this is just a first step in the development of a consistent, coherent, comprehensive view of drugs and their consequences in physical dependency and social harm, it is at least a beginning. There are a number of other examples of cross-silo contact, and more developing all the time. Indeed, these matters are in very rapid evolution.

6. See, e.g., United States v. Hamilton, 428 F.Supp.2d 1253, 1257 (M.D. Fla. 2006). Bills introduced in the 100th Congress, 2007 (e.g. Drug Sentencing Reform Act, S. 1383; Fairness in Drug Sentencing Act, S. 1685; Drug Sentencing Reform and Cocaine Kingpin Trafficking Act, S. 1711) take different approaches to reducing the 100-1 disparity: some lower the punishment for crack, others increase it for powder cocaine.

7. "Young Americans Abusing Caffeine," NewsMax.com Wires, Tuesday October 17, 2006, reporting on the presentation of Danielle McCarthy at the 2006 meetings of the American College of Emergency physicians.

8. David Nutt, Leslie A. King, William Saulsbury, and Colin Blakemore, "Development of a rational scale to assess the harm of drugs of potential misuse," *Lancet* 369 (March 24, 2007): 1047–53.

The Risks of Mishap: Plans without Adequate Bases

While this project has recognized that the lack of consistent, coherent, comprehensive thinking about drugs is at the root of the problem and that very rapid evolution toward greater inter-silo contact is evident, it does not yet advocate the development of a specific plan to correct these difficulties. In particular, though the three strategies outlined above— the autonomist policy, the "drug decision specialist" medical model, or the super-regulatory approach—are informative models, it would be premature to promote wholesale adoption of any of them. This is not because they are wrong, but there is not yet adequate evidence for thinking any of them would be the best choice. Rather, what we must recognize is that across-the-board consistency and coherence is crucial in avoiding mishaps in policy development, and there is far too much work to be done before any single, global plan could succeed without risking making things worse. In particular, when one silo draws on the work of another without understanding it fully, there is a considerable risk of backward motion: misguided policies, bad law, poor medical treatments, escalation of the arms race in sports enhancement, curtailing of religious practice, policies imposed in one area that have counterproductive implications for another. In fact, the most immediate benefit of interdisciplinary communication would likely be the elimination of these backward steps.

It is certainly important to avoid policy based only on anecdote and discipline-limited thinking, as well as policy that interferes with professional practice in many areas. It is also important to avoid specific liabilities, like the primitive thinking about drugs discussed in chapter 2. But inadequate attention to the real issues in drugs and the risk of mishap in policy construction is not always due to disciplinary self-interest or specialty-related greed. It is because some silos do not—and often *cannot*—understand what the concerns of others are. For example, one siloed area of drug concern may wish to promulgate policies designed to reduce addiction, while another might be willing to tolerate dependence (which it does not call addiction!) if other advantages are gained, like analgesia or enhanced sociability. This conflict is played out in the previously seen tensions among pain medicine, alcohol studies, and addictionology.

There are many other such concerns. The legal conception of addiction, for example, is starting to conflict with understandings of choice, voluntariness, and responsibility informed by recent science. But it is not clear in which way this will cut. Is an individual more (or less) responsible for his behavior when he is aware of a genetic susceptibility to a specific drug but he takes it anyway? This has major implications for concerns about common-use drugs, for example, and for some sports-enhancement and illegal drugs.

Fundamental conceptual issues are at the core of many practical dilemmas. Take something as simple as the often-invoked "level playing field," which is used as shorthand for some conception of fairness. In the area of sports drugs, is the level playing field better achieved by banning certain substances or by providing those substances to all? For prescription drugs, do appeals to a level playing field play a similar role? Perhaps not. While increasing the availability of generic prescription drugs seems to level the playing field, it does not seem plausible to restrict those who are well-insured or who can afford the drugs just because others cannot. Are athletes from poor countries who cannot afford the latest steroid drugs akin to elderly citizens who cannot afford the latest prescription drug? And in the area of illicit drugs, is the playing field level because every citizen is equally prohibited from smoking marijuana, or is it skewed because those who need drugs other than marijuana for their medical conditions have legal access while those who could benefit from marijuana are banned from using it? These are difficult questions that do not have obvious answers, but in the search for answers each area needs to examine such similarities. Not only will this help identify when interdisciplinary discussion is likely to be fruitful, but also, and perhaps more important, it may suggest when drawing upon the work of another discipline will only add to the confusion. Whichever is true, interdisciplinary discussion is a necessity.

Drugs and Justice

This project has been looking for an account that would speak to the issue of drugs and *justice*—that is, how to think about issues of drug theory, drug policy, and drug practice in a consistent, coherent, comprehensive way across the board. A contemporary political philosopher, David Schmidtz, has also been seeking an account of justice in a general conceptual sense, not directed to the context of drugs. But it will help here as well, illustrating why the interdisciplinary approach taken here is the way forward.

Schmidtz says that justice is less like a building—the product of a single plan—and more like a neighborhood, not planned in every detail but nonetheless an environment that works, a constellation of related elements that function together. "A good neighborhood is functional, a place where people can live well," he says. "Yet good neighborhoods are not *designed* in the comprehensive way that good buildings are." Neighborhoods can't really be designed, he adds, pointing out that, like movie sets, designed communities "feel fake," as if designed by a single individual.[9]

At the moment, drug theory, policy, and practice are not like either a building or a neighborhood, or even a fake, designed community. A single coherent, consistent, comprehensive view has not yet emerged. There is no unitary "building" here—clearly nothing designed in a unified way across the board. That lack of comprehensive design is obviously responsible for some of the inconsistency and tension uncovered here, though it is not even clear whether comprehensive "design" would itself be desirable. But drug theory, policy, and practice at this point in our history are not even like a neighborhood, a place with related elements that function together. At best, it is more like a series of gated communities, each enclosed within its own bounds, with its own guardhouse, sales office, and security service. Or rather, to stretch Schmidtz's metaphor even further, it is still more like an industrial area, with huge enterprises walled in their own buildings, using their own smokestacks and vehicle fleets, separated off from each other by chain-link fences, punctuated by stretches of asphalt and broken glass. It is indeed more like an industrial wasteland where competing industries do not interact with each other much at all. In this bleak theoretical and practical landscape, we—society as a whole, all of us—can hardly "live well," as a real neighborhood would allow.

It is this condition that needs to be repaired, so that we can move out of a landscape of independent, competitive industries operating in isolation to a more human and "neighborly" model of drug concern. So what would a "neighborhood" model of drug theory, policy, and practice look like? In a neighborhood, people lean over their fences and talk to each

9. David Schmidtz, *Elements of Justice* (Cambridge: Cambridge University Press, 2006), 3.

other; they sit in the same bars or outdoor cafés and tend their children in the same playgrounds; they go to community meetings and work out their problems together. In a really good neighborhood, people respect each other and social interaction transcends race, class, background, occupation, and so on. This need not be a "planned" community—it needs, rather, to be a community that works together.

So what would a neighborhood model of drug theory, policy, and practice look like? Certainly not the bleak landscape of an industrial zone. Rather, those in one sphere of drug concern—prescription pharmaceuticals, for instance—would lean over the fence to talk with professionals, enforcers, and users in illegal drugs, while the dietary supplement industry would talk seriously with, among others, professionals, enforcers, and users in sports enhancement, as well with the "self-use" spheres of OTC drugs, common-use drugs, religious-use drugs, and illegal drugs. Indeed, every sphere would talk with every other. That is a lot of talk, but it needs to be done. Just with the simple schema of seven different spheres or silos described here—prescription pharmaceuticals, over-the-counter medicines, herbal drugs or dietary supplements, common-use drugs, religious-use drugs, sports-enhancement drugs, and illegal drugs—that is nearly fifty conversations, if each talks to each other, not to mention the three-way (and four-way and seven-way) conversations that desperately need to begin. Here is a starter list, personified as neighbors might be, of the interchange that needs to occur:

- Prescription Pharmaceuticals need to talk with Illegal Drugs (and also with Dietary Supplements, Common-Use Drugs, and OTC Drugs) about *self-medication.*

- Religious-Use Drugs need to talk with Prescription Pharmaceuticals, especially in its psychotherapeutic guise, and with Illegal Drugs about *mind-altering drugs,* both those that produce heightened aesthetic experience and those that alter mood.

- Sports-Enhancement and Illegal Drugs need to talk with Common-Use Drugs, especially Alcohol, to talk about *suppression, interdiction, and prohibition.*

- A conversation needs to develop among Sports Drugs, Illegal Drugs, Prescription Pharmaceuticals, and Dietary Supplements—a real conversation, not just a set of mutual posturings—about *enhancement.*

- Every silo needs to talk with every other silo about *relieving pain* and about *pursuing pleasure*, perhaps the two most basic issues in drugs.

This is just a starter list. And what is needed is not just talk, but for neighbors to socialize together, watch their children together, go to community meetings together, and work out their common problems.

Change in the direction of greater justice in drug policy will not be easy. There are many theoretical and practical obstacles to overcome. Among them, it might be argued that across-the-board changes would be too disruptive as a matter of practical reality, or too politically divisive. It might also be argued that although current policy is unjust in the sense of violating the Aristotelian principle that like cases should be treated alike, the weight of history should nonetheless be recognized and the normative force of long-standing policies respected, even if they have come into effect by differing historical routes. It could also be argued that because compromise is essential in a pluralistic society, taking place between sometimes fundamentally different values and views of the world, it will often lead (perhaps always) to inconsistent policies in an effort to accommodate the incompatible concerns of opposing parties. While objections like these must be addressed, they typically provide insufficient basis for simply accepting the status quo. Instead, a real discussion of reasons for policy should begin—*across the board*. This is not to advocate a plan, but this is to advocate for change, perhaps even thoroughgoing in nature. It is not to suggest that all buildings in a neighborhood be designed by a single architect or that particular structures should be built, but it is an appreciation that some ungainly structures must come down and something better should be put in their place. For now, it is more important to recognize how to proceed—afresh, anew, across the board, as if in a neighborhood dedicated to resolving common issues—than what policy conclusions should be drawn. And although siloed hyperspecialization is a large part of the problem, it is also true that this project aims to enrich disciplinary specialization, not destroy it, by considering just what the lessons of a fully comprehensive view of drugs might be for each of the fields involved.

Let's end this exploration into the roots of our troubles with drugs with a call to action or, rather, a set of demands. Think of them as nonnegotiable—these are things a society *must* have if it is to extricate itself from the current untenable situation. It looks like a simple list, but in practice it will be extraordinarily challenging:

- We must make significant changes, not merely cosmetic prunings, in the way we treat drugs—all drugs. *This means scrapping many of the laws now on the books and starting over.*
- We must overcome siloed hyperspecialization when thinking about drug issues. *This means requiring that for all government bodies, expert panels, commissions, conferences, authorship groups, et cetera, professionals from each of the silos of drug concern should be involved—especially when there is talk about such matters as those listed above (e.g., self-medication, mind-altering drugs, suppression of drug use, enhancement, or pain and pleasure).*
- We must avoid *starting* the process of change with a "plan"; rather, changes must arise from much more extensive, reflective interchange about drugs and drug use of all sorts, from prescription pharmaceuticals to illegal drugs. *This means, among other things, resisting politically motivated enforcement and reform measures that have not been thought through with concern for their impact in all areas of drug concern—across the board.*

Good luck to us all. The world of concern about drugs has become so distorted that it will require heroic efforts by professionals in every area, policymakers, enforcers, theorists, activists, and users and consumers of drugs—as, it is essential to remember, virtually all of us are, whether in treating our illnesses, enhancing our health, pursuing pleasure or sociability, participating in religious rituals, pursuing heightened performance in sports, or courting fantasy, pleasure, or death on the streets. This book is intended as catalyst for opening dialogue and deeper, more informed and reflective thought in the pursuit of a comprehensive view of drugs and justice.

BIBLIOGRAPHY

Addiction Treatment Forum. "Frequently Asked Questions and Answers." http://www.atforum.com/SiteRoot/pages/faqs/faqs-November2004-FINAL.pdf

Ainslie, George. *Breakdown of Will*. New York: Cambridge University Press, 2001.

American Academy of Pain Medicine, American Pain Society, and American Society of Addiction Medicine (APAM/APS/ASAM), "Definitions Related to the Use of Opioids for the Treatment of Pain," *Wisconsin Medical Journal* 100(5)(2001): 28–29.

American Medical Association, *Pain Management* series, Chicago: American Medical Association, 2003, online at http://www.ama-cmeonline.com/.

American Society for Addiction Medicine (ASAM), *Principles of Addiction Medicine*, 3rd edition, Allan W. Graham et al., eds., Chevy Chase, Md.: ASAM, 2003.

Bahrke, Michael S., and Charles Yesalis. *Performance-Enhancing Substances in Sport and Exercise*. Champaign, Ill.: Human Kinetics, 2002.

Bailes, Julian, and John McCloskey. *When Winning Costs Too Much*. Lanham, Md.: Taylor, 2005.

Bass, I. S., and A. L. Young. *Dietary Supplement Health and Education Act: A Legislative History and Analysis*. Washington, D.C.: The Food and Drug Law Institute, 1996.

Battin, Margaret P., and Arthur J. Lipman, eds., *Drug Use in Assisted Suicide and Euthanasia*. Binghamton, N.Y.: Pharmaceutical Products Press, Haworth Press, 1996.

Batz, F., P. J. Gregory, K. Hitchens, and J. M. Jellin, et al. *Pharmacist's Letter/Prescriber's Letter Natural Medicines Comprehensive Database*, 6th ed. Stockton, Calif.: Therapeutic Research Faculty: 2004.

Benowitz, Neal L, Peyton Jacob III, Haim Mayan, and Charles Denaro, "Sympathomimetic Effects of Paraxanthine and Caffeine in Humans," *Clinical Pharmacology and Therapeutics* 58(1995): 684–91.

Bhattacharya, B. K., B. Mukerji, and A. Saxena "Behavioural Studies in Fish with Mescaline, LSD, and Thiopropazate and their Interactions with Serotonin and Dopa Archives." *Internationales de Pharmacodynamie et de Therapie* 140 (1962): 327–35.

Blumenthal, Mark, senior ed., *The Complete German Commission E Monographs: Therapeutic Guide to Herbal Medicines* (Tr., from the Bundesinstitut fur Arzneimittel und Medizinprodukte, Germany) (Austin, Tex., American Botanical Council, 1998).

Boaz, David. "A Drug-Free America—or a Free America?" U.C. Davis Law Review (24)(1991): 617.

Bonilha, Leonardo, and Li M. Li, "Heavy Coffee Drinking and Epilepsy," *Seizure* 13(4)(June2004): 284–85.

Booher, Troy L. "Finding Religion for the First Amendment." *John Marshall Law Review* 38 (2004): 473–83.

———. "Scrutinizing Commercial Speech." *George Mason University Civil Rights Law Journal* 15(1)(2004): 74–79.

Booth, Martin. *Opium: A History*. New York: St. Martin's Press, 1996.

Brandt, Allan M. *The Cigarette Century. The Rise, Fall, and Deadly Persistence of the Product That Defined America*. New York: Basic Books, 2007.

Brecher, Edward M., and the Editors of Consumer Reports, *Licit and Illicit Drugs*. Boston: Little, Brown & Co., 1972.

Brendler, T., J. Gruenwald, and C. Jaenicke, eds. *PDR for Herbal Medicines,* 3rd ed. Montvale, N.J.: Thompson PDR, 2004.

Byck, Robert, ed., *Sigmund Freud: Cocaine Papers* [*Über Coca*, 1884] New York: New American Library, 1974.

Camporesi, Piero. *Bread of Dreams*. Chicago: University of Chicago Press, 1989.

CASA. Controlled Prescription Drug Abuse at Epidemic Level. CASA Report, July 7, 2005.

Chessick, R. D., Jean Kronholm, Mortimer Beck, George Maier, "Effect of Pretreatment with Tryptamine, Tryptophan and DOPA on LSD Reaction in Tropical Fish," *Psychopharmacology* 5 (5)(1964): 390–92.

Cohen, Peter J. *Drugs, Addiction, and the Law: Policy, Politics, and Public Health*. Durham, N.C.: Carolina Academic Press, 2004.

———. "Science, Politics, and the Regulation of Dietary Supplements—It's Time to Repeal DSHEA." *American Journal of Law and Medicine* 31 (2005): 175.

Cornelis, Marilyn C., Ahmed El-Sohemy, Edmond K. Kabagambe, Hannia Campos, "Coffee, CYP1A2 Genotype, and Risk of Myocardial Infarction," *Journal of the American Medical Association* 295(2006): 1135–41.

Courtwright, David T. *Dark Paradise: Opiate Addiction in America before 1940*. Cambridge, Mass.: Harvard University Press, 1982.

———. *Forces of Habit: Drugs and the Making of the Modern World*. Cambridge, Mass.: Harvard University Press, 2001.

Crellin, J., and F. Ania. *Professionalism and Ethics in Complementary and Alternative Medicine*. Binghamton, N.Y.: Haworth Press, 2002.

Davenport-Hines, Richard. *The Pursuit of Oblivion: A Global History of Narcotics.* New York: W. W. Norton, 2002.

DiFranza, J. R., and R. A. Lew, "Effects of Maternal Cigarette Smoking on Pregnancy Complications and Sudden Infant Death Syndrome," *Journal of Family Practice* 40)4)(Apr 1995): 385–94.

Drug Enforcement Administration, U.S. Department of Justice/Last Acts Partnership, and Pain & Policies Study Group, University of Wisconsin Medical School. "Prescription Pain Medications: Frequently Asked Questions and Answers for Health Care Professionals, and Law Enforcement Personnel." *Journal of Pain & Palliative Care Pharmacotherapy* 19(1)(2005): 71–104.

Drug Enforcement Administration, U. S. Department of Justice. Notices, "Dispensing Controlled Substances for the Treatment of Pain," See Federal Register 71 (September 6, 2006): 52716–52723] From the Federal Register Online via GPO Access [wais.access.gpo.gov], [FR Doc E6–14517].

Drug Enforcement Administration, Office of Diversion Control, U. S. Department of Justice. Controlled Substances Act Manuals: *Chemical Handler's Manual—A Guide to Chemical Control Regulations* (January 2004): includes *Pharmacist's Manual* (April 2004); *Practitioner's Manual* (August 2006). *Mid-Level Practitioner's Manual*: includes *Narcotic Treatment Programs* (April 2000); *Security Outline of the Controlled Substances Act of 1970.* All online at DEA publications: manuals, http://www.deadiversion.usdoj.gov/pubs/manuals/).

Duke, J. A. *CRC Handbook of Medicinal Herbs.* Boca Raton, Fla.: CRC Press, 1985.

Duke, Steven B., and Albert C. Gross. *America's Longest War: Rethinking Our Tragic Crusade Against Drugs.* New York: Tarcher, 1994.

Duster, Troy. *The Legislation of Morality: Law, Drugs, and Moral Judgment.* New York: The Free Press, 1970.

Ebadi, M. *Pharmacodynamic Basis of Herbal Medicine.* Boca Raton, Fla.: CRC Press, 2002.

Elster, Jon, and Ole-Jørgen Skog, eds., *Getting Hooked: Rationality and Addiction* Cambridge: Cambridge University Press, 1999.

Facts and Comparisons. Guide to Popular Natural Products. 3rd ed. St. Louis: Facts and Comparisons Publishing, 2003.

Feinberg, Joel. *Harm to Others* and *Harm to Self: The Moral Limits of the Criminal Law,* vols. 1, 3. New York and Oxford: Oxford University Press, 1984, 1986.

Fingarette, Herbert. "Addiction and Criminal Responsibility." *Yale Law Journal* 84 (1975): 413–34.

———. *Heavy Drinking: The Myth of Alcoholism as a Disease.* Berkeley: University of California Press, 1989.

———. "The Perils of Powell: In Search of a Factual Foundation for the 'Disease Concept of Alcoholism.'" *Harvard Law Review* 83(4)(1970): 793–812.

Finn, Peter, and Andrea K. Newlyn, "Miami's 'Drug Court': A Different Approach," Program Focus. U.S. Department of Justice, National Institute of Justice, 1993.

Fish, Jefferson M. *How to Legalize Drugs.* San Francisco: Jason Aronson, 1998.

Fishbain, David A. "Chronic Opioid Treatment, Addiction and Pseudo-Addiction in Patients with Chronic Pain," *Psychiatric Times* 20(2) (February 2003).

Fishbain, David A., et al. "Can Patients Taking Opioids Drive Safely? A Structured Evidence-Based Review." *Journal of Pain & Palliative Care Pharmacotherapy* 16, no. 1 (2002).

Fontanarosa, Phil B., Drummond Rennie, and Catherine D. DeAngelis, "The Need for Regulation of Dietary Supplements—Lessons from Ephedra," *Journal of the American Medical Association* 289(2003): 1568–70.

Foster, S., and V. E. Tyler. *Tyler's Honest Herbal.* Binghamton, N.Y.: Haworth Press, 1999.

Gahlinger, Paul M. "The Addiction of Cows." In *Cows: A Rumination,* ed. C. Hileman. Cincinnati: Emmis Books, 2004.

———. "Club Drugs: MDMA, Gamma-Hydroxybutyrate (GHB), Rohypnol, and Ketamine." *American Family Physician* 69 (2004): 2619–27.

———. "Gastrointestinal Illness and Cannabis Use in a Rural Canadian Community." *Journal of Psychoactive Drugs* 16 (1984): 263–65.

———. *Illegal Drugs: A Complete Guide to Their History, Chemistry, Use and Abuse.* New York: Penguin (Plume), 2004.

———. "The Power of Herbs." *Western Journal of Medicine* 170 (1999): 255–56.

Gibbs, Landon S., and David J. Haddox. "Lawful Prescribing and the Prevention of Diversion." *Journal of Pain & Palliative Care Pharmacotherapy* 17(1)(2003).

Gilroy, C. M., J.F. Steiner, T. Byers, H. Shapiro, W. Georgian, "Echinacea and Truth in Labeling," *Archives of Internal Medicine* 163(6)(2003): 699–704.

Goldstein, Avram. *Addiction: From Biology to Drug Policy.* 2nd ed. New York: Oxford University Press, 2001.

Goodman Aviel. "Addiction: Definition and Implications." *British Journal of Addiction* 85 (1990): 1403–08.

Graham, Allan W., Michael Mayo-Smith, Terry K. Schultz, Richard K. Ries, and Bonnie B. Wilford, eds. *Principles of Addiction Medicine.* 3rd ed. Chevy Chase, Md.: American Society of Addiction Medicine, 2003.

Grahmann, Paula H., Kenneth C. Jackson II, and Arthur G. Lipman. "Clinician Beliefs About Opioid Use and Barriers in Chronic Nonmalignant Pain." *Journal of Pain & Palliative Care Pharmacotherapy* 18(2)(2004).

Grant, S., et al. "Activation of Memory Circuits During Cue-Elicited Cocaine Craving." *Proceedings of the National Academy of Sciences* 93(1996): 120–40.

Gusfield, Joseph R. *Symbolic Crusade: Status Politics and the American Temperance Movement.* 2nd ed. Chicago: University of Illinois Press, 1986.

Hansel R., V. Schulz, and V. E. Tyler. *Rational Phototherapy. A Physicians' Guide to Herbal Medicine*. New York: Springer-Verlag, 1998.

Hanson, Glen, and Peter Venturelli. *Drugs and Society*. 6th ed. Sudbury, Mass.: Jones & Bartlett, 2001.

Hare, B. D., and A. G. Lipman. "Medication Use and Misuse in Chronic Pain Management." *Problems in Anesthesia* 4(4)(1990): 561–689.

Harner, Michael J., ed., *Hallucinogens and Shamanism*. New York: Oxford University Press, 1973.

Hasim, Deborah, Efrat Aharonovich, Xinhua Liu, Ziona Mamman, Karen Matseoane, Lucinda G. Carr, Ting-Kai Li, "Alchohol Dependence Symptoms and Alcohol Dehydrogenase 2 Polymorphism: Israeli Ashkenazis, Sephardics, and Recent Russian Immigrants," *Alchoholism: Clinical and Experimental Research* 26(9)(2002).

Heit, Howard A. "Addiction, Physical Dependence, and Tolerance: Precise Definitions to Help Clinicians Evaluate and Treat Chronic Pain Patients." *Journal of Pain & Palliative Care Pharmacotherapy* 17(1)(2003): 15–29.

Hendler, S. S., and D. Rorvik, eds. *PDR for Nutritional Supplements*. Montvale, N.J.: Medical Economics Co., 2001.

HerbalGram. American Botanical Council, http://www.herbalgram.org/herbalgram.

Hora, Peggy Fulton, William G. Schma, and John T. A. Rosenthal, "Therapeutic Jurisprudence and the Drug Treatment Court Movement: Revolutionizing the Criminal Justice System's Response to Drug Abuse and Crime in America," *Notre Dame Law Review* 74 (1999): 439–537.

House of Commons, Culture, Media and Sport Committee, "Drugs and Role Models in Sport: Making and Setting Examples," Seventh Report of Session 2003–04, Vol. 1. London: The Stationery Office, 2004.

Husak, Douglas N. *Drugs and Rights*. New York: Cambridge University Press, 1992.

———. *Legalize This! The Case for Decriminalizing Drugs*. London and New York: Verso, 2002.

Inciardi, J. A., and K. McElrath. *The American Drug Scene: An Anthology*. Boston: Roxbury, 2004.

International Narcotics Control Board, Annual Report, "Abuse of Prescription Drugs to Surpass Illicit Drug Abuse, Says INCB," press release No. 4, March 1, 2006, online at http://www.incb.org/pdf/e/press/2007/annual-report-press-kit-2006-en-4.pdf.

Jacobs, Lori R. "Prescription to Over-the-Counter Drug Reclassification." *American Family Physician* 57(9) (May 1, 1998): 2209–14.

Jaffe, Jerome H. "Drug Addiction and Drug Abuse." In Louis S. Goodman and Alfred Gilman, eds., *The Pharmacological Basis of Therapeutics*, 6th ed. New York: Macmillan, 1980.

Jellinek, E. M. *The Disease Concept of Alcoholism*. New Haven, Conn.: College and Universities Press, 1960, 1962.

Joranson, David E., and Russell K. Portenoy. "Pain Medicine and Drug Law Enforcement: An Important Step Toward Balance." *Journal of Pain & Palliative Care Pharmacotherapy* 19(1)(2005).

Kalivas, Peter W., and Nora D. Volkow. "The Neural Basis of Addiction: A Pathology of Motivation and Choice." *American Journal of Psychiatry* 162 (2005): 1403–13.

Kaplan, John. *The Hardest Drug: Heroin and Public Policy*. Chicago: University of Chicago Press, 1983.

Kessler, Ronald C., S. Aguilar-Gaxiola, L. Andrade, R. Bijl, G. Borges, J.J. Caraveo-Anduaga, D.J. DeWit, B. Kolody, K.R. Merikangas, B.E. Molnar, W.A. Vega, E.E. Walters, H-U. Wittchen, "Cross-National Comparisons of Co-morbidities Between Substance Use Disorders and Mental Disorders," In *Handbook of Drug Abuse Prevention: Theory, Science, and Practice*. Z. Sloboda, W. Bukoski,., eds. (New York: Kluwer Academic/Plenum Publishers, 2003), pp. 447–72.

Klatsky, Arthur L., Cynthia Morton, Natalia Udaltsova, and Gary D. Friedman, "Coffee, Cirrhosis, and Transaminase Enzymes," *Archives of Internal Medicine* 166(2006): 1190–95.

Kumpfer, Karol L., "Special Populations: Etiology and Prevention of Vulnerability to Chemical Dependency in Children of Substance Abusers," in *Youth at High Risk for Substance Abuse*, B.S. Brown, A.R. Mills, eds. Rockville, Md.: National Institute on Drug Abuse, 1987, pp. 1–71.

Kyriacou, Demetrios N., et al., "Risk Factors for Injury to Women from Domestic Violence," *New England Journal of Medicine* 341 (1999).

Lai, Melisa W., Wendy Klein-Schwartz, George C. Rodgers, Joseph Y. Abrams, Deborah A. Haber, Alvin C. Bronstein, and Kathleen M. Wruk, "2005 Annual Report of the American Association of Poison Control Centers' National Poisoning and Exposure Database," *Clinical Toxicology* 44(2006): 803–932.

Lenskyj, Helen J. *Inside the Olympic Industry*. Albany: State University of New York Press, 2000.

Leshner, Alan I. "The Essence of Drug Addiction." Washington D.C.: The National Institute on Drug Abuse, 1997, online at http://www.nida.nih.gov/published_articles/essence.html.

———. "Science-Based Views of Drug Addiction and Its Treatment." *Journal of the American Medical Association* 282 (1999): 1314–16.

———. "Understanding Drug Addiction: Insights from the Research." In *Principles of Addiction Medicine*, Allan W. Graham et al., eds. Chevy Chase, Md.: American Society of Addiction Medicine, 2003, pp. 47–56.

Lipman, Arthur G. "Does the DEA Truly Seek Balance in Pain Medicine? A Chronology of Confusion that Impedes Good Patient Care." *Journal of Pain & Palliative Care Pharmacotherapy* 19(1)(2005): 3–5.

——. "The Federal Ban on Ephedrine Dietary Supplements: An Important Event for Pain Practitioners and Patients." *Journal of Pain & Palliative Care Pharmacotherapy* 18(3)(2004).

——. "What Have We Learned from OxyContin?" *Journal of Pain & Palliative Care Pharmacotherapy* 17(1)(2003): 1–4.

London, Edythe D., et al. "Morphine-Induced Metabolic Changes in Human Brain. Studies with Positron Emission Tomography and [Fla.uorine 18]-Fla.uorodeoxy-glucose." *Archives of General Psychiatry* 73(47)(1990).

Luna, Erik. "Drug Exceptionalism." *Villanova Law Review* 47 (2002): 753.

——. "The Prohibition Apocalypse." *DePaul Law Review* 46 (1997): 483.

——. "The Story of Robinson v. California." In *Criminal Law Stories: A New History of Ten Leading Criminal Law Cases,*" Robert Weisberg, ed. New York: Foundation Press, forthcoming.

——. "War on Drugs." In *Encyclopedia of American Civil Liberties,* ed. Paul Finkelman. New York: Routledge Press, 2006.

——. "'What Is Legal Is Not Necessarily Ethical': The Limits of Law and Drug Testing Programs." *American Journal of Bioethics* 4, no. 41 (2004).

MacCoun, Robert J., and Peter Reuter. *Drug War Heresies: Learning from Other Vices, Times, and Places.* Cambridge: Cambridge University Press, 2001.

Manno, Martin S., "Preventing Adverse Drug Events," *Nursing* 36(3)(March 2006): 56–61.

Marlowe, Douglas B., David S. DeMatteo, David S. Festinger, "A Sober Assessment of Drug Courts," 16(2) *Federal Sentencing Reporter* 153 (2003).

Medina, Jose, and Seymour J. Diamond. "Drug Dependency in Patients with Chronic Headache." *Headache* 17(1)(1977): 12–14.

Meyer, Erin L., Louise C. Gahring, Scott W. Rogers,. "Nicotine Preconditioning Antagonizes Activity-dependent Caspace Proteolysis of a Glutamate Receptor," *Journal of Biological Chemistry* 277 (2002): 10869–75.

McGinnis, J. Michael, and William H. Foege, "Actual Causes of Death in the United States," *Journal of the American Medical Association* 270(18) (1993): 2207–12.

Mill, John Stuart. *On Liberty* [1859]. Indianapolis: Hackett, 1981.

Morbidity and Mortality Weekly Report, online at http://www.cdc.gov/mmwr/preview/mmwrhtml/mm5605a1.

Morgan, Wayne H. *Drugs in America: A Social History, 1800–1980.* Syracuse: Syracuse University Press, 1981.

Morgan, J. P. "American Opiophobia: Customary Underutilization of Opioid Analgesics," *Advances in Alcohol and Substance Abuse* 5(1-2)(1985):163–73.

Murphy, Patricia A., Steven E. Kern, Frank Z. Stanczyk, Carolyn L. Westhoff, "Interaction of St. John's Wort with Oral Contraceptives: Effects on the Pharmacokinetics of Norethindrone and Ethinyl Estradiol, Ovarian Activity and Breakthrough Bleeding", *Contraception* 71 (2005): 402–8.

Musto, David F. *The American Disease: Origins of Narcotic Control*, 3rd ed. New Haven, Conn.: Yale University Press 1973; New York: Oxford University Press, 1987, 1999.

———, ed. *Drugs in America: A Historical Reader*. New York: New York University Press, 2002.

———. *One Hundred Years of Heroin*. New York: Auburn House, 2002.

———. "Opium, Cocaine and Marijuana in American History," *Scientific American* 265 (1991).

National Institute on Drug Abuse, *InfoFacts: Cigarettes and Other Nicotine Products*, online at http://www.drugabuse.gov/Infofacts/Tobacco.html.

Null, Gary, Carolyn Dean, Martin Feldman, Debora Rasio, and Dorothy Smith, *Death by Medicine, Life Extension* (March 2004); online at http://www.lef.org/magazine/mag2004/mar2004_awsi_death_02.htm.

Nunes, Edward V., Maria A. Sullivan, Frances R. Levin, "Treatment of Depression in Patients with Opiate Dependence," *Biological Psychiatry* 56 (10)(2004): 793–802.

Nutt, D. J. "Addiction: Brain Mechanisms and Their Treatment Implications." *Lancet* 347 (1996): 31, 32.

Nutt, David, Leslie A. King, William Saulsbury, and Colin Blakemore, "Development of a Rational Scale to Assess the Harm of Drugs of Potential Misuse," *Lancet* 369 (March 24, 2007): 1047–53.

Oddie, Graham. "Addiction and the Value of Freedom," *Bioethics* 7(5)(1993): 373–401.

Office of National Drug Control Policy, The White House. "Drug Courts," at http://www.whitehousedrugpolicy.gov/enforce/drugcourt.html.

Office of National Drug Control Policy, The White House. *ONDCP Drug Policy Information Clearinghouse Fact Sheet* (2003): 1-8, online at http://www.whitehousedrugpolicy.gov/pdf/drug_datasum.pdf.

Pappagallo, Marco, "The Concept of Pseudotolerance," *Journal of Pharmaceutical Care in Pain & Symptom Control* 6(2)(1998): 95–8.

Passik, Steven D., et al. "Pain Clinicians' Rankings of Aberrant Drug-Taking Behaviors." *Journal of Pain & Palliative Care Pharmacotherapy* 16(4)(2002).

Peele, Stanton. *Diseasing of America: How We Allowed Recovery Zealots and the Treatment Industry to Convince Us We Are Out of Control*. New York: Jossey-Bass, 1999.

———. *The Meaning of Addiction: An Unconventional View*. New York: Jossey-Bass, 1998.

Pereira, Mark A., Emily D. Parker, Aaron R. Fulsom, "Coffee Consumption and Risk of Type 2 Diabetes: An 11-year Prospective Study of 28,812 Postmenopausal Women," *Archives of Internal Medicine* 166 (2006): 1311–16.

Perry, Samuel, and George S. Heidrich. "Management of Pain during Debridement: A Survey of U.S. Pain Units," *Pain* 13(1982): 267–80.

Porter, Jane, and Hershel Jick, "Addiction Rare in Patients Treated with Narcotics"(letter), *New England Journal of Medicine* 302(2)(1980).

Rachlin, Howard. *The Science of Self-Control.* Cambridge, Mass.: Harvard University Press, 2000.

Rich, Ben A. "Thinking the Unthinkable: The Clinician as Perpetrator of Elder Abuse of Patients in Pain." *Journal of Pain & Palliative Care Pharmacotherapy* 18, no. 3 (2004).

Rinaldi, R.E., Steindler, B.B. Wilford, D. Goodwin, "Clarification and Standardization of Substance Abuse Terminology," *Journal of the American Medical Association* 259(4)(1988): 555–57.

Satran, Aaron, et al. "Increased Prevalence of Coronary Artery Aneurysms Among Cocaine Users." *Circulation,* May 17, 2005.

Savage, Seddon R., David E. Joranson , Edward C. Covington, Sydney H. Schnoll, Howard A. Heit, A.M. Gilson, "Definitions Related to the Medical Use of Opioids: Evolution towards Universal Agreement," *Journal of Pain and Symptom Management* 26(1)(2003):655–67.

Schaler, Jeffrey A. *Addiction Is a Choice.* New York: Open Court, 2001.

Schmidtz, David. *Elements of Justice.* Cambridge: Cambridge University Press, 2006.

Schuckit, Mark A., "Longitudinal Study of Children of Alcoholics," In *Recent Developments in Alcoholism*, Vol. 9: *Children of Alcoholics,* Galanter and Begleiter, eds. New York: Plenum Press, 1991, pp. 5–19.

Schwab, Sibylle G., Petra E. Franke, Barbara Hoefgen, Vera Guttenthaler, Dirk Lichtermann, Matyas Trixler, Michael Knapp, Wolfgang Maier, and Dieter Wildenauer, "Association of DNA Polymorphisms in the Synaptic Vesicular Amine Transporter Gene (SLCA18A2) with Alcohol and Nicotine Dependence," *Neuropsychopharmacology* 30(12)(2005): 2263–68.

Selb, Semerl J., and K. Selb, "Coffee and Alcohol Consumption as Triggering Factors for Sudden Cardiac Death: Case-crossover Study," *Croatian Medical Journal* 45(6)(Dec. 2004):775–80; Comment in: *Croatian Medical* Journal 46(1)(Feb. 2005): 148–49.

Senn, Alfred E. *Power, Politics, and the Olympic Games.* Champaign, Ill.: Human Kinetics, 1999.

Shenk, J. W. "America's Altered States: When Does Legal Relief of Pain Become Illegal Pursuit of Pleasure?" *Harper's Magazine,* May 1999, 38–52.

Shirlow, Megan J. "Patterns of Caffeine Consumption." *Human Nutrition/Applied Nutrition* 37(4)(1983): 307–13.

Siegel, Ronald K. *Intoxication: Life in Pursuit of Artificial Paradise.* New York: E. P. Dutton, 1989.

Sourcebook of Criminal Justice Statistics, online at http://www.albany.edu/sourcebook/pdf/.

Stone, J. *An Ethical Framework for Complementary and Alternative Therapists.* New York: Routledge, 2002.

Streatfield, Dominic. *Cocaine: An Unauthorized Biography.* New York: St. Martin's Press, 2001.

Streissguth, Ann P. "Recent Advances in Fetal Alcohol Syndrome and Alcohol Use in Pregnancy," In *Alcohol in Health and Disease,* Agarwal and Seitz, eds. New York: Marcel Dekker, 2001, pp. 303–24.

Szasz, Thomas. "Bad Habits Are Not Diseases: A Refutation of the Claim that Alcoholism Is a Disease." *Lancet* (2)(7767)(1972): 83–84.

——. *Ceremonial Chemistry: The Ritual Persecution of Drugs, Addicts, and Pushers,* rev. ed. Syracuse: Syracuse University Press, 2003.

——. *Our Right To Drugs: The Case for a Free Market.* Syracuse: Syracuse University Press, 1996.

Tarter, Ralph E., Ada C. Mezzich, "Ontogeny of Substance Abuse: Perspectives and Findings," In *Vulnerability to Drug Abuse*, Meyer D. Glantz and Roy W. Pickens, eds. New York: American Psychiatric Association, 1992), pp. 149–77.

Tarter, Ralph E., H. Moss, M. Vanyukov, "Behavior Genetic Perspective of Alcoholism Etiology," in *Alcohol and Alcoholism*, Vol. 1. *Genetic Factors in Alcoholism.* H. Begleiter and B. Kissin, eds. New York: Oxford University Press, 1995.

Tarter, Ralph E., Susan B. Laird, M. Kabene, Oscar Bukstein, Yifrah Kaminer, "Drug Abuse Severity in Adolescents is Associated with Magnitude of Deviation in Temperament Traits," *British Journal of Addiction* 85(1990): 1501–04.

Trebach, Arnold S. *The Heroin Solution.* New Haven, Conn.: Yale University Press, 1982.

Turnbull, Joanne E., and Edith Gornberg, "Impact of Depressive Symptomatology on Alcohol Problem in Women," *Alcoholism: Clinical and Experimental Research* 12(3)(1988): 374–81.

Ungerleider, Steven. *Faust's Gold.* New York: St. Martin's Press, 2001.

Van Dam, Rob M., and Frank B. Hu. "Coffee Consumption and Risk of Type 2 Diabetes: A Systematic Review." *Journal of the American Medical Association* 294(1)(2005): 97–104.

Volkow, Nora D., Hampton Gillespie, Nizar Mullani, Lawrence Tancredi, Cathel Grant, Allan Valentine, Leo Hollister, "Brain Glucose Metabolism in Chronic Marijuana Users at Baseline and During Marijuana Intoxication," *Psychiatry Research: Neuroimaging* 67(1)(1996): 29–38.

Volkow, Nora D., et al. "Long-term Frontal Brain Metabolic Changes in Cocaine Abusers." *Synapse* 11(184)(1992).

Volkow, Nora D., and T-K. Li. "Drug Addiction: The Neurobiology of Behaviour Gone Awry." *Nature Reviews/Neuroscience* 5(12)(2004): 963–69.

Vuchinich, R., and N. Heather. *Choice, Behavioral Economics, and Addiction.* New York: Pergamon, 2003.

Waldorf, Dan, and Patrick Biernacki, "Natural Recovery from Heroin Addiction: A Review of Incidence Literature," online at http://www.drugtext.org/library/articles/narehead.ntm.

Weissman, David E., and J. David Haddox. "Opioid Pseudoaddiction—An Iatrogenic Syndrome." *Pain* 36(1989): 363–66.

World Health Organization, Expert Committee on Addiction-Producing Drugs, annual reports beginning in 1952.

Yesalis, Charles E., and Virginia S. Cowart. *The Steroids Game*. Champaign, Ill.: Human Kinetics, 1998.

Yoy, Robert, with Kirk D. Deeter. *Drugs, Sports, and Politics*. Champaign, Ill.: Leisure Press, 1991.

INDEX